MW01280004

Face To Face

Where Life Meets Reality

By

Tarrance Weaver

xulon PRESS

Face To Face
Where Life Meets Reality
by Tarrance Weaver

Printed in the United States of America

ISBN 9781498412544

www.xulonpress.com

DEDICATION

This book was written for all of the people who are carrying a heavy burden in life.

I want to dedicate this book to Ida Mae Weaver and Wallace Weaver Jr. who always have been and always will be my drive in life; and to all of my family members for loving me when I had no love to give.

Acknowledgements

I want to give a special thanks to all of the people that have played a major role in contributing to this book. I love each and every one of you more than you will ever know. God truly used you in a special way in my life. I specifically want to say thank you to Abe Stamper, Shannon Norman, Robin McKinnie, Kimberly Winfield, and Brandi Gant.

Thanks to Abe Stamper for being more than a manager to me. Thanks for allowing God to use you and guide you into giving me that bracelet on that day. Also, thank you for leading and advising me to seek Christian counseling. God has used you in a mighty way within my life and I am so thankful to have you as a brother among my friends.

Special thanks to Shannon Norman for encouraging me to tell my story. I know that there were countless hours late at night that you were assisting and guiding me through my thoughts over the phone. Thanks for believing in me and walking with me as we made one of my wildest dreams come true. Thanks for every contribution that you have given towards this book and the infinite number of prayers that you have sent my way.

Thank you Robin McKinnie and Kimberly Winfield for never giving up on me. For becoming my Aaron and Hur when I felt like this book was too heavy for me to hold up. You both were there to help close every door behind me that I ventured through as I wrote each chapter. Thanks for every scripture that each of you sent me to help keep my faith going when I felt as if I couldn't take another step towards God. Thank you for helping to hold my head up while telling me to keep looking toward the heavens because that's where my help comes from. I can't thank the both of you enough for all that you have done. I thank God for your roles as my secret ghostwriters at times.

Lastly, I want to say thank you to Brandi Gant. God connected our friendship during a crucial time within this book. You believed in me and challenged me to enter into closets, levels, and emotions within my life that I had not yet dared to examine. You urged me to keep walking as the repercussions of opening some of those doors flew back and hit me in my face. You prayed and fasted me through and also allowed God to use you and your knowledge within my life.

To all of my family and friends that I did not mention by name, I want to say thank you. I know that we all shed a lot of tears while creating this book. It is never an easy task when God asks you to expose your weaknesses, hurts, pains, and family secrets to the world. I truly believe that our victories over the devil will save lives.

What People Are Saying About Face To Face Where Life Meets Reality:

"Just when you think you know somebody well...you find out you truly haven't even scratched the surface. This book was clearly written from the heart. It gives you truths and realities that many of us do not want to face and it gives them to you in perfect fashion…through God's Word. The powerful, personal accounts of my brother Tarrance and the stories of the many others were breathtaking. My dear friend has taken me on a journey that I would have never even imagined. He has come from a life that has made him the outstanding man he is today. If you thought you have struggled, read this. If you thought you were alone, read this. If you thought God has given up on you, read this. Face to Face is where Reality and Life co-mingle with God's written Word. Through this amazing literary journey I have learned that I should not *trust my own feelings because they change. I fully understand that I need to stand on God's promises because those promises will never change*. I have learned that a relationship with God is more than Sunday and Wednesday service. Face to Face Where Life Meets Reality confirms the fact that a relationship with God and faith in His Word will help you overcome any trials and tribulations you may face while showering you with many blessings."

~ Kevin McNeil

"This book made me want to go after my purpose in the ministry. It stirred up what was down on the inside. There was a lot of revelation given to me through this book. No matter what you are going through this book is an encouragement, because it touches on so many aspects of life. This is one that I will go to and read again."

~ Shauntay McDowell

"A truly inspirational book that made me realize the struggles we all go through. I too went through some of the struggles Tarrance went through, but in the end both of us realized how great our God truly is! This book has truly impacted my life and will truly impact yours as well."

~ Sean Quintana

"Reading Face to Face Where Life Meets Reality was powerful. You always think your own life has its ups and downs, but reading this book makes you grateful for what you have. While reading I felt like I knew each individual person and felt myself pulling for him or her. It shows you how amazing our God is and how we can overcome when we rely on the Almighty. I feel like people who need healing will benefit from this book. It is a great read, have tissues ready!"

~ Angela Narr

"Face to Face Where Life Meets Reality is an inspiring book with detailed characterizations. It is an engaging read. The stories are of real people who face challenges in their lives and survive through their faith. It teaches you to live out of faith and not out of fear. As I read this book it made me look upward to the help and source of my strength. I believe it will touch many lives and be helpful to those who read it. Tarrance is a gifted storyteller whom the Spirit flows through and I am looking forward to reading other books that will be written by him."

~ Treatte Males

Foreword

It is my privilege and honor to write this forward. I have known Tarrance since my first couple of days as a college student. We were both attending Evangel University in Springfield, Missouri. I had just moved into Spence Hall, an all-girls dorm, which was directly across the sidewalk form Scott Hall, an all-boys dorm, where Tarrance lived. I walked out the front door of Spence Hall early one afternoon, and as I approached the sidewalk where Tarrance was standing, he gave me a big smile that showed off his pearly white teeth and extremely outgoing personality and he greeted. "What's your name?" He asked this question with his hand stretched out. I don't know where I was originally heading in that moment, but I do know that it was God-ordained because I walked right into a lifelong friendship and into someone who would literally become family to me. We had fun talking and getting to know each other, and by later that afternoon at the university fair, Tarrance was feeling like a matchmaker. He just knew that he had to introduce me to his cousin – Tim. Five years later, Tarrance was standing up as one of Tim's groom's men at our wedding, and from that day on we were truly family as well as friends.

Anyone reading this forward who knew Tarrance in college or the years that followed may be a little surprised to be reading a book about life and faith authored by Tarrance Weaver. Most people would remember Tarrance as funny to talk to, fun to be around, a bit of a rule breaker, definitely hard-headed, and overall a good friend – oh yes, and with his smile and personality – a true ladies man! I actually came to the point where I told Tarrance, "I don't want to have any more friends that are your exes, so don't plan on introducing me to any new girlfriends!" My husband would tell you that Tarrance is the baby of his family, so getting his way and being bossy comes naturally to him, but again, with his smooth personality and charisma most people are more than happy to do things his way. My husband doesn't let anyone boss him around–not even me, but somehow he has always done anything Tarrance wants!

Most people who spent their twenties with Tarrance would not remember him as someone who was walking around preaching the gospel though. As long as I've known Tarrance, he's always been in church on Sunday mornings and even sometimes on Wednesday nights. His soul has always longed to be engaged with the Lord; however, until the beginning of the journey that you will follow him through in this book, Tarrance approached God from the angle of religion and not from the angle of relationship. Looking in from the outside, I can see where this was so natural for him. He grew up in the South – where everyone and their grandma is in church on Sunday mornings and gathered around the dinner table on Sunday afternoons simply because that's the way things are done. I always grew up hearing sermons about the fact that we needed to avoid being "Sunday Christians," but I never really saw that in full clarity until I moved to the South. However, this is the complete opposite of who Tarrance is now. I, for one, am not surprised at all. From the day I met Tarrance, I knew he had a good heart, and he clearly had a ton of charisma and personality that not only made him fun to be with but actually attracted people to him. I had the intuition and a vision then that the Lord was going to turn Tarrance into a leader for Him. I truly had faith that one day he would be someone whose charisma and character would attract others to the Lord instead of to himself. Tarrance and I have spent countless hours together having fun, engaging in deep conversations, praying for each other and our family members, and enjoying friends and life together, so I truly know him and his heart as well as anyone could. I have also been to his hometown, and I have seen where he is from. I married into his family. As a result, I understand him better than most.

I have always been amazed by Tarrance's drive and his many accomplishments, and now I am amazed by his faith and obedience to God. Tarrance's hometown has as much charm and hospitality that any small town in the South possibly could. Aiken is historical and beautiful. However, when you cross through the streets and enter the area where Tarrance grew up, there is also a heaviness in the air. It's not simply for the reason that you are no longer on the rich side of town – it's more. It's the reality that you are in a place where many young people don't form their own dreams and don't ever leave. Instead, they become the next chapter in a book filled with the curses of generational sins such as alcoholism, abuse, and teen pregnancy. Tarrance's life easily could have become one of those chapters instead of the focus of this book. However, that was not God's purpose for him, and even when he was not consciously focusing on pursuing God's purpose for him, he still was determined to find more.

In 2004, Tarrance and I both walked across the stage and received our degrees from Evangel University. Tarrance was the first person in his family to graduate from college! It was a really special day, and there were lots of people from Aiken there to celebrate! Tarrance had brought so much pride to his family. He immediately began a successful career in the IT world. His job gave him the opportunity to travel all over the United States and even to the Caribbean. It also provided him with the means to buy his first home and a new car to park in the garage. Tarrance was always happy to have friends over and to bless others. He has had his brothers and cousins live with him on many different occasions. Tim and I actually had a really fun rehearsal dinner in his backyard the night before our wedding.

In spite of all of these accomplishments, it was evident to me that Tarrance was still searching for more. Tarrance and I have always been close, so we often had conversations about our lives, our goals, and our faith. I knew that he still carried a lot of scars from his past that he didn't ever talk about. I also knew that although it was evident that his soul was yearning for a stronger deeper relationship with the Lord, he was still "sitting in the driver's seat," so-to-say, and he wasn't planning on giving up control of his life anytime soon. I still knew that God had created him to be a leader, so I continued to pray for him and ask the Lord to help him find the courage, strength, and peace to let the Lord be his true source of wisdom and direction. I prayed that I would soon see him surrender all and become the leader I knew he was created to be.

In the middle of 2012 is when it happened! Tarrance came face-to-face with God in an intimate and personal encounter that he would later refer to as his darkest hour. I won't share the details, because he can do that best and you will have the opportunity to live through this experience with him as you read the next chapter of this book. However, I will tell you that Tarrance walked away from this experience completely changed.

When he called me and told me what had happened, I truly had confirmation in my soul that he had completely let go. In his voice and rate of speech there was a distinct mixture of excitement, uncertainty, and peace. I knew that he had not only let God take the wheel, but he had actually completely gotten out of the driver's seat and strapped himself in the passenger side. He was finally ready to see where God was going to take him!

The Lord led Tarrance to request the opportunity to work remotely for a few months so that he could completely change his surroundings and focus all of his off time on strengthening and deepening his relationship with the Lord. It was during this time that the Lord began to lay on his heart the desire to go into ministry. Tarrance began to talk about leaving his job to go into fulltime ministry. It was incredibly refreshing for me to see these prayers answered. The enemy always seeks to discourage believers and discredit what God had done. Tarrance had friends and family tell him that he was truly losing his mind. Some people thought he was crazy to talk about leaving his good job to go into ministry, where he probably would hardly make any money. People teased him and said he must be having an early "mid-life-crisis." Other people didn't believe that the Lord could change someone so fast. They said it would only be a matter of time before he would "backslide." I knew better though. I knew that this was not a change that resulted from a New Year's resolution, a self-help book, or even a personal battle of will. I knew that the truth of the matter was that Tarrance life was forever changed, because he had let go of it and given God full control!

Less than a year later, in obedience to God, Tarrance stepped out in faith and left his job. He stayed with Tim and me in Atlanta for a little more than a month while he fasted and prayed for continued direction and confirmation. During this short time, the Lord connected him with other believers that helped him learn more about his spiritual gifts, his powerful faith, and his purpose. The Lord began to develop the beginnings of this book in him, and He led him to pursue an opportunity to work in ministry in Chicago, where he would continue to learn about God's faithfulness to him, and he would have the opportunity to work with some incredibly strong believers who would mentor him and teach him many of the ropes of ministry.

As I write this forward, I find it funny, maybe even ironic, but I truly believe that as Christians the Lord brings us into close relationships with other believers so that we can take turns being each other's strength, encouragement, and accountability. I had spent years praying for Tarrance. He would seek my husband's advice on different issues in life and mine on various spiritual matters. However, the tables turned. The passion that had been ignited in Tarrance as he came through his darkest hour and surrendered full control of his life created a fiery passion for the Lord that is contagious. This passion began to inspire me. Wait a minute! The cousin and friend that I had prayed for all of these years was now inspiring me, praying for me, and challenging my faith! Yes, this is definitely the work of our Savior!

So I ask you now, are you ready to come face-to-face with the Savior? As you read this book that is most certainly what is going to happen. So get ready to be inspired and challenged to let go and let God have control!

Sincerely,

Kimberley Winfield

"Whoever wants to be My disciple must deny themselves and take up their cross and follow Me."
Mark 8:34

Author's Preface

Face to Face

Where Life Meets Reality

I chose this title for the book because it encompasses our face-to-face encounters with God, life, the world, and our individual struggles. Each story in the Bible mentions how people encountered the presence of God or those of their enemies. Sometimes our worst enemy can be ourselves. Within this book you will encounter my darkest fears and some of my most heartfelt moments. You will hear the heart of a teenager drowning in the ocean of life. You will experience the journey of a boy traveling through life to become a man and some of the obstacles that he had to encounter.

God allowed my path to cross with some amazing people that have also shared their testimonies within this book. A few of the names have been changed to protect their identities, but the power of God is still working through their testimonies. There are multiple testimonies about how others have encountered their worst fears and nightmares. Most importantly, you will read about how each of us had our own unique walks with God and the tough decisions we faced during those times.

By the end of this reading, you will have downloaded a concept into your brain that will hopefully change your decision-making process. This concept is designed to help you think outside the box about the endless possibilities that surround you and the current problems that you may face. Hopefully, it will help you get past your Goliath-sized decisions and focus on your purpose in life. I truly believe that inside every adult is a hurting child in some way, shape, or form. As we grow up in life, some of us choose to walk away from that hurting child and never deal with him or her, and that decision will affect the rest of our lives.

I have heard that it takes a village to raise a child in this world. It is vitally important that we all come together as one family to give hope, purpose, and vision to our future. Even though I am a man, I have to admit that at times it has felt like I was giving birth. This feeling of being in labor has carried on my whole life. Like a pregnant woman, I have carried this bundle of joy inside me, experienced lots of contractions, heavy burdens and pain. Frankly, there have been times when I thought I was going to die from these labor pains. I have misplaced my emotions and feelings on people that did not deserve them. Now that God is releasing this testimony to enter into this sinful world, as any proud father, I hope that this blessing will grow and make a difference in this world.

I'd like to give a special thanks to a group of people that helped me throughout this process and are helping me give this creation the life that it needs. *Face-to-Face* is truly a heaven sent blessing from my Father.

I will discuss some of my family members in this book, but no matter what transpired between us, I love them with all of my heart. I have learned to pray for and love my family, friends, and enemies, no matter the circumstances. I even pray for Joe, because if God can love us after our sins nailed His Son to the cross, how much greater should our love for others be if we are seeking Him.

Tarrance Weaver

Contents

My Darkest Hour

1 Corinthians 13:12

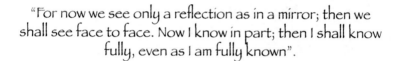

"For now we see only a reflection as in a mirror; then we shall see face to face. Now I know in part; then I shall know fully, even as I am fully known".

One afternoon during the spring of 2012, I found myself sitting quietly in my two-bedroom apartment. I had no clue that reality would soon clash with fate. Suddenly, I realized that I had been running from my past and I had demons to confront immediately as my future was uncertain. I sat quietly on the bed and began to cry uncontrollably, pouring my heart out to God. One would think that if there ever were a time for Him to prove himself to be a living God that would have been the time. The theory of relativity – when a minute seems like an hour and an hour like a minute – came into full effect. This was truly my darkest hour, and it was stretched over a three-day period.

My brother was killed by his father-in-law on December 10, 1994, and I never faced or dealt with the loss like I should have. At the time being a freshman in high school, I could never paint the portrait in my mind of a 12-gauge shotgun shell ripping through the once living body of my brother, my role model, and the only father figure that I had at that time. My heart raced and my lungs gasped for air, because his life had just released it. I have heard that God will never give you more than you can bear, and He would soon test those words on me. Due to my mom losing one of her sons in such a violent way, her future became her past as she lived off the memories of what used to be instead of what was to come.

She became depressed, as most mothers would after such a life-changing event, and relied heavily on alcohol to ease her pain. For a little over four years, she gradually got worse until her excessive alcohol consumption finally took her life on January 22, 1998. During my senior year in high school, I can recall sitting in that hospital room and the awkwardness with neither one of us wanting to talk about it. Finally, in a soft and weakened voice she said, "Baby, come here and have a seat!" calling me to her bedside. I could tell by the trembling in her voice that this conversation would be unlike any other that we ever had. As I approached the right side of her hospital bed, I could see her frail body attempting to lift up and turn on her side to face me. I gazed into her very weak, slightly yellow eyes as she said, "Baby, no one is ever going to take care of you like I have." As any naïve teenager would have done, I fired off with the first thing that came to mind. I said "Oh mom, whatever; you will be alright!" to which she replied "No, listen baby, no one is ever going to take care of you like I have."

It was at that point that I realized what she was saying even though she didn't say it. As my worst fears raced to become my living nightmare, she started coughing and placed a cloth over her mouth to suppress the noise. She would always hide little secrets from me especially the ones that would break my heart. She would never tell me about the results from her previous doctors' visits nor would she discuss how much time the doctors told her she had left. The following day I entered the hospital room and realized that the room was filled with family members. It was then that I was presented with the hardest decision of my life; I was about to decide whether my mom and best friend lived or died. I had to decide whether to turn off her life support machine or keep it on. In a way I was thinking that she could live for a while on the machine and would always be there for me to visit, kiss, hug, and love. It was unclear and I couldn't quite understand why this time was going to be any different from the other two times that she had been in the same position.

The doctor grabbed me by the hand and said that she would not recover this time around. He then told me that the yellowish tint in her eyes and the blood on the cloth from her coughing was an indication that her liver and kidneys had failed. He told me that she was already gone and that all that was left was her shell because the machine was the only thing keeping her alive. I looked up from my eclipsed sunshine giving them their answer, and then I exited the room with a closer relationship with death, hate, and anger towards God. How could He have designed such a perfect world but added me in the equation to be alone in this mean and hateful world without the two closest people in my life?

As I stared at her casket during the funeral, friends and family reassured me with the regular cliché that they were available if I needed anything and that they understood how I felt. How did I feel? I was as lifeless as my mom's body. No one understood the level of pain, anger, loneliness, worthlessness, and fear that I had in me. Unless you've lost your brother, hero and father figure, then shortly thereafter lost your mom, best friend, and your only will for living, you really didn't know how I felt.

There are so many levels in each one of those categories that unless you were me and lived my life, you couldn't truly understand.

Shortly after the funeral, my biological father told me that I was always welcomed to live with him if I wanted. My mother's side of the family was willing to take me in as well, but they suggested that I stay with my father. Neither of those were answers that I wanted to hear at the time. My mother's last words resonated, "Baby, no one is ever going to take care of you like I have." She was right.

They should have embraced me; they should have made the decision for me. However, they didn't, and that was my confirmation that no one understood what I was experiencing at that time. I thank God for touching my Uncle Chester's heart and allowing him to take in a son. Uncle Chester was married to my Aunt Martha–my mother's eldest sister–and he became the father figure that I was searching for; I also became the son that he never had.

It was now years later and I found myself in my darkest hour. I sat for three days in my room, crying and confessing all of my hurt, fears, and sins to God but still felt alienated by Him. I was hoping to hear a deep voice or to see a burning dresser, like the bush with Moses, but nothing happened. As the silence of my past screamed loudly to a point where I could not bear it anymore, I slowly picked up my sub compact .40 caliber Springfield Armory pistol and placed it to my head. I took a deep breath and exhaled very slowly. As the next couple of seconds of my life moved slowly through my head, it was then and only then that I could hear birds chirping outside of my window. My right hand trembled with the gun in it. I knelt on my right knee facing the bed, eager to meet my fate when something came over me and said "Pause!"

The Pause Concept

1 Samuel 12:16

"Now then, stand still and see this great thing the LORD is about to do before your eyes!"

I have to give credit for this concept to our Heavenly Father. During the summer of 2013, I was asked to share some knowledge–or my heart–with some kids at a school in Chicago for about ten or fifteen minutes. As we approached the school, Bishop Spencer Jones told me that the first class was going to be a group of third graders. I began to panic because I had no clue how third graders look and think. So I stopped and prayed before I entered the room. I prayed, "Father, please help me because I do not know any third grade lingo, and I am not sure how useful I can be in this environment–Amen." As I entered the classroom all of the little eyes turned and faced me, and I thought, "Man, they are way bigger than what I had imagined." In that moment, as I stood in front of this class of about twenty, getting ready to be introduced I heard God say, "Just relate to them and give your testimony."

I really wasn't sure if I could do this, but it was too late to leave. As I started sweating, I introduced myself. I told them that I grew up in a neighborhood similar to theirs here in Englewood. I began to tell them about my brother WJ and how he was killed. I also told the class that he had three little kids named Britania, TJ, and Raheem. After telling them this information, I asked them, "Have any of you ever lost a close relative or friend?" I was surprised to see that over 75% of the class raised their hands. This next part was God taking over my mind. I asked them, "Do any of you have a PlayStation, Wii or PSP at home?" and they all answered, "Yes." I went on, "Well, what does that triangle in the middle of the PlayStation controller do if you press it while you are playing a game and you have to walk away?" They answered, "Pauses it." I then asked them, "What does it do when you come back to the game and press it again?" They answered, "It will allow you to un-pause or play the game." I explained to them that you could take that same concept and apply it to your life. For example, when I was in about the fourth grade I had a friend who wanted to get some candy from the store.

Once we made it to the store he looked at me and asked, "Do you have any money?" My reply was "You're the one who invited me to the store. Don't you have money?" He said, "No, but I am going to get some candy!" I stopped my story at that point and asked the kids if they knew what he was about to do, and they all shouted, "Steal it!" I told them that it was at that moment that I heard a little voice that said, "Do not do it!" I think that we have all heard that little voice at some time in our lives. Some of us refer to it as the little angel and devil sitting on our shoulders. Others say that it's our conscience guiding us through the decision.

I asked them, "Do you want to know what I did? I paused, and I asked myself three questions. What would my mother do? What would my pastor do?" and of course since we were in the classroom I asked, "What would my teacher do?" Then I asked the kids, "Would my mother, pastor, or *your* teacher want me to steal the candy?" They all shouted, "No!!!!"

After talking about this concept of "pausing," I continued telling the class the rest of my testimony. I told them that the guy that shot my brother received sixteen years in prison, but he got out in eight years. Several years later my niece, Britania, came to Missouri to visit me for the summer. Well, when the summer was over, I drove my niece back to her mom's house in North Augusta. I pulled into the yard and grabbed her bags out of the car and walked into the house. I put her bags down inside of the living room and headed towards the kitchen to speak to her mom and brothers. When I rounded the corner and walked into the kitchen, I spoke to the family and started to back out of the kitchen. Then, as I turned around to exit the kitchen, I found myself staring right at Mr. Joe! Time paused for what seemed like hours even though it was only seconds. My adrenaline started to rush as my facial muscles started to contract. I started to give thanks to God because this was the encounter I had been praying for. As I stared into his eyes, these thoughts rushed through my head. "*It's not fair that you only served half the time that you were given. Not only did you kill my brother, but because of your actions my mom's reactions caused me to lose her also!*"

Over the last eight years, I had visualized millions of sick and twisted ways to get even! The final thought running through my head as I stared at Mr. Joe was, "*You may have paid your debt to society, but you owe me your life!!!*"

As Mr. Joe stared at me I am sure he had thoughts running through his head, also, like *"I have served my time in prison, so my slate is clean." I knew this day was going to come when I would encounter one of WJ's brothers; now*

I will have to kill again or be killed! Now that I am a free man, I don't owe Tarrance or his family anything. All I want to do is live the rest of my life out as a free man without looking over my shoulder!"

At this point every muscle in my body started to twitch and every living cell started to scream, and that's when I heard that little voice in my head saying, "Don't do it!" So I PAUSED! I asked myself these three questions. *"Would my mother want me to kill him? Would my pastor want me to kill him? Would my brother want me to kill him?"*

As I stood there in front of this classroom of young children, I was filled with wonder and curiosity about what their reactions would be to these questions that stopped me in my tracks that day. I vividly remember my gut reaction. In that moment I thought that my mom would have wanted me to kill him so that I could get revenge for all of the pain, suffering, and loss that he had inflicted on our family. However, in the very next moment I immediately knew that those were my thoughts and not hers. I knew that my mother would want me to live my life to its fullest potential, because she could no longer do the same. I knew she would want me to allow him to live and let God be his judge, to finish college and get my degree, and to live my life in a way that would honor her memory and God's will.

As I finished telling this part of my story, I stood there in the classroom and wondered whether these young children would have had the same sinful gut instincts that I vividly remembered having that day, so I asked them if they were in this situation would their mother want them to kill this man? To my amazement about 98% of the class had that very same sinful reaction, and the others said that I should at least "hit, kick, or fight" him. As my heart poured out to them, I told them that in this type of situation there was no way that you could limit your anger to just a hit, kick, or punch. Once you start to engage in this situation, then you have already passed the point of no return. I reminded the kids that the only reason that I wanted to kill this guy was because he killed my brother. If I engage with him or kill him, then someone will probably want to kill me. Plus, there is a possibility that my niece will want to kill the person that kills me, and her brothers will try and kill the person that kills her. Before you know it eight or nine people are dead, and it was unclear why the first two people truly engaged in the violence in the first place. If Mr. Joe would've paused and thought about the three questions, my view on life would be different than what I have experienced.

Now to the second question of whether my pastor would want me to kill him. Even though my eyes could only see red at that time, I knew that the answer was–No! I knew that my pastor would point me to Romans 12:19 which says, "Do not take revenge, my dear friends, but leave room for God's wrath, for it is written: It is mine to avenge; I will repay says the Lord." You see, it's easy to do what people expect of you in a bad situation, but it's hard to step out of line and dare to be different. My pastor had the insight to know that had I gotten revenge, I would have received instant gratification, but I would have also received long-term suffering. In Romans 12:2, it is written, "Do not conform to the pattern of this world, but be transformed by the renewing of your mind. Then you will be able to test and approve what God's will is—His good, pleasing and perfect will." So again my curiosity got the best of me, and I asked the kids if their pastor would want them to kill the guy that killed their family member, and they all shouted, "NO!!" So I tip my hat to all of the shepherds that are leading their sheep in the right direction and to the fact that one lost sheep is just as important as all the others.

Now I find myself facing the class asking them what they would have done if their brother had died. "Would your brother want you to kill that guy?" Again, I was shocked at the number of hands that confirmed my worst fear. At least ninety-eight percent of them said that their brother would want them to get revenge. So I told the class that their way of thinking was not necessarily wrong, but here's what my brother would want: My brother would not want me to get revenge, because he would want me to grow up and be successful in life. He would want me to be there for his kids and be the father figure in their lives, and walk his daughter down the aisle when she gets married because he is not able to. Give his sons advise when they are at a cross road in their lives. To hug, kiss, and tell them that I love them because he can't.

Some of you may ask why I choose to ask myself what my mother, pastor, and brother would do in those situations. Well, I have three slots labeled from most important to the least important among the people in my life. Now depending on the person, they may have a number of different people in those slots. My mom was the most influential person in my life. She gave birth to me and cared for me with all of her heart. My pastor is constantly feeding the spiritual side of my life. My brother was someone that I always looked up to in my life. So those are the top people in my life to help me make really good decisions. Now depending where you are in your spiritual walk in life, you can place whomever you want into those slots. For example, if you have a really close relationship with God, you can place God the Father, God the Son, and God the Holy Spirit in the slots. If you haven't developed a true relationship with God yet, then you can place friends, family, or super heroes and role models in those areas. The point of asking yourself those questions are to get you to think outside of your box so that you can hopefully see past the wall or those obstacles that are causing stress in your life. Their purpose is to show you that there are other choices, a fork in the road, and a better life beyond your challenges.

So, I shined a little light in the darkness of the children's minds. Just like the children, you were able to experience what it is like walking in my shoes for a day as you read this story. I only talked to you about one experience with the third graders. I have talked to classes from the third grade through the college level. As I find myself visiting more schools and centers, and talking with more people, I noticed that we all have something in common with one another. We all have a history in life. We all have lost someone or something, loved or have been loved, and cried tears of joy or sadness at one point in our lives. It would break my heart to see innocent tears running down the children's face in the middle of the concept speech. I would soon find out that the tears were not shed for my pain, but for the history or present times in their life. Some of the kids would raise their hands and tell me about the pain in their lives.

They would talk about being raped, molested, and beaten. Other kids would talk about witnessing people being shot, stabbed, and hurt. Also, they would share thoughts of hurting themselves and how they have been bullied by adults and peers. I would catch myself relating to their pain even though our experiences were different. Their innocent little eyes would gaze into my eyes looking for answers to overcome the hurt and pain in their history. My heart would break into thousands of pieces because deep down inside I am thinking that they are stronger than I could ever be in those situations. It is at that point that God would flood my mind with His wisdom. I would posi-[illegible] concept just right in their life so that their history [illegible]k against itself and alter the view of their future.

This pause concept is not only designed to help prevent people from making mistakes they may regret later, but it can also be used to invoke good works or deeds. For example, I was mentoring a teenager one weekend, and we decided to go into a gas station to purchase a couple of items. Once we made it inside of the store, he realized that he forgot something in the car, and he needed to go retrieve it. In returning back inside of the store, I noticed that he didn't hold the door for the seasoned lady walking in behind him. So I asked the teenager if he noticed the lady walking in behind him, and he said, "Yes, the lady in the white sweater." I proceeded to ask him why he didn't hold the door for her to enter into the store, and he said, "Well she was like five steps behind me." He started debating the situation of why he wouldn't have to wait. Once he was finished I just asked him to "Pause," and he smiled. He proceeded to say, "Yes, my mother, pastor, and grandma would want me to hold that door for her." Over a period of time, I started to notice a change in his decision-making skills.

In the next couple of sections of the book, I will talk about, and try to define, what it means to be a good parent, pastor, and role model. Hopefully, you will walk away with a better understanding of how to better choose the people that you want in your slots or help others to make wiser decisions in life. After those sections, you will start to notice that there will be a section closing each chapter that gives you a chance to reflect back on opportunities where that person could have paused before and after their incident. I will provide one example and there is a blank space for you to write your own example if you so choose. They are just examples and your conclusions may differ from those listed within each chapter. Just keep in mind that they are there to help walk your mind through its first true encounter with the pause concept.

Good Parenting

Proverbs 17:6

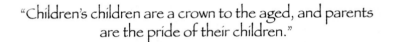

"Children's children are a crown to the aged, and parents are the pride of their children."

There are different forms of parents: biological parents, adoptive parents, godparents, and spiritual parents. What is a good parent? I think most people would agree that a good parent is one who puts their kids' needs before their own and is involved in their kids' everyday life. A good parent will have the courage to correct their kids' wrong doings and the wisdom to discipline them within the boundaries of our society and our spiritual Father. It is written in Ephesians 6:4, "Fathers, do not provoke your children to anger, but bring them up in the discipline and instruction of the Lord." So we should apply discipline and instruction of the Lord. Also, in Proverbs 22:6, "Train up a child in the way he should go; even when he is old he will not depart from it." A good parent is willing to grab their kids by the hand and walk them through life, while explaining the mistakes that they have made in their own life. Another aspect of a good parent is one that allows just enough rope in the relationship where they will find their own independence in life, but enough to catch them before they fall. A good parent will explain to kids that most mistakes in life are there to help sharpen their minds and make them more prepared for life as long as they learn from them.

I truly think that the real definition of a good parent lies in the eye of the beholder. I think that we have too many different backgrounds, cultures, religions, and beliefs to unify on this subject. We may not all agree on this topic or see eye to eye, but we can all agree that we want our kids to have amazing lives. Some of us want our kids' lives to be better than what we have experienced in life, and others want their kids to grow up to be like them. Ultimately, encouraging our children to seek happiness, accomplish goals, and strive to fulfill life's purposes while in search of that one true love is a template that we all can use.

I would say that despite the circumstances I was dealt and the life that I was birthed into, my mom was a great parent. At times she worked multiple jobs just to make ends meet. That taught me that at times in life I might have to sacrifice myself for the good of the group. It also taught me how to work hard in life to get what I want. There were times when we didn't have power at the house and she would pull out the kerosene heaters, and we would all gather in the living room to stay warm. We would nail quilts and bed covers over the doorways to keep the heat in that particular area. At the time I was ashamed of the situation, but again, it taught me some valuable lessons. I learned that in every bad situation you can find some good, if you are willing to take a closer look. I learned that true love is about giving more even when you feel as though you have given your all. It is about making the most out of the little bit that you may have. It is about standing back up with a smile and looking at the world and asking, "Is that all you got?", even when you can't take another blow. It's about keeping a smile on your face even when you have just experienced the worst. You see, those moments sitting around the kerosene heaters and camping out in the living room for a couple of days were some of the best days of my life. I never knew that I was experiencing hard times, because my mom's love would pour out in those moments and the quality time that we experienced was priceless. My mom, two older brothers and I would all snuggle up and tell stories. The only downside to this was going to school the next day smelling like kerosene (chuckle).

I realize one thing as I am sitting here writing this story, that we were all alive at that moment, healthy, and full of love even though life had us by the hairs on our necks. There were also times when I was out of line, like most kids, and my mother would whoop me, but again I would not take those moments back because they made me into who I am today. So if I had to ask myself, who is an example of a good parent? My answer would be Ida Mae Weaver. She gave me the best that she had and expected way more from me. She taught me that life is not always fair to us but to always look at the bright side of things. Most of all, she taught me to never just look at the good in life for life lessons, because you can learn just as much from the bad. You can learn just as much from a bum or drug addict as you can from a successful businessperson. Basically, life lessons learned from both a businessperson and a bum are equally important.

I have learned that God is good and faithful just as He has promised. Now, it states in Philippians 4:19, "But my God shall supply all of your needs according to His riches in glory by Christ Jesus." I have to admit that he did supply me with Uncle Chester to fill that fatherly role when WJ died. He didn't stop there; He also supplied me with Mia Davidian (Momma Mia) when my mother died. As His glory unfolds everything just seems to fall into its rightful place in my life. Momma Mia is my angel. Neither one of us knew what God's purpose was in each other's lives at that time. Our lives and up bringing were total opposites, but our spirits were very much alike. I was black and she was white. She was accustomed to the good life, and I was from the hood. Our life and relationship were similar to the movie "The Blind Side" except I didn't go to the NFL. On many occasions I would sit down at the dinner table with her and her family and it felt awkward. Here was a perfectly good working model of what a family should look like–a father, mother, and kids having dinner together. Everyone would talk about their day and at times key decisions that would influence their futures. While growing up, that atmosphere wasn't an option for me, but God allowed me to be a part of theirs at certain times. At the time I did not realize it, but I had no dreams, goals, or desires in life. I had been too distracted by the negative things in my life that I never answered the question, "What do I want to be when I grow up?" My only goal was to graduate from high school. Mia and her family gave me a breath of fresh air and God used them to tear down my barriers in life and to teach me that life is so much bigger than what I had seen. They taught me to think outside of the box, to realize that the only restraints that are on my life are the ones that I am applying, and not to become a product of my environment. Each hug given to me from that family assured me that my dreams are attainable. They encouraged me and reminded me that I am not alone in this journey.

Good Shepherds (Pastor)

Matthew 18:12-14

"What do you think? If a man owns a hundred sheep, and one of them wanders away, will he not leave the ninety-nine on the hills and go to look for the one that wandered off? And if he finds it, truly I tell you, he is happier about that one sheep than about the ninety-nine that did not wander off. In the same way your Father in heaven is not willing that any of these little ones should perish."

In the month of July of 2012, I can recall sitting at work at my desk a few months after my darkest hour encounter, praying to God. I said, "God please guide me to where you want me to be in life. God, I am not sure if this type of person still exists outside of the biblical days, but if so bring them to me. Let my mentor be a person that seeks You with such passion and truth that everyone will know his heart. Let them be in your Word and of your works 24 hours a day. Father, I need more than a Wednesday and Sunday preacher! Let me see Your living hand over his life and a relationship between You and man that is beyond desirable. Let them be of good integrity, great importance, and truly understand the meaning of humility. Let this man be about helping people and saving people's lives."

Within the next couple of months as God took the heart of my prayer and started shifting it through the atmosphere, things became uncomfortable. These changes were so uncomfortable until the point that I tried to help Him out. I thank God that for every door that I tried to open, He closed it so that I would be on His schedule. A year later, I was talking to a friend about wanting to be a missionary, and he gave me the phone numbers of two preachers who could assist me. I took the numbers and stored them in my phone with no intentions of calling them. I had prayed and God had answered it for me, but I was afraid to move! As I internally battled with taking a leap of faith and trusting Him for what I had prayed for, I begin to panic. I have noticed that it is always the first step that hinders your faith-building relationship with God. When we pray and God answers, we tend to pause and become hesitant. Some of us turn away from our blessings in life. It's almost disrespectful when we ask our Father for something, and He provides it, but then we don't want it. It's a good thing that our God is a loving Father.

This reminds me of when I had my first encounter with a zip line course about a year ago. I was at a Christian youth camp and I found myself standing on the platform contemplating jumping. The instructor was very supportive in telling me that I could do it, and everything would be ok. She soon realized that her repeated countdowns from three were not the answer to my problem. She turned and looked me in my eyes and said, "Where is your confidence in God?" For a moment, I could feel her confidence and faith in God. For some strange reason her eyes told me that she was 100 percent confident that God would protect me. I broke eye contact because the little six-year old stuck on the tree swing obstacle directly behind the zip line, started to scream at me. Apparently, I was holding up the line. The moment I looked down towards the ground, my faith went out of the window again. I felt as if I was in the tallest tree in the world. I felt like I had nowhere to go but forward because the obstacles behind me were just as intimidating. Once again, I found myself stuck in life. Eventually I told the instructor to push me when I least expected it, and she replied, "No!" and said, "This is reflection of your faith in God so trust HIM." So three minutes later, I took a deep breath, closed my eyes, and jumped. In the beginning they couldn't get me to jump until I took the leap of Faith. I couldn't wait until I made it to the end to start the next obstacle. The little kid waiting for the platform lost all of his bodily strength trying to hold on to the swing, while I built up the courage and took a leap of faith. Once we were both on the ground, he was the first one to give me a congratulatory hug. Satan will always try to create distractions in your life, "You intended to harm me, but God intended it for good to accomplish what is now being done, the saving of many lives."–Genesis 50:20

Now as I stared at the two numbers in my phone, I felt that deep down in my heart that one of these two numbers was the answer to my prayer. I never called either of the numbers, so God told His shepherd to go out and find His lost sheep. Two weeks passed by, and my phone rang while I was at work. I stepped outside to answer it, and it was Bishop Spenser Jones, one of the two numbers, searching for God's lost sheep. After making the initial connection, I avoided the next seven phone calls in hopes of not having to make the leap of faith. I didn't really want to have to quit my job, move, and step out on faith! Once God has an agenda, He will see it through. My Shepherd never gave up on me and is now walking me through life. To make a long story short, I quit my job and stepped out on faith, and God has blessed every step of my journey.

I am now living in one of the roughest areas in Chicago against all odds. My personal goal in life was to make it out of the rough areas and never return, but God's plan was different. He was using my trials and tribulations as preparation for my purpose.

What I have noticed in life is, just because you have made one leap of faith doesn't mean that the leaps will become easier. It does not mean that there will not be fewer or future leaps of faith. It gives me the courage to look back and say that I made it and God provided. It gives me the strength to stand on my own faith and look at the other first time zip liners and say, "I will not push you because this is a faith builder, so trust in HIM!"

God created a soul-winner when he designed Bishop Spencer Jones. There aren't too many people who don't know him as a Pastor, a God-sent father to the fatherless, and a mentor. I have seen God use him to create fires inside of people that the average person would have given up on. I have noticed while working under his teachings that part of the reason why the violence is taking over the world is because we are all hurt or broken. We have a system of hurt and broken souls trying to help and guide the hurt and broken...the blind leading the blind into darkness. We need God's laborers to rise up and help guide the hurt and broken into God's light. Since every Christian has a testimony, depending on the stage of their walk, we can possibly call it the "Healed guiding the Hurt and Broken."

The definition of a shepherd is one who cares for and guides a group of people as a minister or teacher. (According to the Free Dictionary by Farlex)

As I walk with Bishop Jones through this part of my life, he reminds me of the stories that I have read about Moses. Moses was very passionate about his people. God gave him a great task of freeing the Hebrews. In Exodus 12:40 it is written, "Now the sojourning of the children of Israel, who dwelt in Egypt, was four hundred and thirty years." God freed his people after four hundred and thirty years, keeping his promise to His faithful. Moses was known as a religious leader, a prophet, lawgiver, and teacher/rabbi, though most importantly I see him as a shepherd. Moses had a calling in his life to help guide his people to the Promised Land. To free them from the old sins and move them into the blessings of our God!

If you have had the pleasure of meeting Bishop, then you have felt the warmth of his spirit within his hugs. Similar to Moses he had to make vital decisions and face a lot of oppositions in his life. God has carried him from Poplar Bluff, Missouri, through the Vietnam War, and into Chicago. I think of Chicago as the desert before the Promised Land as we build our trust in our Lord God! I feel as though Bishop, just like Moses, can hear/feel the moans and groans in the hearts of Gods people's. On numerous occasions I have been in the middle of a conversation with him, and he walks off to witness to a soul. Bishop is forever faithful and witnesses to every living soul. On some days, I am glad that the corners and sidewalks are empty, so that we can make it to our destination on time. On those days, I haven't figured out if he has witnessed to everyone and no one's soul needs to be saved or if everyone is hiding. Bishop is up at 3 a.m. every morning praying over our lives while we are asleep. In Luke 22:39-46 it talks about Jesus while He prayed in the garden. It reads, "Jesus went out as usual to the Mount of Olives, and His disciples followed Him. On reaching the place, He said to them, 'Pray that you will not fall into temptation.' He withdrew about a stone's throw beyond them, knelt down and prayed, 'Father, if you are willing, take this cup from me; yet not my will, but Yours be done.' An angel from heaven appeared to Him and strengthened Him. And being in anguish, He prayed more earnestly, and

His sweat was like drops of blood falling to the ground. When He rose from prayer and went back to the disciples, He found them asleep, exhausted from sorrow. 'Why are you sleeping?' He asked them. 'Get up and pray so that you will not fall into temptation.'" Little did we know that we were about to encounter a multitude of miracles that would lead up to the ultimate miracle, miracles varying from restoring an ear to fulfilling the role of our Savior.

I would always believe that Jesus had the power to perform those miracles in our lives because He was the Son of God. Since Jesus was a part of the trinity, He came into this world with all power in His hands. It would later be revealed to me through prayer and wisdom that I need to read between the lines. I discovered that Jesus was able to perform those miracles every day because He would wake up in the premature hours of the morning and pray like our lives depended upon it! Due to the content of His prayer and condition of His heart, God the Father honored Jesus by filling His cup and allowing miracles to over flow upon our lives. I can tell you that Bishop's prayers have worked miracles within my life.

To be honest, sometimes having a shepherd or role model is not easy in the beginning, especially with me being a boy and evolving into a man the best way that I knew how. I felt as if I knew it all. To be honest, I made it through my younger life without having a man (or role model) guiding me 100% of the time. I had accomplished everything that was on my "to do list" in life. I had put myself through school, purchased my own house and car, and travelled all over the world. So at times, Bishop and I would bump heads, and I would become so frustrated. One thing that he would do is invite me down to his office and pray over any differences, if any occurred during that week. Normally, by the time we got to that point, I was mad! I really didn't want to pray. I felt as if I was right, and he needed to see things from my point of view on those particular issues. I have to admit that this same attitude that I was displaying towards the Bishop is the same one that I had developed towards God at times.

When things weren't going my way and I was upset, frustrated, or mad. I didn't pray, give thanks, or praise God as if I was hurting Him. The truth is that I was hurting myself because God wanted me to handover that pain instead of carrying it around and being mad at the world. The Bishop could see that imperfection inside of me and was mentoring to that area in my life. I didn't want to listen to him mainly because he would use old, traditional methods to resolve a modern day problem. To me, that was like taking the choice of driving a 1968 Ford mustang over a 2013 Lamborghini. To me it was a no brainer that the 2013 Lamborghini is newer and faster. Still, I would always pray when he asked me even though I was mad. He would go into this really long prayer over my life, and I would use John 11:35, the shortest verse in the bible, "Jesus wept." Amen! It seems that one of the hardest things to learn in life is to unlearn what you have learned. I was a know-it-all, and in order for me to position myself just right under God's glory, I had to change. I am sure that Bishop noticed that trait in me from the very beginning since he has mentored many people. He probably realized that he needed to pray for me like he has never prayed before. Well, as God's ears heard Bishop's prayers, something started to change inside of me. I started to notice that the fight was never with Bishop, it was always between the old and new versions of myself. It was like Bishop would give me a word that would stir up and start a controversy inside of me. I truly felt like Paul when he talked about 2 Corinthians 5:17 (NIV) "Therefore, if anyone is in Christ, the new creation has come: The old has gone, the new is here!" Through my transformation, I was able to see that it was the blessings of God that were bestowed upon me and coasted me where I have arrived at today. God showed me that the 1968 Ford Mustang has its strengths, also. It is a classic. It has endured the past, proven to be true over past decades, and strong enough to still exist. Our legacies were built upon their backs and we still have a lot to learn. Some cars were built for speed and others were built for cruising but both will get you from point A to point B!

It almost seemed like Bishop lived his life from the prospective of day to day, because tomorrow isn't promised to us. He ministers to every sheep, and it doesn't matter if they are not of his flock. Ultimately, his goal is to make sure that everyone one makes it to the Promised Land.

If you have a shepherd in one of your slots as the three people that will help influence you to make better decisions, then I hope you make wise decisions in choosing your shepherd. There is only one true shepherd that every pastor should use as a role model and that's Jesus Christ. I hate to say this, but not every pastor is a good shepherd. Pastors are humans just like we are and make mistakes. When looking for good shepherds there are some good qualities to look for. A good shepherd seeks God first. They are willing to help shepherd other flocks because everyone belongs to God. They are willing to be the first person to pray for you in the morning, and the last one to say "amen" at night. You should always be able to relate to, rely on, and believe in their walk with God. I thank God for my shepherd, because I was one lost sheep! I have since learned that I didn't accomplish any of the things above, but it was through God's grace and mercy that I was blessed with those items and opportunities.

Good Role Models (Teachers)

Mark 1:22

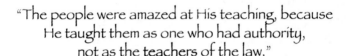

"The people were amazed at His teaching, because He taught them as one who had authority, not as the teachers of the law."

Months after my brother died, a lot of emotions started running through my body. I truly didn't know how to control these feelings. It was the middle of my freshman year of high school, and my grades started to drop. I started getting into a lot of trouble at school. I would sit in the back of the classroom and daydream about how my life used to be. I would reminisce on all of the memories that my brother and I shared together. He taught me so many lessons in life, because he had already gathered the experiences being a couple years older than me. My mind traveled back to a time when I was ten years old and WJ was teaching me a lesson in life that caused him to scream at me.

I can recall on that day the heat sizzled around my cousin Keith and me as we stood in the backyard. The grass was starting to turn brown from the incredibly hot and dry summer we were enduring. On that day, there was a slight breeze stirring, but it still wasn't enough to make much of a difference in the scorching temperature. Keith then said, "Come on, Tarrance, it's your turn." I knew it wasn't a good idea, but he had just done it three times in a row. How much trouble could we possibly get into? I bent down slowly and pulled up some grass to make a little pile. Then, after a small hesitation, I reached out to take the match from Keith's hand. As I bent down to light the grass, thoughts of what could happen swirled around in my head. Then, it was on fire. We patted it out as Keith said, "Okay, two more times now." I pulled some more grass and lit it again, becoming a little bolder this time. The third time I lit the grass on fire, Keith said "Let's see what happens if we leave it a little longer." After all, we had been able to pat it out quite easily the last five times.

Suddenly, as the pile of grass started to burn, the breeze picked up, sweeping the fire along with it. I watched in slow motion while the fire started to spread. Desperately, we tried to put it out. When we realized we couldn't stop it, we decided to run away. As fast as our ten-year old legs could carry us, we ran to the front of the house, sat on the porch steps, and folded our hands in our laps, trying to pretend nothing had happened.

The fire cut a large strip across the back yard, consuming it in flames. Fortunately, my older brother WJ, happened to look out the window. He raced outside as the breeze picked up even more causing almost a quarter-acre fire now. He reached the water hose in record time, unraveling it and turning it on almost simultaneously. As he sprayed the flames, his thoughts raced between anger at us for lighting the fire and silent prayer that he could get it out. After what seemed like an eternity, the flames started diminishing and the ground became a soaking wet, charred black mess.

Once the fire was completely out, he stomped to the front yard. "What did you think you were doing? You should have known better! If I hadn't seen that fire out the window, what could have happened? It could have spread to other yards, caught houses on fire! What would you do if the house caught on fire? Tarrance, you have to think about things before you do them!" The ringing noise in my eardrum from him yelling at me transformed into the classroom bell and brought me back into my reality as the bell interrupted that part of my daydreaming process. As I stood up and started to walk out of my freshman classroom, I started to smile because my brother was right once again. I needed to learn and think outside of the box to encompass the full view of the picture and not just the details that were so blatantly clear to me. I had to challenge myself to become a thinker, because I was smarter than what I proved on that day. I knew that I should have listened to that little angel on my shoulder telling me not to light the grass on fire.

I could also recall when multiple family members and friends told me that I needed to be strong and hold it together for my mom's sake. So that's just what I did. I suppressed all of my feelings deep down inside of me until I reached the point of numbness. They were pushed so far from my reality until I didn't even cry at my own brother's funeral. I could remember staring at his casket as he lay there in his black suit, white shirt, and black tie. His right hand was resting on top of his left wrist. His eyes were closed as if he was in a resting state. My mom made sure that he had his glasses on his face so that he looked as much like himself as possible. I was fully engaged with my surroundings. My mind started giving his chest movements as if he was just sleeping. I watched everyone approach and give their last respects to my brother. The moment came when my mother had to say her last goodbyes and she fell apart. On the inside, my emotions were boiling like a pot of water sitting on a red-hot stove with the dial set on high. Tears would bubble up in the corner of my eyes as she was crying out loud, but I withheld them from showing. I did exactly what I was told to do; be a rock for my mother. Naturally three years later, when my mother died, I suppressed more pain deep down within my inner most being. I felt like I needed to be strong for my niece and nephews. I felt as though I couldn't shed a tear, because that would show that there was weakness in this suffering life. I truly miss WJ and my mom with all of my heart, although it has been over a decade since I have last seen them alive.

There have been times in my past where I have been caught between a rock and a hard place in my life. Times where I really and truly needed my family to help me get through the quick sand that was devouring my every thought. As I prayed about those issues that I was facing and fell into a deep sleep, at times, my brother or mother would visit me in my dreams. WJ would give me advice or walk me through my situations. My mom and WJ may not always visit in the same dream, but their presence always allowed me to wake up with a smile on my face and a warm feeling in my heart. Now I know that some psychologists would say that it was the creative part of my mind creating these dreams or illusions, and that it truly never happened. Honestly, they could be right, but here are the facts I believe as a Christian. God uses dreams at times as a way of giving knowledge, wisdom, or warning signs to people about their future multiple times throughout the Bible. In Numbers 12:6 He said, "Listen to my words: When there is a prophet among you, I, the Lord, reveal myself to them in visions, I speak to them in dreams." Now I am not stating that I am a prophet, but I have also read in the Bible where God has used angels to warn people or give them advice. My God is a God of endless possibilities and cares enough about me that He often sends His angels to visit me in my dreams giving me hope, comfort, and a piece of His love. I have said all of that to say this; even though part of my family passed away years ago, I can feel their presence at times. I think that they work harder now guiding me than they did when they were alive.

One of the reasons that I chose a teacher as one of my options to use in the pause concept is because a very special teacher went out of her way to make a difference in my life. Kathy Carlyle took the time to step outside of her day-to- day job and made a few phone calls that altered my life forever. She was one of the many teachers that I had throughout the day during my senior year in high school. The moment that she heard the news about my mom passing away she embraced me. At the time in my mind she was just an ordinary teacher, but when the time presented itself she was an extraordinary teacher. Even though she had her own life to live she sacrificed her time to help me through my rough period in life. I figured that God was speaking inside of Mrs. Carlyle about my state of mind. I figured that He had given her a spirit of discernment where she could tell that my spirit was in an uproar, and that a suicidal spirit was resting on me. Later, you will read about that spirit in the chapter titled "The Unspoken Killer." To this day, I am not sure what she saw inside of me or what made her intervene, but I am so thankful for her. God still proved to me through Mrs. Carlyle that He will continue to stand firmly on His word. The Bible states in Jeremiah 29:11-14, "For I know the plans I have for you," declares the Lord, "plans to prosper you and not to harm you, plans to give you hope and a future. Then you will call on me and come and pray to me, and I will listen to you. You will seek me and find me when you seek me with all your heart. I will be found by you," declares the Lord, "and will bring you back from captivity. I will gather you from all the nations and places where I have banished you," declares the Lord, "and will bring you back to the place from which I carried you into exile." Mrs. Carlyle took the time to contact Momma Mia and convinced her that I was worth saving and investing in. Without that one kind act from her, I can truly say that I don't think that I would be here writing this book for you today. I know that everyone loved Mrs. Carlyle, and I am not sure how many lives she saved over her teaching career before she retired. I owe her more than I can ever repay. For all of the teachers out there, please never give up on the children that are placed in your life for a short period of time. You may not understand the quality of life that those kids are experiencing while they are at home, but you do value the concept of a better life. The one decision that you make to invest a little something extra in someone's life may start a ripple effect and the results may be unseen at first, but the blessing will be undeniable and immeasurable. So here's a special thanks to Mrs. Carlyle and all of the past, present, and future teachers that may have spirits like hers.

Understanding God's Forewarning

God has a way of revealing Himself to each and every one of us. He loves all of His children. Some of us aren't in a place in our lives that we can hear, feel, or understand His glory. In Genesis 37:5-8, God revealed parts of Joseph's future to him in a couple of dreams. "Joseph had a dream, and when he told it to his brothers, they hated him all the more. He said to them, Listen to this dream I had: We were binding sheaves of grain out in the field when suddenly my sheaf rose and stood upright, while your sheaves gathered around mine and bowed down to it.

His brothers said to him, do you intend to reign over us? Will you actually rule us? And they hated him all the more because of his dream and what he had said." Yes, God gave Joseph some of the knowledge about his future, but Joseph didn't have the wisdom to present it to his family. That caused a lot of turmoil in his family. Just like Joseph, God gave me a dream so I tried to handle my situation a little differently. Even after everything had come to pass, I still was afraid to tell people of that encounter, because I was afraid of the repercussions from man. I didn't know if people were going to think that I was crazy for revealing this encounter. Years later, I realized that if I had the chance to do it all over again, I would, only to see if I were to change my reaction and see if it would have provided a different outcome. Maybe it would've given me an opportunity to ask my brother some questions that would've given me more knowledge into the unknown. As you turn the page into the next chapter, you will see how God revealed His presence in my family's lives.

God's Forewarning

Daniel 1:17

"To these four young men God gave knowledge and understanding of all kinds of literature and learning. And Daniel could understand visions and dreams of all kinds."

For a while I was angry with God because I figured that he had turned his back on me. In Matthew 27:46 and Mark 15:34, Jesus shouted in a loud voice, "*My God, my God, why have you forsaken me?*" Some Christians think that the cry was Jesus in His purest form because He felt betrayed by man and deserted by God. I felt like Jesus did in that hour of darkness, because man had betrayed me, and I felt like God had deserted me and left me feeling alone in this world. It seemed that God took the two most important things in my life away, and although God had a resting place for them in heaven, He was also preparing me for what was to come in my future. One night in November of 1994, I went to bed like most high school freshmen. I would soon find out that this night would serve as an anchor to my faith and is why I trust in God.

I went to sleep and had what I thought was a dream. In this dream I was standing off to the side and watched the scenes unfold from a third person's perspective. What I witnessed was my family living their normal day-to-day lives. My mother and I were living in the same apartment on Carver Terrace, and then suddenly a great sadness fell upon me. What I saw next had me scared and made me pray for things that I shouldn't have prayed for to happen. What I dreamt about was my brother getting shot. I couldn't see which brother it was that was shot or who shot him, but it felt so real. It scared me so much that I woke up in a panic. My heart was racing, and I was out of breath just as if that were really happening. Once I realized that it was just a dream, my heart rate started to calm down, and I tried to make sense of it all. As I lay in my twin-size bed, I realized that this dream was different. It was almost like I was awake, but I brought part of the dream into reality with me. I could still visualize everything happening including a lot of the minute details. It was then that I got out of bed and onto my knees to pray to God for it not to happen. This next part I am almost ashamed to admit and I have only told a handful of people about how my heart turned cold on that night. I was so confused about why this dream felt so real or why it felt like a vision. I had never had a vision from God before that time, but I knew that something was different about this dream. So I prayed, "If this was a vision and it has to come to pass, please GOD don't let it happen to WJ. If it has to happen, please let it happen to my older brother Cornell." You see, Cornell and I didn't have a close relationship at that time, and WJ was more of my shelter from the world. Cornell was the oldest brother and he left the house when he was about sixteen to start and raise his family. So, we didn't have a lot of the earlier memories together, because I was about 5 years old when he moved out. Whereas with WJ, he assumed the role of the "man of the house" in my life and helped mom raise me even after he moved out with his own family. He took the time to explain life to me and walk me through it. WJ corrected all of my wrong doing with discipline and consequences while keeping my best interest at heart.

He taught me how to fish, hunt, defend myself, and appreciate life. So that was the reasoning for my prayer to God after waking up from that dream, even though it wasn't right. Growing up, I was taught that if you dream about fish, it means that someone in your close circle is pregnant, or if you had a bad dream about someone, you don't tell them or it may come true. I know that it is a superstition, but I think that everyone's life involves a little superstition through family traditions. With that said, I was afraid to tell WJ about the dream, so I never did. A couple of weeks passed by, but my anticipation because of that dream never went away. I knew the time was near when my brother started talking and acting as if he had the same dream. What I mean is, he would come into our mom's room and sit on the edge of her bed every night and just talk. These talks were different from the perspective that it was for five nights in a row from 12 a.m. until about 3 a.m. I would normally pass out while they talked. WJ would say things like, "Mom, please don't let anything happen to my kids. Do not let other men raise my daughter." My mom would tell him to stop talking like that and to go to bed, but he insisted as if he knew something that we did not.

December 9th is a day that will be etched into my brain forever. That day was cold and the clouds were very grey. The weather was misting most of the day, and there was this strange presence to that day that I had never felt before. My brother left my place that night about 10 p.m. and as he walked out of our apartment, he told my mom, "Remember to take care of my kids if I do not make it back." There was a knock at the door at approximately 1 a.m. that startled us. My mom asked me to get the door, because she could not move due to a sudden pain in her upper back. So I answered the door, and it was my cousin informing us that we needed to come with her because there was a lot of police activity at Joe's trailer. I went back into the room where my mom was and told her what I had just heard and informed her that we needed to leave. My mom couldn't physically move her body for about 15 minutes because she was in so much pain. Once the pain subsided we started our journey over to Mr. Joe's single wide trailer. I can still visualize the scene, as we drove down the main road in Shiloh Heights, the neighborhood where the event took place. I could see an infinite number of blue and red lights off in the distance to my right as we approached the trailer park. Slowly, we made a right turn off of the paved road onto the dirt road that would soon lead us up to his trailer. The distance from the main road to Mr. Joe's trailer was about 200 yards; it was the longest ride I'd ever taken into the unknown. Due to the amount of police cars that were there, we had to exit the car and walk another 60 yards to his location. Once we were there, our curiosity grew with every passing minute, because no one was giving us any insight into what was going on. The only information that we had was that there was an altercation at this residence. As my mom and I watched the police officers scurrying in and out of the trailer, we became restless and leaned on the car behind us. There were thousands of questions running through my head as we tried to make sense of this situation.

Where was WJ? What had he done this time? I wonder if they got into a fight or something and did WJ win? I don't see WJ; they must be in the trailer talking to him or maybe he is already at the jail. Man, he has done it this time! Mom is going to be pissed when she talks to him! Hmmm... You see, my brother was not a stranger to trouble and by no means perfect, but the fact remains that he is my brother and I would love him no matter what he had done. During the process of my mind speeding up and rambling on with questions, my mom's mind was slowing down and processing her environment. Suddenly she leapt off of the car that was once helping to support our weight and she screamed, "OH LORD! NO, NO, NO!" My heart started to race again, because I could see the panic on her face! So I asked her, "What is wrong?" She said with such fear and defeat in her heart, "This is a coroner's car." So then she proceeded to tell me that they are the ones who transport the dead bodies to the morgue. All of a sudden my body was ambushed by fear, panic, rage, and pain. I thought to myself, "My God, what has WJ gone and done this time!" I started evaluating my surroundings with a purpose at this point. Then I started focusing on this police cruiser sitting off in the distance near the car that we had just gotten out of. I could see the crown of what seemed to be a head in the window. As my mom sat in this state of panic near the coroner's car staring intensely at the front door of the trailer, I could not take my eyes off of this one particular police cruiser. I glanced at my mom once more before I started walking slowly towards the cruiser. With every step towards this car I became overwhelmed with sadness from the thoughts of Joe's family being mad at WJ and my family.

I couldn't imagine how Joe's daughter was going to cope with losing her father. I was gazing at the ground trying to process all of these thoughts in my head as I walked the sixty yards back towards the car to see WJ. I noticed as I approached the cruiser that his head was leaning against the back seat. At this point, I found myself nearing the rear door on the driver's side of the car with very little sight, due to the really bright flashing police lights on the cruiser. The silhouette of my brother turned slowly and looked at me, and it was then that reality slapped me in the face. Mr. Joe was staring at me! I could not move my feet, scream, or even begin to process what was happening or what I was seeing. As I glared at him with his hands bound in the back of the car he had a look on his face that I will never forget. There wasn't a killer's scowl or an emotionless face as one would expect. It was almost as if he was searching for forgiveness with regret. As reality started seeping back into my mind, tears started to form in my eyes as I looked back at his trailer where the coroner's car was now backing up to the front door. I started to run back up to the house and yell to my mom, "It's WJ, Mom!" and at that time she responded, "I know, baby," and we watched helplessly as they brought the black body bag outside and placed him in the car. I remember staring at his outline in the body bag realizing that a death can rob a person of their hope, security, love of life, happiness, dreams, view of invincibility and replace it all with darkness. This darkness is a seed that would grow in time into an uncontrollable rage, devouring the concept of a good life and giving birth to revenge and more contagious seeds!

As the coroner closed the door to the car, I glanced back at the police cruiser again with an overwhelming sense of darkness and anticipation at the idea of our paths crossing again. It wasn't until after we went back to my mom's best friend's house that I realized my dream had morphed into a vision. What God showed me a month prior had come to pass, but God had ignored all of my prayers that I sent to him about saving WJ. Now that I am older, I realize that God was preparing me with the vision, warning me with WJ's prophecies, and then confirmed everything with my mother's back pain. Remember I mentioned we heard a knock at the door and my mother was in so much physical pain she couldn't move? That was the first time she had ever experienced back pain. There is a certain connection that a mother has with her children that is difficult to explain. How could she feel a sharp pain in her back the moment she woke up without having an inclination that her son's life was in trouble? How could she feel the pain in her upper back in the very spot that he was shot? Some might call it a sort of telepathic link between parents and their kids. Some might call it a coincidence that it happened that way. Others might not believe that it even happened at all.

What I do know is that our Father's love for His kids is so profound that He subjected His Son to die for our sins. In the beginning, I mentioned how in Mark 15:34, Jesus shouted in a loud voice, "*My God, My God, why have You forsaken Me!*" It was almost as if God the Father turned His back on Him. Maybe God didn't abandon Jesus, but turned His face away because He couldn't bear seeing the pain on His face, but only wanted to focus on the pain that They felt and shared together. Maybe He was gathering the full experience of life from the human's point of view and confirming a mother's love for her son!

Pause Insight before the encounter:

- WJ could have followed his gut instinct and stayed home.
-

Pause insight after the encounter:

- Trust that God knows what he is doing even if I can't answer the "Why" questions.
-

Challenging Love

To give your whole heart is to love as if there is no tomorrow. It can be a risky yet rewarding task. Not every heart will be broken nor will it be cherished for its true worth. Most hearts are fragile and only expect what is desired from them (Love). In some cases, once you have given your all and you have been let down, it's hard to love again. Some of the purest love is supposed to come from your family. I have heard that true love has no boundaries. I think that is false, because every relationship has its boundaries. One or more of those boundaries may be violated at some point in time throughout that relationship, and then comes the true test. If that love can endure or weather the storm, it is then that the test or trials of life should strengthen your relationships instead of tearing them down. Within this next chapter you will read two accounts of love from two separate hearts. You will have the chance to first listen to my heart as it defines love, and then later on in the chapter you will hear Tiffany's heart as it tries to maintain. While these are two totally separate situations and encounters, there will be a similar outcome.

Love Doesn't Love Me Anymore

Genesis 37:4

"When his brothers saw that their father loved him more than any of them, they hated him and could not speak a kind word to him."

I think that at times God has a funny way of demonstrating His love for us. Sometimes in life we tend to build a wall around our heart as if it was the city of Jericho. From the perspective of the people of Jericho, it took a lifetime to complete the wall but only seconds for it to fall once the Israelites started shouting. Now with our emotional walls that surround our hearts, it's just the opposite. It feels as if it takes a lifetime to tear the wall down, but only seconds to build it. It is almost as if we have the wrong concept of life. In the book of Joshua 6:1 it is written, "Now the gates of Jericho were securely barred because of the Israelites. No one went out and no one came in."

Walls are designed to protect our innocence, love, insecurities, passions, and our hearts. Due to the anger that I had towards God and the abandonment by the world, I created my own Jericho. In my city, I would only allow certain people and family members near my heart at times, and even then I was evaluating them and trying to determine what their angle was on my life. It always seemed like my past relationships would fortify the gates to my heart like the people of Jericho, and my heart would not allow anyone in or out. I was constantly waiting for people to make one wrong move so that I could be alone in this city. My thought process was if I pushed everyone out of my city, then I wouldn't have to entertain the presence of love, hurt, rejection, and death. I felt as if the world had chewed me up and spit me out, and I was at my wit's end. I would constantly test the durability of my friendships in hopes of pushing them away. I figured that it was easier to quit love than to have it drop me again. I was ready to take on the world, like David took on Goliath.

Now, the story of King David that I am so used to hearing is about a future king who is about to take one of life's final exams, if I may say. You see, David had been studying for this test his whole life by being a shepherd. God isolated him as a shepherd so that man could not place the fear of bears and lions in his spirit. While caring for his sheep, David would learn to watch and evaluate his threat, develop the courage to attack, and conquer his enemies. So when it came time to take the final exam, David didn't hesitate. The bible was clear that David was a man after Gods own heart, but let me play devil's advocate for a second. What if it was just the opposite? Could David have been afraid of life and what lay ahead? Could he have been full of the "what ifs" in life? What if King David arrived too late to fight, and Goliath challenged someone else? Was there fear in his heart as he approached Goliath? Did David wonder at any time why he should die for his people or what have they done for him? Why did he choose five smooth rocks instead of just one? Could his concept of love, faith, and trust have been as fortified as my city?

I think that these questions could create the image of a natural being walking in imperfection. See, we tend to think that because he received God's blessing that nothing could have happened to David. History has shown us that King David was human and made lots of mistakes. To be honest the Bible is full of stories about people that have made mistakes. We are drawn in by those stories, because we are far from being perfect. It's the living Word, and it gives some of us comfort to know that someone else has made similar mistakes throughout life. There were times when God was in the process of punishing David, while David was punishing himself for his actions. There are times in our lives when we take on the spirit of David (punishing ourselves) when we can't control our surroundings.

For example, after WJ's death my mother punished herself until her death, because she felt like she should have done something. She could visualize the five nights when he came in the room and talked about life as if it was about to end. She felt like she let her son down and should have done more to prevent his death. I am sure she was thinking, "*Take me Lord and not my son!*" My mom tried but could never bounce back from her failure. There are times in all of our lives that we feel as if, "Had I been there to protect them, then they would still be here," or "Had I gotten there a couple of minutes earlier or stayed a little while longer, I could have helped." Seeds of darkness will be planted in the absence of your heroic efforts.

Right after my mom died, I could never understand why I did not matter enough for her to live for me instead of dying for him. I could never understand my mother's pain, because we were on different levels in life. She was 46 and her life was ending whereas, I was 19 and my life had only begun. Well, she took the road of drinking to fill the void in her heart. Every rising of the sun always brought the pain again. Everyone has a way of dealing with the hurt in his or her life. I needed companionship. I would go into relationships with girls knowing that I was going to use them and wasn't going to let them into the walled city of my heart. In relationship after relationship I would find myself hoping to fill my void, but I always felt empty once they left. I always felt the need to be in someone's company and was always afraid to be alone. I was in search of love in all of the wrong places. I was looking horizontally instead of vertically.

I have a friend, who through her life experiences, took on the spirit of David. Tiffany is an amazing girl who grew up in the Midwest. She had a pretty normal life with amazing parents. At times she would grab life by the horns and live on the edge. She would do things that most kids would do when they are trying to find their identity in the world. Follow this journey through her eyes.

When I was about thirteen years old, I started making bad decisions. My cousin and I thought it was fun to meet people in online chat rooms. Sometimes we would even meet them in person. All of our friends were way older than us, so we learned about the party world really early. We were already drinking and partying with the best of them when we were barely teenagers. It wasn't as if anyone knew though. Our parents were oblivious.

At least, they were until the year I turned 15. One day in April, my cousin, my sister, and I went "shopping." The only problem was we didn't use money to purchase the items we took from Target that day. I remember the officer who arrested us saying that he felt sorry for whoever had to ride with my dad. Of course I was the one that rode with him. It was the most uncomfortable ride of my life. It was never my intention to hurt my parents. I never dreamed I would disappoint them so badly. Between the time, embarrassment, and cost of that one decision, my parents continued to stand behind my sister and me. They were there through all of it: court, the juvenile officer, fines and six months of probation.

Then on June 24th, our lives were altered forever. My sister and I agreed to spend the night at my aunt's house with our cousin. They lived in a two-bedroom grayish/tan color house with blue shutters. It had a fairly large living room that all of the girls agreed to sleep in. My aunt was letting a boy from the youth group stay over. Since there would be a person of the opposite sex attending this sleep over, my cousin decided to join the rest of us girls. She decided to give him rights to her room for the night so everyone would feel right at home. We all decided to stay up late watching a comedy movie. We were all sitting on the couch for the first part of the movie, and then my sister and cousin decided to fix a pallet on the floor in hopes of becoming a bit more comfortable. Well, as night gave way to the morning, everyone fell asleep except for me and the guy that spent the night. I have to admit that I thought he was cute and it seemed that we both had eyes for each other. Well, one thing led to another and we ended up in the empty bedroom. I realized that things were moving a little faster than I wanted them to be at that moment in time. My conscience started speaking to me saying, "This isn't right, STOP!" I repeated it out verbally, but in a soft tone that wouldn't wakeup everyone in the house up. He ignored it and kept pursuing his inner most desires. So I started repeating it over and over to him while trying to push him away. I started begging him to let me go, but he wouldn't! With tears flowing out of my eyes, helpless and over powered. I never thought that I would have found myself in this position. I laid there crying and focusing on the ceiling while repeatedly pleading my case. All I could think about was my family sitting in the next room and this is all my fault. I was screaming on the inside and crying uncontrollably on the outside. Why did I have to follow him into this room? What did I do to deserve this? Is this really happening? It took me a while to make the connection that I was raped that night!

The next morning, he left before anyone woke up. I felt numb. I didn't know if I should tell or not. After all, wasn't it my fault? I put myself in that situation. My sister and my cousin could tell something was really wrong. They riddled me with questions. At first I thought it would be better to tell them it was consensual. After all, it was better than all the negative attention that might come from telling the truth. I finally asked my sister if she would take me to see our youth pastor's wife. She opened the door and I asked her if I could talk to her. I started to cry as they continued to drill me about what happened; the truth came out. As the youth pastor's wife asked over and over "Did he rape you?" I decided to confess. That confession brought a lot of tears and shame on my part. One of the counselors from the youth group called a prayer line as the youth pastor's wife packed me up to take me home to my parents and tell them what had happened. I remember thinking on the drive that this was already a much bigger deal than I had wanted to make it.

When we got home, Marsha called my mom. My mom and my aunt came immediately. I was unable to speak, so Marsha told them what had happened. As they cried together, they decided that we needed to call the police. When the police came, they asked tons of questions and eventually found him and took him to jail. In the meantime, I had to go to the emergency room and humiliate myself even more by having them go over my entire body with a fine-toothed comb. No one could possibly know what it feels like to be violated and then hours later be violated again in the name of justice unless you have been through it. It was the worst experience of my life. They took pictures of my entire naked body, did a full exam, pulled hairs from everywhere, all while my family was sitting in the waiting room. I felt so embarrassed and ashamed. I didn't even want to face them when I came out of that room. When my dad tried to give me a hug, it was everything I could do not to shake him off. It wasn't because I was upset with him, but rather because I was hurting so badly and I just didn't want to be touched anymore, because every touch felt like a new violation.

I remember feeling so isolated, so lonely. Even when I was with my family and friends, I still felt like I was completely alone. I was an outcast. No one wanted to deal with or acknowledge what had happened to me, and I couldn't seem to relate to anyone anymore. Then on July 4th, I realized that something really had changed with my family. I was sitting by myself the whole night, since my cousin had gone to a friend's house, and when I did go near my family, my grandpa said something really mean that hurt so badly I had to cry. When we went home, I told my mom that the family was acting really weird and asked if she knew why. She didn't at that moment, but it wasn't long until we would.

A few days later, my grandpa called my dad and said that we all needed to get together and talk. My dad agreed, knowing that this had been difficult for the whole family. When we got to their house, I found out that my cousin had told my aunt about the internet chat rooms, the people we had met, the partying we had done, and the family had decided to blame it all on me. Not only that, but because of my prior actions, they had decided that I was lying about the rape. They weren't willing to listen to anything I had to say about it. They had made up their minds that I was a liar and a troublemaker.

My dad told them not to speak to me that way and took me home. It has been 10 years now and they still don't talk to each other because of that one event. I still struggle with feeling like it is my fault that my dad lost his whole family. My parents were harassed for years because of that decision. My aunt would yell out car windows at my mom when she saw her in town, and my grandpa said horrible things to my dad. I remember my grandpa leaving a message on our answering machine, stating that my sisters and I were not welcome at his house anymore. My father looked at us and made sure we knew that he would stand behind us, no matter what, as he turned his back on the family he had grown up with to protect the family he had created. That was the most alone I had ever felt. Not only had my body been violated, but the people I trusted to stand behind me as protectors, as family, had turned their backs on me. People I had spent my entire life with rejected and abandoned me when I needed them the most.

They say that when a woman is raped, she tends to either draw into herself by avoiding sex and relationships altogether, or forget her own value and become promiscuous. The state appointed a counselor to ensure that I could heal from the trauma. The only problem was, that counselor had some bad advice. He told me that it was my right to use and abuse people until I felt like I had healed from the abuse I endured that night.

I took him at his word. I became the promiscuous damaged girl, looking for love anywhere I could find it and trying to find value in myself, while keeping my emotional distance from anyone of the opposite sex. I continued to try to appease the pain of what had happened by using people rather than actually dealing with the underlying emotions.

Then, in 2007, my grandmother found out that she had cancer. I was devastated. I knew that we had to make things right before she passed on. I called their house one day to see if there was any way I could visit her. Grandma told me that she would have to ask Grandpa. Grandpa grabbed the phone and started yelling at me, making it very clear how unwelcome I was, and then he hung up the phone.

I was so broken. I knew my dad wouldn't get to see his mom before she died if this wasn't resolved. However, when

I told him how I felt that it was my fault he didn't have his family he just hugged me and told me to never feel that way.

Grandma died in June. I can recall sitting at the funeral and feeling so out of place. It should have been a time when family came together to comfort one another, and instead, it felt as if the wedge was driven even deeper between us.

I think the most difficult thing in a situation like this is learning to forgive. It's not only the person who committed the crime. I had to figure out how to forgive my family for abandoning me. That was more painful than the rape itself in so many ways, and I am still learning to forgive myself. I put myself in a situation that was easily volatile, and I still blame myself for it on occasion. I know it isn't my fault, but it takes daily reminding still to believe that. I have heard that forgiveness is a choice that you make every day, and some days I just don't feel like reliving it enough to forgive myself.

Although Tiffany has had a very rough life, God has shined his light in her life and allowed her to see that her testimony will help others heal. In Geneses 50:20 after Joseph's family mistreated him, he said, "You intended to harm me, but God intended it for good to accomplish what is now being done, the saving of many lives."

God has allowed Tiffany's weakness to become her strength! The very issue that changed her perspective about life, bruised her spirit of trust with men, and devoured her happiness is now her gift to life. The situation that sent her into a tail spin and made her feel so dirty and ashamed is her voice and inspiration to all of the other hurt, abused, and silent voices out there! She helps convey knowledge to young men that may have rage similar to that of her aggressor that NO means NO and to pause and think, which is the central concept of this book.

In the beginning of this chapter, I talked about how God sometimes has a funny way of demonstrating His love to us, and how circumstances at times force us to build walls. One may ask, "Why did the people of Jericho build this wall, and what were they trying to hide or protect?" I would say that they experienced life only in the physical form instead of walking in the true spiritual form. I think that due to the psychological wars they were fighting with their enemies and themselves, that they first built an emotional wall. Once they were being attacked with verbal threats as well as by relentless armies, they started to seek a more promising refuge behind the physical wall. Jericho figured that if they built this wall high enough, no man could get over it and wide enough that no man could go around it. It will be humanly impossible for anyone to penetrate Jericho's city on an emotional or physical level. I think that we can all relate to this story at some point in our lives. As humans, our survival skills kick in, and we try to do things on our own. We feel as though we don't need God and our man-made walls will protect us physically and emotionally.

Personally, I figured that if I isolated myself physically from the world and shut down emotionally, I was safe. I felt like my personal city was human proof! If I had to guess, I would say that Tiffany's personal city was human proof, also. Needless to say, just like in the city of Jericho, God sent someone into our lives to tear down our walls. He took over our personal cities and has full control over our lives. God has always had the keys to our cities. We were right about the fact that once our walls went up, it was humanly impossible for man to penetrate our cities, but we left out one of the most important factors- "The God Factor!" God had to press pause in our lives, allowing the destruction of our physical and emotional walls so we could surrender and rise again in HIS name within his Spiritual wall!

Pause Insight before the encounter:

- Tiffany should have screamed and woke someone up.
-

Pause insight after the encounter:

- Tiffany should not have kept all of the blame inside of her body for all of these years.
-

Understanding My Reality

In life we are taught as kids that the world is our playground and the sky is our limit. I can remember being asked as a kid, "What do you want to be when you grow up?" and "What do you want in life?" My answers were always similar to all the other kids' answers, "The President, a doctor, or a lawyer." Now there's nothing wrong with those careers, because we need all of those people in the world. A world without those three would be a world filled with chaos, sickness, and evil. Okay, well maybe it would be ten times worse than that which we experience today. I mean we are experiencing the end times, right? Well, the three careers above help to provide world order, healing, and justice. It wasn't until I became an adult and I prayed for my purpose that God revealed it to me. He helped show me that I could accomplish everything on my list in life and still harbor brokenness deep within. He allowed me to see that my purpose was His calling, and my dreams would transpire through His visions.

I would later learn through His Word that there was a career that I overlooked. For a kid it would be less desirable because it doesn't have all of the fortune and fame displayed in the media. It is the only career where HE is your mentor and will teach you, guide you, and answer all of your questions until the day that you die. He leads by example and His resume should simply say, "Over qualified, yet under estimated." There was a retirement/promotion party that He gave for Himself and His twelve disciples. HE was going back to Creator status but they were being promoted to be presidents, doctors, lawyers, and authors. At this party He provided a toast and they broke bread and drank from His cup before He announced His surprise gift to everyone. He advised them that they would be receiving the Advocate, the Holy Spirit, shortly after His promotion. He said that once He gets in His new office, He would ask His Father to provide this Gift in His name. This Gift would accompany the twelve disciples to go out into the world and help to provide/guide people within the realm of world order, healing, and justice. With the understanding that the world would one day make an author out of me, He allowed me to see the intricate details within a couple people's lives and present them to the world.

The Reality of it All

Colossians 2:17

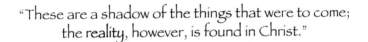

"These are a shadow of the things that were to come; the reality, however, is found in Christ."

At times it was really hard for me to look at life and see all of the blessings that were bestowed upon my life. There were days when I would look in the mirror and be a stranger to the person who was staring back at me. I would smile on the outside, but I was in complete disarray on the inside. I can remember walking in the park on a warm summer day, and as the wind danced with the kites in the sky, it would grace me with its presence from time to time. I can recall stopping to sit on a bench as my legs grew tired from the sun stealing my energy. As I sat next to the pond where the ducks were practicing their takeoffs and landings, I started to people watch. Not in the sense of being a creepy guy but in the sense of being on the outside looking in. See, when we look at life from this perspective, it's like we are the artist and they are the blank canvas, and we can paint any picture of their lives that we want. We can create any scenario that we want because the beauty of it all lies in the eye of the beholder. Well, as my eyes swept from my left to my right, there was a couple getting ready to walk by, and I remember thinking that I wished I was that guy. From my point of view they were a young couple and looked as if they were so in love. It almost seemed as if they only knew of "the concept of life and love" as being safe– as each other's best friends with their lives joined at the hip. Only that moment in time mattered to them, because in their minds, they were the only two in the park. It was almost like I was watching a movie, because they looked as if they were in perfect harmony as they moved gracefully out of my view. As I got ready to sign my name on the bottom of that portrait, because it was completed when they walked out of my view, my normal reality started to flood my thoughts as I searched for another canvas. The next portrait that walked into my view was a family, and I remember looking at the little toddler thinking that it would be nice to have a clean memory slate again. To have no recollection or the knowledge that a boo-boo or an ouchie could lead to my first encounter of pain. Hurt, pain, and fear have no boundaries, friends, or acts of being prejudice, but at some point will violate everyone and everything as it brushes through our lives. Sometimes life has a way of challenging our morals and beliefs, making us react differently. Again, as they walked out of my sight, my mind was flooded with my day-to-day reality that I am not them, and my hurt and pain still existed in my heart.

The reason I have told you about that day in the park is so that you see that at times we all want to find happiness in others or we want to, at times, be someone else. Sometimes, we look at others overlooking their problems, hurt, and pain so that we can envy them. It was easy for me when I was going through the storm to focus on the good in others and only see the bad inside of me. I want to encourage you and tell you that those storms don't last long, and there is always someone waiting on the other side for you. In Psalms 30:5, King David had just come out of his storm and realized that God still loved him even though he didn't deserve it. The second half of verse five says, "Weeping may endure for a night, but joy cometh in the morning." In that verse God is telling me that I will have some trials and tribulations in my life, and I will scream about them from the mountaintops as my testimony to help others get through their storms.

God allowed me to cross paths with a girl who was truly an angel in my eyes and she began to bless me by telling me about her trials and tribulations. As she told me this story, I could see that she was in the midst of a storm and that God had his loving arms around her. So I am going to let her tell this from her point of view.

My name is Anna and here is my story. Looking back, I regret the day when I made the decision to leave my parent's house early to find my independence in life. I felt as though I rushed it instead of embracing it. My parents were trying to preserve my innocence of life, love, hope, and the pure relationship that I had with my Heavenly Father. They weren't being over-protective. They were trying to guide me through life because they knew how difficult life is. My mother, as a pastor, knows all too well what the devil's plans are. John 10:10 states, "The thief comes only to steal and kill and destroy; I have come that they may have life, and have it to the fullest." I wish I had truly understood the depth and power of that verse as a teen.

1 Peter 5:8-11 teaches us, "Be alert and of sober mind. Your enemy, the devil, prowls around like a roaring lion looking for someone to devour. Resist him, standing firm in the faith, because you know that the family of believers throughout the world is undergoing the same kind of sufferings. And the God of all grace, who called you to his eternal glory in Christ, after you have suffered a little while, will himself restore you and make you strong, firm and steadfast. To Him be the power forever and ever. Amen." Little did I know that this verse would become reality in my life!

At 18-years-old, I was attending community college and trying to figure out what I was going to do with the rest of my life. On our last day of vacation, I noticed a Memorial Day service on TV. Seeing the Army band come marching down the road mesmerized me. I recall saying to my mom, "That would be fun to do." My mom's response was, "Well, as directionless as your life is right now maybe it would be the best thing for you." In my mind I was referring to marching in a band as I had been a musician most of my school career. To her, this was an opportunity to get my life on track.

I had just received a letter of academic probation from college, thus finding out that as a freshman I wasn't compatible with college. As I continued to search for direction, I took her sarcastic advice. I joined the Army in February of 2003. Little did I know that I would never be prepared for what my future had to offer me! No Bible lesson, no Sunday school song, nor guidance from mom and dad could prepare me for what was about to happen to me in the next six years of my life. The first nine weeks of basic training were tough, but I endured. During those nine weeks, the Army had taught me the true definition of respect. I realized that I had been disrespectful to my parents. God was heavy on my heart and had me call my parents and ask them for their forgiveness. Being the gracious, loving parents and true servants of God that they were, they forgave me.

As my career steadily progressed for the first time, I realized what it meant to be an adult and to take on real responsibility. I received word that I was about to get deployed to Iraq. Our country had just invaded Iraq and we were going to set up permanent communications in Iraq for the soldiers that had been there during the invasion.

My boyfriend of four months was being deployed with me to Iraq. He wasn't a Christian and to be honest, I hadn't been acting like one either. My heart was being neglected. I was ignoring God's voice. Once I made it to Iraq, I figured that since I was going to be here a full year, I needed to get involved with church. I joined the chapel services as a part of the praise and worship team. I never completely turned my back on God, but I would soon have my faith tested. I have seen and experienced things that no one should ever have to experience.

Early in the deployment, we were all on our base trying to stay cool. The temperature on that day was between 115 and 130 degrees. It was a day just like any other day in Iraq where I did my normal daily communication activities. All of a sudden the mundane humming of the generators was shattered by the sounds of the enemy fire ripping through our base camp. BOOM! The first one startled me because this couldn't be happening again. See, we had been under fire for nine months straight and every day the attack seemed different. Some of us started running to take cover and others ran to engage with the hostiles. Suddenly, everything slowed down in my mind. My destination was about 30 yards from the truck I had been sitting in all day. With every explosion of a mortar, my heart would skip a beat; I took a deep breath not knowing if it would be my last. I was closing in on the 30 yards as fast as I could, but it felt like I was running in slow motion. As I ran for the hard side building I could hear the mortars whistling and knew danger was right behind me. The ringing sound in my ears was muffled by the screams of the wounded and the shouting of my fellow soldiers telling everyone to take cover. I paused for a moment just inside the building, standing behind a wall of glass, watching the terror unfold on the other side of the compound wall from where I worked daily. My world felt like it was at a standstill. The steady *ring of my eardrums crossed paths with an eerie silence. I glared at the tile floor in the "safe" building and it was at that moment I blacked out. A dark cloud had settled on the camp that day, and it would follow all of us for the rest of our lives. Seven people lost their lives during that attack. Seven mothers and fathers would be receiving a knock on the door by an officer and Chaplin to learn their children/ loved ones would not be coming back home alive. Seven American flags would be given to seven American families during the twenty-one-gun salute.*

As I came out of my blackout, I found myself in our Brigade Command Sergeant Major's office trying to piece together what had just happened. Could the very same God that I have known my whole life allow such a thing to happen? How could I hold firmly to the concept of a loving God when I had just seen my fellow soldiers hit by enemy fire near me? Where was He when I needed Him the most? Why do I feel so much hurt and pain, and will it ever go away? "Are you angry with me Father? Why won't you answer me!?!"

My faith was being tested. "God I don't understand, I grew up in your church my whole life, was that not enough? It wasn't until I became an adult that I realized that You were not just a building or a place that I went to on Sundays. It took me a while to realize that You are alive, and I could talk to You every day, and have a personal relationship with You; a relationship that would change my life."

God knows that I have practically lived at church my whole life starting the Sunday after I was born. My family and I have always been the first ones there and the last ones to leave. I was not a stranger to the Good Book. I have read the Bible from cover to cover. I was a part of every group that a kid could join at the church while growing up. I was involved in every Christmas play up until I graduated from 6th grade. "God! You are no stranger in my life."

At this point in my life, I adopted two very different versions of myself: There was the Anna before I enlisted into the military and the one after. The Anna before was directionless and clueless about life (but aren't all teenagers?). I have to admit that back then I was happy and full of life, and I was eager to see what was around the next corner!

The other version of Anna has a different perspective on life. The first day of my enlisting into the military, I started a transformation that I will never be able to reverse. I became a super hero in so many aspects. Once I put on the uniform, I would no longer be a civilian. I looked different, I walked different, and I talked different. I am Army Strong. From day one I was taught how to strengthen my mind, body, and soul. I was taught that real super heroes have no weaknesses and show no pain. You are to only smile when asked, do what you are told, and not to think but react because that's what our superiors are for. You are taught that emotions are tools of the incompetent and no super hero uses them. If we were to be honest, all of our fictional heroes are built and designed around our military. They have all of those characteristics and more when they are in their uniforms and seem to be balanced citizens when back in their civilian clothes. I will let you in on a little secret... Normal does not exist once you put on the uniform. I have seen, done, and heard things that I wish I had never been a part of. I have done things that I can't take back.

At times I hate being a soldier, but I love my country. Do you see now that I have all of the characteristics of a super hero? There were even times when Clark Kent didn't want to be Superman. Here is something you may not know about being a super hero. We all have our own weaknesses. Superman's weakness is the green kryptonite that is always stored in some remote cave on another planet. Well, my weaknesses are the demons that I have created that follow me throughout life. I have them stored in a dark closet in a remote place within my mind, but sometimes they escape and my PTSD (Post Traumatic Stress Disorder) takes over my body. I have nightmares, headaches, and I can only see the evil in the world at times. I am afraid to sleep and jump when I am awakened. So being looked at as a super hero isn't so bad if you can carry the burdens of the world. I hold onto 2 Timothy 2:4 that says, "No one serving as a soldier gets entangled in civilian affairs, but rather tries to please his commanding officer." My God and my parents always told me to respect those in authority over me. As a soldier, this verse took on a whole new meaning. God is and will always be my commanding officer. (HOOAH!)

Anna's story is an amazing story because just like Anna, when you ask God a question be prepared for the answer. The attack that she told us about earlier was during her first of two tours in Iraq a little over 8 years ago, and it still haunts her today. As she prepares to leave for her third tour, I ask that you pray for her because she has since realized that God was all around her that day keeping the remaining soldiers safe. You see God is the creator of super heroes, and it is written in Hebrews 13:8, "Jesus Christ is the same yesterday, today and forever." And in Psalms 55:22 it is written, "Cast your cares on the Lord and He will sustain you; He will never let the righteous be shaken." First, God wants to take care of your yesterdays through your repentance and his forgiveness. Secondly, He wants to take care of your today by building a hedge of protection around you keeping you clothed in his grace and mercy. Lastly, He wants to go before you and fight your battles in life just like He did with the Israelites while leading them into the Promised Land.

I bet that you would agree with me when I say, "God used a special kind of mold when He created Anna and the rest of our super heroes!" We understand that through our childhood memories, every village has a hero and every hero has an arch nemesis waiting to try and take over! I thank God that through our dedication, hard work, and persistence the good guys always prevail. So let us tip our hats off to them and the service that they have provided for our country!

I truly believe deep down in my heart that God needed seven more angels in heaven on that day, and I know that Anna was grateful to have served with angels of that caliber!

Pause Insight before the encounter:

- Anna could have paused and listened to her parents instead of rushing out into the world to find her independence.
-

Pause insight after the encounter:

- Instead of focusing on the loss that occurred during the attack and allowing that memory to control her, Anna could recognize God's presence and protection that was with her and the rest of the soldiers who survived that day and let that memory inspire her to continue to seek God's will for her life.
-

Entering the Gray Area

Within this next chapter I will be discussing the gray areas in life. I feel as though Christians are trending towards settling in the worldly ways. I know that the older generations of the Christians are stepping down, and we have a new front emerging. The traditional style of preaching and reaching the youth is changing, because they are more geared towards the technology that is surrounding them. I would say that their attention span is shorter due to the way our social media has been conditioning them. Everything has to be short, sweet, and to the point. Anything outside of about 25 minutes is crossing over into the youths' Instagram, Twitter, Facebook and texting. We are in a society where we have to be politically correct and don't want to offend anyone. It has gotten to the point where instead of everyone listening to what God is feeding the shepherd, now some of the shepherds are ignoring God's message and are listening to what the sheep are feeding them.

Well, I believe that the Bible is very black and white when it comes to worldly and moral issues. It is our human nature to try and test our boundaries, to create the desire to feel good, and fix our own problems. When we step out into this territory we are walking into our gray areas.

Now, please allow your mind to open for a brief moment as we walk into this next chapter. In this chapter, I will refer to your "journey" as in life itself or being alive. I will refer to your "destiny" as in Heaven, or after the human body has died. Finally, whenever you see the word, Father, I am referring to God or our Heavenly Father. So, now let us enter into the next chapter.

Gray areas

Galatians 1:7

"Which is really no gospel at all. Evidently some people are throwing you into confusion and are trying to pervert the gospel of Christ"

One morning, I was driving to Atlanta from Chicago for a vacation. I started my journey out of Chicago at 4:00 a.m. to beat the morning traffic. I realized that I was following a car going east on Interstate 80 with speeds up to 75 miles per hour. Since the speed limit was 65, there was no need to panic just yet, because we were the only two cars on the road. Plus, there were at least three car lengths between our cars. I am not a morning person so my brain was still asleep at this time in the morning. Let's be honest, even our feathered alarm clocks were still in their coops at that time in the morning.

Suddenly, the car in front of me vanished and before my mind could realize what happened, I had a collision with a heavy blanket of fog. My heart dropped into my stomach as my eyes searched fruitlessly trying to adjust to the fog! There was a 10-foot visibility range, and I wasn't sure of the location of the first car! My first thoughts were: Did I just enter a realm of heaven? Please God not like this, dying alone in a car wreck! In the midst of my panic and rage growing as deep and wide as my adversary, a familiar calmness took over my body. I now know that God was about to save me like he has countless times before. Then my eyes settled on my cell phone and I could see the road on my phone's GPS. Since it was an 11-hour trip, I had entered the address, so I would not get lost on my journey. I never thought that particular action would save my life. I can recall thanking God for his creation of advanced technologies on that morning! As I slowed down, I looked at my phone and I could see that the road was still straight. Traveling within this gray area gave me an understanding that God and I would become really close during the next ten miles of my navigation through this valley. As I clenched my steering wheel, I sat up in my seat, and began to pray. I felt like David in Psalms 23:4, "Yea, though I walk through the valley of the shadow of death, I will fear no evil: for thou are with me; thy rod and thy staff they comfort me." That verse has spoken wonders into my life during my struggles. Some of you are thinking, "It was just fog, Tarrance, calm down!" Well, I think it was a signal for me to enter into God's kingdom and have some one-on-one time with Him. I think that God creates little pockets throughout our days for us to give Him our time.

When I am scared, I give Him my time, or when I have done something wrong, I repent during that time. If you haven't caught on yet, His rod and staff was my GPS system on that morning. It was the rod and staff that lead me out of my troubles. One thing that I have realized during my years of living on this earth is that everyone encounters gray areas at some point. Some may not be as obvious as my fog story mentioned above. You may experience it on a moral level instead of a physical one. According to the Free Dictionary by Farlex – gray area is defined as an intermediate area; a topic that is not clearly one thing or the other. As I reflect on this definition and my life, there have been a lot of gray areas in my past. I am not perfect and I would, at times, alter my reasoning – giving justification for my actions – hence creating gray areas.

For example, most people claim to view life from a black and white perspective. I am not talking about from a race standpoint, but from a moral point of view. Everyone has that friend asking for advice because they are struggling with a moral issue in life. If you do not have that friend, chances are you may be the person we are talking about in this chapter. In that profound moment in time we can give very black and white instructions on what to do to resolve their issue. It states in Proverbs 28:5 "Evildoers do not understand what is right, but those who seek the Lord understand it fully." It almost feels like God can speak the remedy for their confusion into our hearts. I am only speaking from experience here in this chapter. I have been on both sides of this fence and, at times, it's a real struggle. I have always been able to tell others how to get out of their messes and fix their problems, because I was a spectator.

The moment I am walking through the valley of the shadow of death, my gray areas emerge. These gray areas are designed by our minds to justify our actions at that time. Now what's interesting is, since every human is considered to be unique, no two gray areas will be the exact same. A prime example would be with identical twins. They look exactly the same, but they are different people. Most twins will walk through life as one but will have two separate views on life. At times, twins rely on each other more than their own mother. Even though you may not see the physical, mental, or emotional difference at first, just be patient and it will emerge. Once you pull out the magnifying glass and examine their lives, not only will you find the differences but you will also find the gray areas between them.

You can know a person your whole life and never find the boundary lines of their gray areas until that time occurs!

Life revolves around choices that we make on a day-to-day basis. The choices we make help mold us into the people that we are evolving into today. Not every choice will compliment your future and shine on your past, but I hope that they help guide you through your gray areas. As Christians we don't have gray areas right? (*smile*) I mean the Bible gives us clear instructions on what to do in life based on the successes and failures of the previous generations. We all know that Moses came from a broken family and, against all odds, he would be considered to have lived a very successful life. There is a whole book about him in Exodus explaining his journey and encounters with God. Then, in the book of Genesis, we learn about Adam and Eve and how sin was birthed. It talks about how Eve coaxed Adam into eating the fruit against God's will. That story provides truth that the devil will try to come between God and man or man and woman to create division or betrayal. Lastly, in the book of Luke, chapter 22, verses one through five, it talks about how Judas, one of Jesus's disciples, made the decision to embrace his gray areas in life for 30 pieces of silver. The referenced people that were mentioned earlier-Moses, Adam and Eve, and Judas- have been freed from this world for some time now, but their stories are being re-lived at this very moment.

I don't believe that it's ever God's will for us to make the wrong decision when we are confronted with a gray area, but I do believe that when we do, He can redeem us from that decision or choice and then use our testimony to sway others from making the same errors.

God has blessed me with the opportunity of crossing paths with the family in this next section. Throughout their heartaches and pain in life, they wanted to bless the world with their testimony. While interviewing the family, I felt lead by God to tell the story through the eyes of one of their daughters, a very special young lady. I pray that her story touches your heart just as much as it has touched my heart.

My name is Harmony, and here is my story. I hear that life is a journey you take to make it to your destiny. Growing up, I had one older brother and two older sisters. My grandparents are preachers, and my mom and dad grew up under their teachings. Reggie, my dad, decided to become a deacon in the church in search of a closer walk with God on every level in life. Liberty, my mom, also works in the church as an accountant for my grandfather. I was told that she would lie in her bed countless numbers of hours with her eyes closed, at times with Reggie's head pressed against her belly listening. They were listening to my heartbeat as our heartbeats would form a rhythm of life. I was told that's how I received my name Harmony; our hearts would beat with one accord. I really don't have a whole lot of time to tell you this story, so you will have to pay close attention.

I can recall being in my mom's belly, and I could feel my brother and sisters touch as they would talk about life. I would push and kick back, but they couldn't feel my attempts, because I was so small at that time. One day, I overheard my Father and mother talking about how I almost didn't make it.

The story goes something like this. My mom and dad have been married for eight years now and have a really strong Christian foundation. My brother and sisters are in church every Wednesday and Sunday. I was told by my Father that my mom has issues with her body, and she was advised by the doctor that every childbirth would be risky and she would progressively get worse. Plus, if she continues getting pregnant, she will soon be birthing funerals. So, with me getting the short end of the stick, I was chosen to be the fourth child. Go figure, right? Well, I was told that John (the oldest) was the first miracle baby because he was supposed to have been born with brain problems. I was later told that Judy (my oldest sister) had complications during her birth as well and Justice (my sister before me) had heart problems and may not survive.

Well, my family prayed until they had prayed her through her birth, and she is still doing great. God is a loving GOD who loves His children. It states in Luke 18:15-17, "People were also bringing babies to Jesus for him to place his hands on them. When the disciples saw this, they rebuked them, but Jesus called the children to him and said, 'Let the little children come to me, and do not hinder them, for the kingdom of God belongs to such as these. Truly, I tell you, anyone who will not receive the kingdom of God like a little child will never enter it.'" It clearly states that God loves every child and each child is as important to Him as His first. Well inside of Heaven, God the Father carefully hand picks each and every one of the kids to enter life or this journey. Earlier I mentioned that within Luke, God the Son was laying His hands on the children and blessing them while they are on their journey. God the Holy Spirit helps to guide, protect, and constantly remind them that He loves them. I realized later that God put His special blessings on my birth.

As I kept listening, my mother talked to my Father about how she was so afraid that I would have life-threatening injuries if she proceeded with this pregnancy, how life is not fair that she has this illness and suffers daily and is now faced with giving birth to a life that may suffer also. At one point, my life was in the hands of the council (my mom, dad, and the doctors). My parents discussed all of the possibilities of my outcome. They even approached my grandparents with their ideas and were advised to pray and ask for guidance from God. It was discussed how she was harboring the idea of an abortion. Well, since I am only in the pre-stages of my journey I have my whole life ahead of me to learn life's lessons. I have heard that life evolves from love. To be honest, if life is love than I can't wait to live.

I think that my mom was in search of answers that were already staring her in the face. My story seems to have a lot of similarities to that of Jesus' and how His life was up before a council to choose his fate. Well, the story doesn't stop there. Liberty started talking about this one particular time they went to the doctor's office for a check-up. They performed an ultrasound to see how I was doing, and they could see that I had developed heart issues, and they thought I may not survive. I wasn't worried because, if my sister Justice could make it, than I could make it, too. As they were listening to my heart beat, I could tell that something was wrong. My heart beat was fine but my mom's heart beat was out of control for some reason. I felt my sense of joy turn into sadness. I could hear Reggie crying in the room saying, "No!" and I could hear Liberty saying, "She was not able to bear the thought of it!" Reggie then pressed his body up against ours, and I could hear teardrops and footsteps leading out of the room. As our hearts raced, I waited anxiously for the next sound of comfort. Ahhhhh!! At last, I felt my mom's touch as she began to rub her belly in a circular motion. Ahh, the nurturing feeling that I have been waiting for. Wait! Why is she still crying? What is all of the movement out there? OUCH! What is this, and why am I beginning to feel this pain in my body. IT HURTS SO BAD!! Liberty, I mean Mama, please answer me! Please close your eyes and just listen! Listen to the Harmony of your body! All of a sudden I could hear my mother scream, "NO! I can't do this!" and a soft voice replied, "Just take a deep breath and calm down. This part of the childbirth is normal." I can hear my mom say, "But I have changed my mind." Again, the soft voice replied, "I am sorry, Liberty, it is too late now. We passed the point of no return when you took the medicine."

Due to the rapid increase of pain in my body, I began to fight. I started kicking, pushing, screaming, but nothing prepared me for what was about to happen! Liberty then cried out, "I have made a mistake, and God will never forgive me!"

My Father told me that Judas also tried to give the 30 pieces of silver back to the council, but it was too late and things were already set in motion!

Just in case you have forgotten my name, it was Harmony. I am the fourth child of my parents.

Just like Moses, I had an encounter with God. My Father sat me on His knee and told me a story about my journey in life that lead me to my destiny. He told me that just like Adam and Eve, my parents were told not to do something, and they ignored the warnings. My Father talked about how his fallen angel took advantage of Liberty's heart. He spoke of how the doctors gave Liberty the same exact news that my mom was given with her previous kids; that they would not survive, but she decided to turn and walk into her gray areas instead of seeing His truth. They told her that I had a bad heart and probably wouldn't survive this birth. That she would probably be giving birth to a funeral.

My Father talked about all the times that Liberty prayed asking for an answer and He would send John, Judy, and Justice into the room as a reflection of His truth, faithfulness and an answer to her prayers. The only problem was Liberty didn't see it from that point of view! To her, they were only a disruption to her silence and peace of mind as she sat and waited for God's reply. God then told me that due to the gray areas in Liberty's life, she talked to Reggie and convinced him that it was the right thing to do and that everything would be ok! Does that story sound familiar?

Yes, I am still comparing my journey to the life of Adam and Eve. As my Father tells this next part of the story to me He starts to cry. He takes His hand and lifts up my chin and looks straight into my hazel brown eyes and says, "My Son was betrayed with a kiss, and you my child by a hug given from Reggie to Liberty. He then says, "The kiss that He received was to show that He was the chosen one. Now the hug that was given by Reggie to Liberty was to show his confirmation of her/their decision."

If you haven't figured it out yet, the hospital that we visited on that day was an abortion clinic. I was born that day into my destiny and not my journey. Due to the advancement of technology in the world, my parents were able to seal my fate before my journey ever began. The very thing that my parents were trying to prevent (birthing a funeral) is the very thing that took place but in the worst possible way. I felt like the lady with the issue of blood that was cured of her illness just by touching the hem of Jesus' garment. I felt if I could have touched the hem of this life, then a miracle would have been performed. My Father loves fixing the broken and making them whole again.

I asked my Father to send an angel to Liberty and let her know that I forgive her and to please forgive her sins. He told me that it has already been taken care of. He also told me not to worry because she will always remember me as her fourth child and that she will keep track of my birthday until the day she joins us. Now, I can't wait until our destinies collide so that I can hug, kiss, and tell her how much I love her! My Father told me that my sacrifice will almost divide this family, but my story will bring life to the world. My Father allowed me to see Reggie sitting in the waiting room with his head down and fingers clasped together, so I asked my Father to send another angel to touch Reggie's heart and to let him know that I forgive him, also, and to remind him that when things get too heavy for him, he should close his eyes and listen to the rhythm of our heartbeats. I could tell by his body movements and the drops of water on the floor that he was crying, debating, and pleading for my life. Reggie, please understand that since my Father is love, that I am loved.

I think that was a powerful story about Harmony. I chose to tell this story from her point of view to give all of the babies who have been aborted a voice, because their fate was sealed before their journey started. I feel that God also wants us to realize that we should give every child a journey before their destiny. God says in Genesis 1:27-28 "So God created mankind in his own image, in the image of God he created them; male and female he created them. God blessed them and said to them, 'Be fruitful and increase in number; fill the earth and subdue it. Rule over the fish in the sea and the birds in the sky and over every living creature that moves on the ground.'" I guess that, at times, in our journey we tend to lose focus in our gray areas in life and focus on the underlined word above. Yes, we were made in His image, but we tend to make God-like decisions and, to let the truth be told, that is what has gotten us in the predicament that we are in today! Ever since sin was birthed into the world, we have been trying to draw closer to Him like we once were. John 14:6 states, "Jesus is the way, the truth and the light". It states in John10:10 that "He came so that we may have life, and life more abundantly." There are a lot of people in the world who have taken on the spirits of Liberty and Reggie to have an abortion in the midst of their gray areas. If you are one of them, then I just want you to know that God truly loves all of his children, including you!

I will end this chapter with the audible sound pouring from Reggie's heart. "*As I sat in the waiting room of the abortion clinic, fingers clasped together, a million and one things racing through my mind – I couldn't help but to repeat over and over in my head, "This isn't right, this isn't right, this isn't right, this isn't right..." My wife sat next to me with a sorrowful look on her face. You could tell she was torn mentally and emotionally. What a decision to make! Do I take the chance and have a potentially still-born baby? Or do we have an abortion. Who wants to take that multiple-choice test? No one!*

I recall my father-in-law calling to check up on us right before we were called to the back of the clinic to finalize our decision. I could hear him asking my wife, "How is Reggie holding up?" And as soon as she said, "Not good," I just broke down crying. Not just tears streaming down my face, but an audible grown that could be heard by others in the waiting room. It was a legit cry. It was a grown man crying, with tears, noises, snot and the whole nine yards. Shortly after that my father-in-law began to pray over the phone and offer us some words of comfort. I still didn't feel right with the decision we were about to make. I gave my last plea and asked my wife to forget the whole thing and just head back on the highway. She said we had come too far and the decision was made. Right then and there, the most eerie, random thought popped into my head. It was as though my psyche sat beside me and asked a very real, very poignant question. He asked, "What are you going to tell your baby when you see her in Heaven? How are you going to explain this very moment?" The crying continued even more. After a few minutes had passed, I heard our name being called, and we headed to the back to make a decision that I will regret for the rest of my life!"

Pause Insight before the encounter:

- Always seek God's wisdom and shift through the details of your circumstances and God's answer may be staring you in the face.
-

Pause insight after the encounter:

- Realize that a decision of this magnitude will always affect someone in life. It will either affect your kids, spouse, family, and even yourself. Most of all, it will affect the life that was given to you by God.
-

Approaching My Angel

Angels have always intrigued me, ever since I was a little boy. In fact, some people say if a baby is staring at the ceiling and laughing it sees angels. The definition of an angel according to *The Free Dictionary* by Farlex is, "A typically benevolent celestial being that acts as an intermediary between Heaven and earth, especially in Christianity. A representation of such a being, especially in Christianity, conventionally is the image of a human figure with a halo and wings or a guardian spirit or guiding influence." In Luke 4:10 it is written: "He will command his angels concerning you to guard you carefully."

I think that we all view the angels as the good guys and the demons as the bad guys. Most of the baby Christians would say that the angels report to God and the demons report to the devil. What we have to understand is that Satan was once a good angel also. At one point, Lucifer was one of the most glorious of God's angels before he was cast out of the Heavens. In Job 2:1 it is written, "On another day the angels came to present themselves before the Lord, and Satan also came with them to present himself before him." Satan wanted to be equal to or greater than our God. Together with the other rebel angels they tried to take over heaven. One of God's toughest archangels, Michael, and the others protected the heavens and won the battle. So they cast Satan down into Hell where he resides and is in control.

Today, we flip a coin, with heads representing the good angels and tails representing the bad. It lands on heads, so I will discuss a couple of encounters with God's good angels that I have had the privilege to see or hear about. I understand that not everyone believes that angels exist or because they have not had an encounter, their minds cannot perceive the notion. In Matthew 19:26, Jesus looked at them and said, "With man this is impossible, but with God all things are possible." The awesome part about God is that he has no limitations. He can perform any miracle that he wants.

There are a lot of stories in the Bible where God's angels assisted or intervened in humans' lives. In the world there are countless accounts where they have performed what we call miracles in our lives. So, as I pray going into the next chapter, I just thank God for what He has done in my past, present, and future. I ask that He builds up a hedge of protection around me and let his angels protect the gateways into our lives. I ask these things in Jesus' name, and Amen!

My Angel

Hebrews 13:2

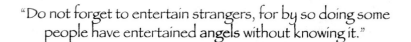

"Do not forget to entertain strangers, for by so doing some people have entertained angels without knowing it."

I can recall late one warm summer night in Springfield, Missouri a couple of friends had the great idea to go bridge jumping, and we all decided to go. As we approached the bridge I can remember thinking that this was a crazy idea. It seemed that everyone was eager to jump because it was a familiar thing for two people out of the four. We exited the car and walked hastily over to look off of the edge of the bridge. The soothing sounds of nature reassured me that everything would be ok. By using the moon's reflection on the water I could see that we were about four or five stories above the water. It seemed as if the water was silently moving through the riverbeds concealing its true depth and inner parts. Suddenly without warning, everyone stripped down to their swimming wear. Since this was my first time jumping off a perfectly good bridge, or any for that matter, I was still hesitant about doing it. Casey and Jen decided to prove to me that there was nothing to fear and climbed on the ledge in making preparations to jump. The onlookers started the countdown and off Casey went into the darkness. As I took in a deep breath searching in the lucent areas for any sign of hope, I saw her head emerge out of the water and cheers filled the air. Casey then shouted, "Be careful because I was barely able to touch the bottom! But you guys will be fine." Well, that sealed the deal on my short-lived adventure, especially since I wasn't a seasoned swimmer like the others. I mean, I can swim but only if my destination is in a close proximity.

John and I watched as the two girls continued to jump off the bridge a couple of times before I decided to walk down a grassy trail to the river side, leaving John on the bridge watching the view from the top. Once I made it down there I could remember looking up thinking, "Those girls are crazy!" I soon found myself admiring the view and skipping rocks in between jumps, whenever I could find a rock worthy of breaking my last record.

Casey screamed, "Look out below!" and jumped into the river, but now I saw it from a different view. As she swam to the shore she said, "I think I will climb up the bridge rails to the very top of the bridge and jump." My reaction to that statement was, "Please don't do that, because that is crazy!" and as she walked past me up the grassy trail she said, "Oh it will be fine, Tarrance! Just live a little!" Once Casey made it to the top of the bridge, I noticed that she approached John. I figured that she was trying to convince him that he needed to stop being a chicken and jump with her. Apparently what she said worked, because he placed the items in his hand on the ground. John started climbing up the sides of the railing on the bridge to the very top of the bridge. My eyes widened because here is a guy that would not jump from the lower level but will attempt to do the unthinkable. As they climbed the additional two stories and stood on the edge, my heart started to race. All I could think about was Casey's first jump and how she said, "Be careful because I was barely able to touch the bottom! But you guys will be fine." Now here they were adding an additional two stories on top of the first level. It really didn't make sense to me, but apparently John had to be manly and take the challenge.

The two of them locked hands and took a step closer to the edge in preparation for jumping. They stood there looking like two crazy daredevils, but it was a stupid move if you were to ask me. Again, I had this feeling that something bad was going to happen, and I could almost feel it in my gut. I could hear the little angel on my shoulder screaming, "DON'T DO IT!", but I guess the devil was on their shoulder screaming, "Do It!" I knew there was nothing that I could do to stop John from jumping with Casey, because he had a huge crush on her. As my last attempt to communicate my worst fears to them, I yelled, "Don't do it!" I knew that my words fell on deaf ears when they acted as if I did not exist.

Suddenly, I noticed that John turned and looked down over his left shoulder at the bridge. I could see the silhouette of three figures, but I could not make out the gender or any other details. My first thoughts were for Jen's safety since the two figures were standing beside her. Hopefully, they were just supporters and maybe they were giving them some tips on how to land in what seems to be shallow water that was not made for a five-story jump. From the bottom of the bridge, I could tell something was wrong when John turned all the way around to face them. I immediately got a weird feeling about the situation so I made my way up the grassy path to the top of the road. As I started walking towards the bridge, I could tell that the two silhouettes turned out to be a man and woman. I was about ten feet away from the couple and Jen. I turned and looked up at John and Casey as they started to descend down off the railings of the bridge. I asked them, "Is everything ok?"

and John replied, "Yeah, it's fine." Within that half of a second my eyes refocused in front of me, and the couple was gone. I turned 360 degrees looking for them in every direction and there was no sign of them. It took John and Casey less than thirty seconds to climb down and the bridge was about seventy yards long and twenty feet wide and had lights. There were about six light poles, three on each side of the bridge running the full length. As I approached the area where they were standing, I only looked up for a half of a second. There was no humanly way possible that they could have moved without me hearing them. They couldn't have jumped into the water without a splash, plus they were fully dressed. Lastly, we timed it that it would have taken about 25 seconds to speed walk to either end of the bridge. It was as if they had just disappeared. After John checked under the bridge and realized that they were not there. I asked him, "What did they say or want?" John said, "They came and told us not to jump and told us a quick story about someone jumping and dying off of a bridge similar to this one, and then the couple just disappeared."

Still to this day I am not sure what happened to those people or angels. I am so thankful that God penciled my friends' name on the list for those angels to save on that night. I am glad that angels work late hours and know just what to say. Let's think outside of the box for a second; had the angels been running late or had the wrong directions to the bridge, this story could have had a different ending and the devil may be receiving the credit for this encounter. This story still gives me the chills when I think about it. I am reminded of what King David said in Psalms 91:11 "For He will command His angels concerning you to guard you in all your ways." Well, I still thank God for allowing me to have that encounter to help strengthen my faith. We all decided on that night, they were angels sent there by God to prevent anything bad from happening.

In Genesis 28:10-22, it talked about Jacob's vow at Bethel. It talked about how he laid down and God shared a vision with him. During this dream it is written in Genesis 28:12, "Then he dreamed, and behold, a ladder was set up on the earth, and its top reached to Heaven; and there the angels of God were ascending and descending on it!" If you truly believe in the Father then you truly believe in his powers and angels. He went on to say in verses 13-15, "And behold, the Lord stood above it and said: "I am the Lord God of Abraham your father and the God of Isaac; the land on which you lie I will give to you and your descendants. Also your descendants shall be as the dust of the earth; you shall spread abroad to the west and the east, to the north and the south; and in you and in your seed all the families of the earth shall be blessed. Behold, I am with you and will keep you wherever you go, and will bring you back to this land; for I will not leave you until I have done what I have spoken to you."

I truly believe that the blessings that were spoken upon our forefathers are still flowing over His righteous people today. When our Lord said, "Behold, I am with you and will keep you wherever you go." I truly believe those words with all of my heart. As you have read over and over throughout this book, the devil had me isolated in the darkest corners of my life. God's light opened doors in new dimensions in my life that only my heart could have desired, and my mind could not even comprehend.

For example, this next story about God's truth is going to reflect just that. I have had the privilege of knowing Amber for a number of years and have seen God's hand in her life. This experience showed me just how strong of a hand God had in her life.

As I turned the corner to enter into Amber's hospital room, the all-so-familiar smell of this place brought back so many memories from my past. There is no other smell in the world like that of a hospital. It seems to be the mixture of sterilization, hope, fear, and that horrible food. Of course being the friend that I am, I came bearing gifts of a more desirable meal of soup and crackers from her favorite restaurant. As we exchanged greetings, I sat in the chair next to her hospital bed. Amber began telling me a story of how God and His angels were working in her life. As she told me this story, my body began receiving chills up and down my spine as God's love poured over her life. I don't want to get ahead of myself in this story, so I will let Amber start from the beginning.

If you were to look inside of a dictionary under my name, Amber, you would notice that I am named after a jewel. The color of this jewel is referred to as a warm-honey shade. This color holds true to my heart as well as towards my life, love, and my family. My family is the center of my life as God surrounds us. I don't believe in religion, but I wholeheartedly believe in a relationship with Him. Growing up, my grandparents' love and affection would soothe my worries and fears in life. I can recall times in my childhood when my grandma (dad's mom) would take her small, fragile, soft hands and stroke my earlobes and tell me that everything would be ok. I can also recall at times my grandfather (stepdad's father) would take his rough, very large hands and place them on my leg and tell me not to worry and that he would always be there when I needed him. Since then they have both gone on to be with our Lord and Savior. I can recall the very first time that I truly needed their physical touch. It was when my best friend, Brandy, was in a terrible wreck. I can remember the hurt and pain of knowing that I had just lost my other half. We were only fifteen at the time. The car that she was inside of was t-boned by a police officer that was in a high-speed pursuit of another car. This police officer did not have his siren or flashing lights on during the chase. As she sat in the back seat of the car within her boyfriend's arms, she never knew what hit her and went into a coma never to recover. I would visit her body daily in the hospital looking for the slightest change, any sign of hope that I would get my best friend back. They said that she would have been in a vegetative state of mind had the family not made the decision to pull the plug! I can recall the loneliness settling in my spirit. Years passed and finally I rekindled my relationship with love. This time instead of it just being on a family, or friendship level, it surpassed that and encompassed all of those inside of one person, the love of my life–Raul. Well, a few years passed by and our love grew stronger with every passing moment.

During that time, I also started noticing pains in my stomach area. I would go to the doctors and have tests run on my body, but the results were always the same. I would always receive a clean bill of health. So months would go by and the pain in my body would become stronger. The symptoms went from mild pains to severe pain to the point that I could barely move. My mom took me to the hospital and to our surprise, we received shocking news. My doctor advised me that I had an infection in my body and would need to have immediate surgery. They told me that my gallbladder would need to be removed. However, once that was removed, the issue was still lingering. I spent 11 days in the hospital, and my problem was still haunting me. So, I decided to learn to live with the pain, and hopefully, one day it would eventually go away. Six years went by and my pain level once again reached the point that I could not bear it anymore, so I decided to visit the hospital again. The doctor then told me that I had another infection in my body and would need immediate surgery yet again. Due to this infection in my body, I would need an exploratory surgery because my white cell count was extremely high. The doctors did a microscopic surgery and discovered that my uterus was pressed to the back of my body wall. Once they had opened my body up on the operating table he said, "It looked like a war zone inside of my body due to the infection." They found a huge cyst that had burst inside of me and noticed the inflammation on my ovaries, fallopian tubes, and appendix as they scraped my uterus off the back of my abdominal wall. Now my dreams of providing a family to the love of my life were shattered. How could this be? Why me? How can I tell him that our only way of a family will be through an adoption agency? Do I choose health over family or keep the infection with all of my parts. Risk my life to provide a family that may grow without me?

The doctor allowed my family to come into the room and see me, but Raul was on the road working and would not get back in time. What if I don't survive this surgery? I need to have Raul here with me! I want to feel his warm lips one last time before they make these life-changing moves in my body. The doctor told me that they could not wait any longer. They proceeded with the surgery, and when I finally awakened, I had excruciating pain in my legs. It felt as if my ankles had been split open with a razor blade. I wasn't sure why that was happening, but I was told that I was screaming at the top of my lungs after the surgery to take the leg cuffs or pumps off. They were supposed to help keep the blood flow moving during and after my surgery. I was in the hospital five long days before the surgery and two days after. Finally, I was released to go home no longer the woman that I was when I entered the hospital. Honestly, I felt like I wasn't even half the women that I was on the day I was admitted in the ER. I could not bear the thought of staying one more night in that hospital, and I longed for my normal environment and the peaceful atmosphere of my three cats. Once I checked myself out of the hospital and arrived home, I immediately started taking the pain pills to subdue the pain levels that had held my body hostage only to find out that this was the wrong medicine and that I would have to head back up to the hospital the very next morning. Once I got to urgent care again, I realized this issue was much larger than I anticipated. The pain in my legs was increasing. They performed an ultrasound scan of my legs. The tech rushed out and told me that she was sorry to be the bearer of bad news, but the scan confirmed the blood clots in my leg. I felt so helpless during the time of taking the meds and hoping the blood thinners and the shots would dissolve the blood clots. I was told to keep a close watch for any of the symptoms confirming them passing through my heart.

The next day, I had an appointment to have the staples removed from my stomach from the surgery prior to these past encounters. Once I sat on the table to have them removed, I noticed that the blood clots started to pass through my body. I had a sudden pain in my chest, and it felt as if someone was squeezing my heart, a shock up my spine of pain, as my heart started to race. I looked at Raul as I told the doctor that I wasn't feeling good. Raul then told him my symptoms and advised him of the blood clot that I had heard of the day before and he gave me meds to stop the vomiting and to help with the pain. I left and went home. It was snowing outside and the roads were slick as we drove home. Once we made it home after getting the medicine, I laid in the bed. My goal was to relax as I took the medicine as Raul called other doctors in a panic in hopes of convincing me to go back to the hospital. The medicine made my body numb, I felt helpless and I knew that something was terribly wrong. I managed to work my way inside of my living room and sat on the couch. I laid there and dozed off. Raul decided to fall asleep on the floor next to me. I guess a couple of hours went by when I felt this presence that was all so familiar to my heart. I was awakened to the soft tugs of smooth fragile hands on my left earlobe, the roughness of my grandpa's hand rubbing my right knee, and Brandy's hands stroking my right hand.

As I opened my eyes in response to that, my cats were walking frantically over my chest and would not leave me alone. I had a strange sense that I needed get to the hospital quickly. I attempted to brush one of them off of me. Raul was awaken from my movements and attempted to help me remove the cats, but they hissed and moaned at him. I thought that was weird at the time, because that has never happened before. So as the cats surrounded me again, I would soon understand their wisdom, and what they were trying to tell me. Once again, a sudden sharp pain hit my chest, as I closed my eyes, clenched my teeth and held my breath in hopes of it passing. I let out a cry so loud that it sent Raul racing outside to scrape the snow and ice off the car in preparation for our speedy departure for the hospital. Upon my arrival, they rushed me in the back to do a scan on my chest with an idea of what was happening but wanted to make sure. A doctor came into my room and informed me that I was having heart attacks. I was told that 16 blood clots passed through my heart and nine were now resting in my right lung and the other seven were resting in my left lung. I was told that any one of the sixteen could have killed me.

I found myself staring in disbelief about the news he was giving me and also impatiently waiting for his solution or remedy for my problem. Again, I was told I would be receiving a medication that would hopefully dissolve the clots. I asked the doctor, "I will be okay, right?" and his reply was, "I can't answer that question because this situation is very severe. Any of the 16 blood clots passing through your heart could send you into cardiac arrest, but I will do my best!" After those words, all hope left me and fear settled in my heart. Internally, I was crying and screaming and pleading with God. On the outside, I was trying to stay strong for my family and Raul who was inside of the room with me. As the doctor walked out of the room, I was sure that I would soon meet my fate.

My family gathered closer to me and Raul's mother climbed in the bed next to me. I remember feeling loved as the medicine launched me into a state of relaxation. I eventually dozed off on them and slept for a couple of hours when I woke up the room was empty. So I closed my eyes and prayed until I fell asleep again. Well, I must have been asleep about thirty minutes before I felt the presence of people touching me again. So as I slowly opened my eyes and looked around, I noticed that again the room was empty. This was the same presence that I felt at my house while I was sitting on my couch, but there was something different about it, also. It was as if the hands that they were laying on my body were full of prayers! I could once again feel my earlobes being rubbed by my grandma's soft hands, knees stroked by my grandpa's rather large yet rough hands, and Brandy's soft strokes on my left hand as I heard soft whispers, but I could not make out what they were saying. As I sat with my eyes staring at the ceiling trying to make sense of this but loving the presence of these familiar spirits, an amazing peace fell over me and the voices and touches disappeared. With a smile on my face, I knew that God had heard my prayers. In the next couple of days as I waited fearing for my life to see if this medicine worked, my mind wrestled with the pros and cons of the medicine working, life, and the outcomes of this situation. My life must have passed through my mind about a million times thinking about all of the things that I had not done in life. I was ambushed with anger and questions that may never be answered until I reached Heaven. I am only in my late 20s and I feel cheated. I have always lived by the honor code in life. I have righted all of my wrongs in life and, have no enemies. I don't go to church, but yet I pray every day. Is that it God? Am I being punished for not going to church and believing in a relationship instead of religion?

I was released, once again, with high hopes and little faith to head home and wait! I needed to wait and see if the infinite amount of pills decided my fate. Months went by with me anticipating the due date of my next checkup to see or confirm my worst fears. Every minute situation would create fear in my heart. If I had the hiccups, sneezed, coughed, or had all three cats fighting for my attention, I would fear that the pain was going to accompany those actions. I figured that any one of those may launch a blood clot to my heart, or maybe the cats are forewarning me again! The day arrived that I had to visit the hospital for my checkup. As I walked into the doctor's office, they were all surprised to see me still in good health and fairly good spirits. It was almost as if they had seen a miracle happen when I entered the room! Let's face it, the odds were stacked against me, and no one and I mean, "NO ONE" expected me to still be alive, including myself. They took me in that back room and commenced to scan my body for the location and the number of blood clots. I stared intensely at the nurse's face as the results came back. I can recall every inch of emotion being written on her face as she looked at me. As her words fell on deaf ears, my face became emotionless. As she repeated her response, tears started to run down my face as Raul hugged me. I must have shed about a hundred tears in that room before the nurse walked out puzzled.

The nurse's exact words were "I cannot seem to find any blood clots in your body. I have looked everywhere and they are not present. Your lungs and veins are all clot free!" The tears that I displayed on that day were of joy and sadness. Joy because I can now see my future and that God heard my prayers. Sadness because I had very little faith and only high hopes! I felt as if I should have been sitting among the disciples in Matthew 16:8-10 when Jesus asked, "You of little faith, why are you talking among yourselves about having no bread? Do you still not understand? Don't you remember the five loaves for the five thousand, and how many basketfuls you gathered? Or the seven loaves for the four thousand, and how many basketfuls you gathered?" I should have never doubted His love and powers. When we are going through our storms in life, we tend to focus on the here and now instead of the miracles from our past or the powerful testimonies in our future. Tarrance always reminds me that, "God loves fixing the broken and that every encounter with our God or the world should be considered a faith builder!"

I know that this is only the beginning of His works in my life and that I will encounter a number of obstacles in my life that will try and detour me from my faith in Him. Just like it is written in Matthew 16:17-18, "Jesus replied, "Blessed are you, Simon son of Jonah, for this was not revealed to you by flesh and blood, but by my Father in Heaven. And I tell you that you are Peter, and on this rock I will build my church, and the gates of Hades will not overcome it.'" I will stand firmly on my newly found rock of faith and help build God's church. The miracles performed in my life during this chapter helped me realize that my trials and tribulations in life were needed to give purpose to my testimony!

Pause Insight before the encounter:

- Amber could have gone to different hospital to get a second opinion when she first started having issues with her body.
-

Pause insight after the encounter:

- Embrace life and cherish every moment of it as if it is your last.
-

Approaching the Unspoken Killer

Within this chapter I will talk about evil spirits and refer back to my darkest hour. I know a lot of you were left sitting on the edges of your seats wondering what happened after the pause. I will get to that point in a second. I want to talk about the devil for a brief moment. According to the Merriam-Webster Dictionary, the devil can also be considered as the "Personal supreme spirit of evil often represented in Jewish and Christian belief as the tempter of humankind, the leader of all apostate angels, and the ruler of Hell." He manipulates your mind and wants to rob you of all of the good in the world. He makes your life such a living hell until his evil propositions here on earth almost seem enticing.

I was down on one knee with tears and snot running down my face, pleading with God and tempting the Devil. I said to God, "If you don't show yourself to me soon God, I am going to do it!" I truly thought that was the end for me. I had lost all hope, desire, and will to live this life anymore. I know that you aren't supposed to demand anything from God or yell at God, but again, I wasn't in my right frame of mind. My heart was dark. Satan had robbed me of my joy. I had every intention of pulling that trigger, but God had bigger plans. When that spirit came over me and said, "Pause," I knew that feeling all so well. I slowly put the gun down and picked up a pen and pad, and before I knew it, I had made a list. It probably wasn't the kind of list that you are thinking about. It wasn't a list of items that I was leaving my loved ones or my farewells. It was a list of the order or what would be the order of my life. I listed out about ten things on this list, but I will only share one of them with you. Number one and at the very top of the list was "Your will be done!" I know a lot of you think I am out of my mind right now, but something truly came over me. It was almost like a test of my faith.

As you have read in the previous chapters, I had already had visions, and confirmations that God is real, but I wanted to run in the worldly realm. I can truly tell you that I put down my grandma's faith, and on that day I picked up my own faith. At that time, I felt like something physically died inside of me, and I was spiritually born again. I have always heard that if you try and save a drowning man, there is a possibility that you both will die. You can save him, but you have to wait until that right moment when he has tired himself out or is just about to give up hope. Then he will have less fight in him. That's what God did to me. He allowed me to run for a while and then called me into the ministry. I view life differently now. I found out that once you have an encounter with God, and I mean a real encounter, there is no turning back.

Now to finish the story, after I made the list, something inside of me told me to get up and burn the list in my room. Kind of like a vow to God and secrecy between us. I was still broken on the inside and still very lost in life. Here is the great part about God, even though we may give up on God, He will not give up on us. He provided my ram in the bush. What I mean by that is, He proved Himself to be truthful! So the next day I went into work, and the moment I sat down at my computer there was an email from my boss, Abe Stamper. I could only think, "What now?!" "If it isn't one thing, it's another. The blows from the devil won't stop coming!" So I proceeded to make my way into his office, and he told me to close the door behind me. I did just that before I sat in the seat across the desk from him. He started to tell me that the reason he called me in his office was to give me something. I took a deep breath and could only image a brown box to gather my belongings from my desk, especially after the dark weekend that I had just experienced.

He then extended his right hand and gave me an item. With sweaty palms I reached out with my right hand and retrieved a bracelet. As I started to read the inscription, he proceeded to say, "These bracelets were ordered three weeks ago and they just arrived today. I wanted to give you one." So I looked back down at the red bracelet, and it read "Psalms 23:4 – Stay Strong!" on one side and the other side it said, "For You are with me!!" Tears started to form in my eyes, and I was speechless. My mom use to always say, "He may not be there when you want Him, but He is always right on time!" God knew three weeks prior to me having these evil thoughts that I would need that bracelet on that day because He is perfect. I always keep it on my wrist as a constant reminder of His unfailing love. In Acts 1:7-8 it is written, "He said to them, 'It is not for you to know the times or dates the Father has set by his own authority. But you will receive power when the Holy Spirit comes on you; and you will be my witnesses in Jerusalem, and in all Judea and Samaria, and to the ends of the earth.'" He is the author and finisher of our faith as it states in Hebrews 12:2, and He is constantly proving that to me on a daily basis.

As we step into this next chapter, always remember to pray. Pray for yourself, loved ones, friends, strangers, and your enemies. You never know what trials people are experiencing in life. We should always remember Ephesians 4:26-27, "In your anger do not sin, Do not let the sun go down while you are still angry, and do not give the devil a foothold." Let's take away the devil's credit and recognize where our help cometh from!

The Unspoken Killer

John 8:44

"You belong to your father, the devil, and you want to carry out your father's desires. He was a murderer from the beginning, not holding to the truth, for there is no truth in him. When he lies, he speaks his native language, for he is a liar and the father of lies."

In chapter one, we talked about my darkest hour and how I arrived there. In this chapter, we will talk about suicide and why I refer to it as the unspoken killer. It seems as if we are afraid to be proactive with this topic. As parents we treat the topic like a book and set it on the same shelf as the book about the birds and the bees with high hopes of never having that talk with our kids. Most parents think their kids are too young to know about this topic or that if their child has thoughts of suicide, then it is a reflection of them being bad parents. Sometimes they are afraid to open their child's mind into something that will possibly consume their every thought. As adults, we always compare the present times with our past and how we were raised. We have to realize younger generations knows more about suicide and sex as adolescents than we did as teenagers and adults.

Suicide, the unspoken killer, walks in the shadows of our mind, planting seeds within our sorrows. Growing up, you were probably told never to talk to strangers. Suicide is a stranger to all of us, but it will try to befriend the majority of us. Its constant presence will make you think that, "It is not so bad." It will display some level of comfort in our minds and eventually tell us that there is no other way. Its voice is constantly whispering in your ears saying, "Do it!" The unspoken killer convinces your mind that no one else understands and that you are alone. It is when you are alone and at the lowest point in your life that it embraces you. During its visits to water the seeds that have been planted, its alternative motives are to determine when it will reap what it has sowed. Just like weeds that grow in your gardens, the thought will always come back. Destructive thoughts may come to us all at some point in time. There is no boundary of life that it will not cross. It shows no discrimination against any friendly faces, races, genders, ages, or social classes.

To be honest, that night wasn't the first time I found myself in darkness. The very first time I had an encounter with suicidal thoughts was when I was a teenager. It was a couple of weeks after my mom passed away. I was dating my high school sweetheart at the time and was very much in love with her. The love that we shared here on earth was no comparison to the love that I had lost. I had my good days and bad days. The average person could not tell the difference between the two. I can recall asking my uncle to borrow his Mustang GT. He was very proud of that car and had invested a lot of time and money into making it fast. He gave me the keys so that I could attend the high school basketball game. That was out of his character, but I figured it was because he felt sorry for me and what I was experiencing. I could tell that the parking lot was full as I approached the school. The only parking available was in this field attached to our football practice area. I parked the car there and attended the game.

Once the game was over I walked out of the gym and started my approach to the car. I had no clue that the spirit of the unspoken killer would be waiting for me in the car. The moment I sat down and started the car part of me really started missing my brother and mother. I could hear it saying, "Everyone that loves you dies. You are incapable of being loved and no one loves you. You are alone in this world, so join your loved ones." As I pressed the clutch in and shifted into first gear, I can remember pressing the accelerator all the way to the floor as I slowly released the clutch. Now things were in motion. My target was a big oak tree at the end of the field. The tree was about two hundred yards away, and I was approaching it fast. I speed shifted into second gear as tears started to roll down my cheeks. As I started screaming with about one hundred yards to go, closing my eyes in hopes of seeing my mother and brother, I reopened them on the other side. Suddenly, I felt this presence of love and warmth that took over my body. It was new to me because I was angry at the world, and I had turned my back on God. That presence made me feel like everything was going to be okay. I know it was through my family's prayers and the love of our Father that I was spared. When that peace comes upon me, I feel like Paul and Timothy when they wrote the letter to holy people in Philippi. In Philippians 1:3-6, "I thank my God every time I remember you. In all my prayers for all of you, I always pray with joy because of your partnership in the gospel from the first day until now, being confident of this, that he who began a good work in you will carry it on to completion until the day of Christ Jesus."

I am not sure why God intervened on that night. As I was driving towards my destiny, I missed the tree by two feet because God detoured me back to my journey. At times I wish I knew why and how God chooses certain people to reveal His presence to, or what my mission in life is. I am constantly reminded of a tragic event that took place about a year before my mom died. One of my family members made a couple of careless decisions that almost killed everyone in our single wide trailer. Once again, I was face to face with destiny, but this time resulting in a physical encounter with God. I will save that story for the next book, but I can tell you something that God told me before I started my journey back to my reality. He said "I have to send you back because you have something to do!" I wish I knew what that was or if I am walking in that realm of my life now. We all will experience different walks of life inside of our unique journeys. His love is tailor made for each and every one of our lives.

Let me be clear about this part of my life. I have to be honest with you that I am very ashamed to even mention that I have thought of or even took the steps to attempt suicide in my life. In fact, I was talking to God as I was writing this book to see if there was any other way than exposing my past or sacrificing myself in this book. I felt like His reply was, "Had there been any other way to save the souls of the multitudes, I would have taken that route, also!" I guess since He did not see any other way except for me to be sacrificed, I say, "Here I am Lord!" I am not proud of the things I have done. I am not trying to encourage anyone to dance with the unspoken killer in hopes of having an encounter with God! That's not what this book is about. It is about us realizing that we are not alone in life, and we need each other. It is about pausing and realizing that you don't have to focus on the obstacle in your life, but you can look past it and see your dreams, and goals in your future.

I Samuel 12:16- sums it all up for me, "Now then, stand still and see this great thing the LORD is about to do before your eyes!" To me the words "stand still" mean pause. I feel as though suicide, violence, and death seem to be at an all-time high. Even though there are many people who claim that we are experiencing what is considered the end times, we need to remember that our God loves fixing the broken, and He will conquer the impossible, providing an infinite number of possibilities.

If I want to be honest with myself, I have to realize that my mom's death was surrounded by depression and that lead to the door of suicide. Due to Joe's actions, my mom's reaction was the bottle. I have recently come to terms with the phrase, generational curses. I have lost a couple of family members this way. To let the truth be told, she committed suicide by the bottle instead of by a knife, car, gun, or pills.

We all know that no one sin is greater than the other, but sin is evil and God separates himself from sin. I think depression is the hallway leading to the unspoken killer's door. We know if we commit suicide that it is an act against God and what He stands for. God is the one who should ultimately decide if someone lives or dies. Thou shall not kill is listed as number six on the list of the Ten Commandments. The act of suicide is considered self-murder.

I realized that my hurt and pain became unbearable after my mom's death. It was at that point that seeds of darkness were planted in my sorrow. Most people have never looked at drinking and doing drugs as suicide, but it is if you are using it to cover your pain and sorrow. Not every depressed person thinks of suicide, but every suicide victim was once depressed.

There are so many different types of depression and scenarios that can ultimately lead you to make the wrong decision. Here is a common scenario that occurs every day.

You don't realize it is happening until it is too late. God has allowed me to cross a number of lives throughout my journey with Him. I was blessed with the presence of a young lady that will help give us some insight about her scenario.

Hi, my name is Blossom and I have a story to tell. I write with tears in my eyes… as the end of a dream comes to a more abrupt and painful halt than I could ever have imagined. As you may have seen on Facebook, my new status is "single." I have heard the stories being shared and know there is a lot of speculation, so I thought I would let you all in on my "side of the story."

The story begins in November of 2006. Two people met each other. Technically we met before this point in time, but we had never really connected. We went to Franklin, Tennessee, for a leadership conference and in the weekend we spent there, we had already fallen in love. He was so charming, and he was attractive. He had overcome so much. His background was so similar to mine. He had been through it all, and he had conquered. He was so strong, so happy, so outgoing. I just knew he was the one. With pasts as similar as ours, how could we not have the same views on life, right? We had both been abused as children, both came from broken homes, both were lonely and seeking direction and guidance… We both wanted to make something of ourselves, had ambition and a drive and desire to succeed. He was perfect. He was the man I had made a list about. He was my dream come true, my Prince Charming, come to rescue me. I had this nagging feeling in the pit of my stomach that something wasn't right, but I decided to ignore it. After all, it was just the rest of my life I was thinking about.

We dated for almost three months. Several people warned us that we were moving too fast, and we needed to be careful. What did they know? They had only been our best friends for years. And still, that nagging feeling continued to bother me.

We decided to get married. Quickly. No rings, no proposal, just a spur of the moment decision. Now the nagging turned into screaming. Something was not right. Why was he in such a hurry? Why was I? Did we know it couldn't last? What did we still not know about each other? Maybe we should try premarital counseling. I made the suggestion, and he agreed. We went to one session. He decided that he didn't see what the point was. We had each other and with pure determination, we would make it through anything. After all, we were obsessively "in love" with each other.

January of 2007 brought a speedy wedding, hastened by our desire to be with each other. We still had no idea who the other person was in the slightest. The first few months were pure ecstasy. We enjoyed every moment we could together. Soon I was fired from my job for spending too much time at home with my (as I discovered after the wedding) unemployed husband.

We were evicted from our home and moved in with his mother and stepfather in March of the same year. They were great to us, and allowed us to stay until we could get on our feet, which happened in the middle of the year (June or July). We moved into our new home with excitement. Things were changing for us, and the house wasn't the biggest news we had! We had just discovered I was having a baby! We were so excited, so full of hope and life and love... and we thought nothing could bring us down.

My pregnancy became much harder as it progressed and by the last month, I was on bed rest, but still chasing our dreams with my infallible husband. We stayed out late nights, driving long miles and working as hard as we could to get to our perceived goals (which neither of us had set for our family).

I had my son on April 9. For the first month, I felt like it was all a dream... But then, when he was 5 weeks old, we were evicted from our home once again, and life came crashing down around us.

We moved back to my mother-in-law's house, and still, they were very supportive and did everything they could to help out. However, I wasn't managing well. I was angry. I was hurt. The perception I had of my husband before marriage was giving way to reality. He wasn't a good provider, he wasn't responsible, and he was nothing like the promises I had believed from his mouth. We no longer even slept in the same bed.

The hopes and expectations I had when I said "I do" were slowly crumbling beneath my feet. As we continued to plunge further and further into debt, we stopped communicating little by little.

In October of that same year, several of my friends held an intervention and helped me leave the man I loved. We still saw each other on a daily basis, but I found that when I was apart from him, I missed him like a drug and felt like my life couldn't continue. The following March, we reconciled. He re-proposed (since there hadn't been a proposal the first time around), and it was so romantic. He said, "Sometimes learning in life is like learning to ride a bicycle, you might fall down, but as long as you pick yourself up and continue to try, eventually you WILL learn. Give me a second chance to ride this bicycle with you," and I was hooked. I thought, "He has such a way with words, and he is so extraordinarily charming. No matter his flaws, he is the man for me."

The distance between us continued to grow, however. Instead of the flowers and honey I had been promised, we found ourselves spitting vinegar at each other. Soon, our decisions led to the devastation of our family. We were still trying to figure out the issues that had haunted our lives, still working on the financial mess that had landed us once more in a bad situation, still figuring out how to communicate and who we were as individuals. I struggled daily with whether I should tell him the awful things I was going through, what would happen if I did, and how I had become a victim instead of a fighter...

We were evicted yet again in December of the next year, and moved once more into his parent's house, although this time it was the house next door instead of a bedroom in their home. I found out in January that I had a brain aneurysm, and although it was extremely small, they weren't sure if they would have to operate or if it would work itself out. I started looking for wigs and praying for hope. I was stressed out, angry at my life, and hurting more than I could recall ever hurting before.

The days wore on. He drank so much on his birthday in January that I was cleaning up vomit and urine for days. I was only a remnant of my former self. My entire life was focused on preventing people from seeing the irresponsibility and pain that were normal in our relationship. As we celebrated Valentine's Day, we both knew there was nothing loving in our relationship. We attempted to make it a romantic holiday and ended up sleeping as far away from each other as possible. I found out I was pregnant on February 15.

Finally in March, I broke down. I admitted myself to the psychiatric ward of the hospital for suicidal thoughts and ideations. I didn't want this child. I didn't want any form of life. I was tired of everything- tired of pretending, tired of just breathing instead of living, tired of being verbally harassed and abused at every turn. I made an adoption plan for the baby in case I couldn't keep her. It was the most difficult time in my life, and I went through it with a husband who didn't believe in me and wasn't even sure he wanted to be in the hospital room with me when I delivered.

He tried so hard to be supportive, but he started drinking even more heavily and between his job and DJ'ing at parties, he wasn't home much. I tried hard not to be needy and weak, but I was. All I wanted in the world was to feel like I had someone who would fight for me, and instead, he mocked me, abused me and shunned me. That was the first and deepest cut... and they continued to come after that.

I look back now and realize that he was probably as hurt and as needy as I was and both of us were digging an emotional debt that we would never be able to recover from. By this time I was feeling so abandoned and alone that I didn't know what to do or where to go. Bruce's drinking problem continued to get worse. He was feeding off the alcoholism displayed by his mother on a daily basis. They enabled each other and encouraged one another in their destructive habits.

One day his mother attacked me. I had chosen to feed my son hummus and vegetables instead of the pasta she made for dinner and she (in her drunken stupor) found that reason enough to shove me into a table, causing my 36-week pregnant belly tremendous pain and starting a "threatened miscarriage" to quote the doctor's words.

I called Bruce to tell him that I was on my way to the hospital, but he was already too drunk to do anything. His first response was "well, what did you do to make her hurt you?" It wasn't what I wanted from my husband who was supposed to be my protector and caretaker. My friend drove me to the hospital, staying with me and giving me the support that should have been my husband's role.

I decided in those few moments between speaking with police officers and doctors and nurses, that I couldn't take this anymore. I would never live with Gloria again. I asked my friend if we could stay at her house. Being the amazing person that she is, she welcomed us into her home with open arms, but Bruce had other plans. He refused to move with me, choosing to stay with his mother and feed his habits over feeding his family. I should have known then. I should have listened to the naysayers and the people telling me it was time to give up on our marriage, but I was determined to make him love me. I was determined that I could be worthwhile one day.

I found a new house within a few weeks and invited Bruce to move back in with me. A month later, our beautiful daughter was born, but her father had been absent during her birth. He didn't even come near me the entire time I was in labor. Still to this day, I attribute my peace in that situation to my Heavenly Father. My friend and doula also had a lot to do with it! I don't know if I would have made it through without her staying at my side, reminding me to breathe and smiling reassurances over and over again.

That summer I had to have a few surgeries due to complications with my health. Because I had been isolated for so long, I was unable to find someone to care for the kids. The first surgery went okay, and although Bruce didn't stay home with the kids, he did have his mother come and stay with me. No matter how stressed I was by her presence, I was still grateful for someone who was capable of picking the kids up since I wasn't.

The second surgery was a scheduled surgery. He didn't even come to the hospital with me. He left as soon as I got to the house and went to a party. His "gig" went late and he wound up being way too drunk to drive, so he stayed out overnight the night of my surgery. When he got back in the morning, he passed out. Since I had taken a cab from the hospital, I hadn't stopped to get my pain medication. I was hoping he would get it for me when he came home. However, since he was so out of it, when I tried to wake him, he told me to do it myself. When I proceeded to inform him that he hadn't brought our car home, he told me that I could just ride his bicycle. So I did. I rode a bike the 2.5

miles to the pharmacy and picked up pain medication. I took a pill when I got the medicine from the pharmacy and another when I got back to the house. I knew that between my pain level and the medication in my system, I wasn't in my right mind, but I didn't realize how out of it I was until I looked back a few weeks later.

When I got home, the kids hadn't been fed, the house was destroyed and my brand new baby and three-year old son were completely unsupervised.

For the first time in my marriage, I lost my temper. I forgot to trust God. I forgot to pray. I didn't think. I went in like a momma bear. I started yelling at him. I have no idea what I said to this day, but I cannot recall being that angry at any other point in my life.

In response, he rolled over and told me to get out and leave him alone. He informed me that I needed to quit being such a woman and toughen up.

So I did, but not the way he was expecting. I threw a book at his head and DEMANDED that he get up and help my half-crazed, tortured, weak, medicated self. In response, he picked me up by one arm and threw me out of the room and locked the door. So I went through the other door. Still angry, still yelling, still out of my right mind and over-medicated in a feeble attempt to deal with the pain.

The next part is a bit of a blur, but I remember I ended up on our dining room floor, hurting even worse. He told me he wanted a divorce, and that I was psycho and he didn't want to have to deal with me anymore. I was devastated. All I had wanted was a little help, and I had ended up in a physical altercation with my husband while in my home with my children. It was a situation I had promised myself since childhood that I would never find myself in again.

All I could think about was how I had failed.

I had failed myself. I had been weak. I had been a victim, and when I tried to be strong, I had failed again. I had promised myself that I would never raise my voice. I would never be a screaming maniac, no matter the situation. I had promised myself that I would never be a violent person, especially if I had children. I knew that life could be lived without violence, and I had absolutely failed some of my strongest convictions in life.

I had failed as a wife. I had hurt the one person in my life who had managed to not abandon me. My husband no longer loved me. He was through with me and he had informed me more than a few times that he deserved better. Obviously with the way I had behaved, he was right. Anyone deserved better than the temper and fighting that were happening in my house. I blamed myself for it all.

I had failed my children. This was the hardest to deal with. My children deserved the world. They deserved only happiness and sunshine. They didn't have to grow up in a home where there was drama and violence and yet, I had just journeyed down that path with them. It didn't matter that they were upstairs when it happened. They still could feel the atmosphere of the household. They would still see the bruises, the broken items in the house. They would still see that mommy was a failure.

My emotions were overwhelming. I was swallowed up by despair. In my state of mind that day, I had failed at life. Everything seemed hopeless. I had tried to spare my children from the horror I knew as I child, but I had failed at that too. History was repeating itself.

I could not see the point of continuing with this life. I had no friends, I had no close family, I had no husband that cared anymore, and I felt my children would be far better off with someone else to raise them than this wreck called me.

I took a notebook and wrote out all of the financial information, passwords, and special dietary needs of the children. I wrote letters to my mom and kids. I calmly walked back into the house and handed it to Bruce, explaining what each thing meant.

I then went to my neighbor's house, asked her to keep an eye on the kids and walked away with only my bottle of pills.

As the sun started to move to the high noon position, I found a secluded area in a nearby alley. My thoughts continued to overwhelm me. I opened the pill bottle and counted them slowly. Twenty-five pain pills remained, meaning I had already taken five that morning. I didn't stop to think. I started swallowing them by the handfuls. I finally stopped when the bottle was gone.

I walked until I found a tree, and I laid down under it, hidden by some shrubbery from anyone driving by. As I drifted in and out of consciousness, I remember feeling so peaceful. I just knew that everything was going to be okay now.

Then my neighbor found me. Still to this day, I don't know how, but suddenly there she was, sitting beside me, asking if I was okay. I said I had never been better and that everything was going to be great for my kids now, and asked her politely to leave me alone. At least that is how I remember it.

She had never seen me in a state like I was and worried about the fact that I had asked her to keep an eye on my kids without any sort of time frame. I was usually very responsible about that type of thing. So she did as I asked and went home, but on the way, she made sure to call the police and informed them that she thought I had attempted suicide and told them where they could find me. Soon I woke to lights from an ambulance and police officers attempting to make me sit up. My time of peace had come to an end.

They loaded me in the ambulance and took me to the hospital. I don't remember much once I was there, except telling them that I didn't want my husband to know where

I was. A few women from my church came by. I remember that, but hazily. They pumped my stomach, and I came around eventually. They admitted me into the psychiatric ward and all I could think about was my failure. I couldn't even commit suicide properly, and I couldn't believe that I had FAILED again!

I was so angry with myself, with God, with my husband, and with life. I spent a week there. I would have stayed a lifetime if it weren't for my children. They came to visit me a few days into my stay, and I realized how important it was that I stay with them. They were dirty and unkempt, and my daughter's eyes were turning yellow from her dietary needs not being met. I decided then and there that I had to live for my children. I had to give them a life that I had never had a chance of living. I decided no matter what happened; I would never find myself in such a dark place again. And if I did, I just had to remind myself that my children really did need me. When I was released from the hospital, I stayed a week with my friend Sara from church. She begged me not to return to Bruce, but when I saw that he was already talking to other women and that he didn't care about me anymore, I decided I had to "win him back" for my children's sake. So, I went home to my husband and children once more. We again attempted to try for the fairytale that we had dreamed of when we said those first "I do's." I determined that I would not give up on my life, my kids, or my marriage.

Everyone that was standing on the outside of my marriage looking in on it, thought that I was a fool for trying to hold on to my marriage. I had people in my life who cared, who were trying to warn me that it would only get worse, but I wouldn't listen. Bruce and I continued to struggle. Our lives were going in opposite directions. He found solace in the bottom of a beer bottle while I took comfort in my church family. I cannot thank God enough that they were there when things hit rock bottom.

Bruce came home one night around 8 pm. He was already so drunk that he passed out when he got home. Emotions running high, I proceeded to put my kids to bed, get dressed up and go out to meet some friends. I was determined that if he could have a good time, so could I. Was it wrong to be in that mindset? Absolutely! Was I wrong for leaving my kids at home with a passed out drunk? Unquestionably! But I was past the point of logic. My emotions, my hurt, my anger had taken over, and I was determined to exact my revenge.

I had a few drinks over the next few hours. I had fun talking with old and new friends alike, and when I closed the car door to begin my drive home, I remember thinking "I can see why he enjoys this so much." I wasn't anticipating the wrath that was awaiting me.

I pulled up in the drive, stepped out of the car and walked up to the door. As I opened the door, he was standing there. He didn't seem so drunk anymore, so I said hi. He reiterated with "give me the keys." I handed him the keys, and he walked out the door. It was about 2 a.m. by now, and knowing that he was angry, I decided to sleep in my daughter's room, so that (hopefully) he wouldn't yell and wake her up.

Still to this day, I don't know what time he came back. All I know is that I was abruptly awakened by him pulling the covers off of me, throwing them in the rocking chair and screaming "Get up, you lazy b&^h!" I rolled over and put the pillow over my head, hoping that if I just ignored him long enough, he would go away.*

Unfortunately, it didn't happen that way. Instead he grabbed my arm and dragged me across the floor to the hallway. I remember fear starting to curl around my heart as I realized that he was intent on harming me. I yanked my arm away, running to my bedroom, slamming the door and climbing under the covers like a child afraid of an imaginary monster. Only the monster wasn't imaginary. The monster was the man who had taken a vow to love and to cherish, to honor and protect me. As he burst into the room and grabbed the blankets, I recall the terror I felt in that moment. When he took my right arm and threw me against the wall like a rag doll, I realized I had made a terrible mistake.

My mistake wasn't in going out to have a good time with my friends that night. No, my mistake had been to believe in him with all I had even when everyone was warning me that he couldn't be "saved." My mistake was thinking that I could change him and save him when he didn't want to be saved. My mistake had been to think that because we were married, he loved me. My mistake had been thinking my children needed a father in the home more than I needed a husband to cherish me.

As his 210 pounds settled on top of my 100-pound frame and his hands wrapped around my throat, I looked into his eyes and realized that I was going to die that night. It would take a miracle to save me. As I watched his eyes, they suddenly changed and he exclaimed "You need to clean the f&^%#g house, you B%^h!" I attempted to concede, knowing this was my chance to get away. The air was cut off though. I couldn't even breathe enough to sputter okay. I thrashed around on the floor, silently begging him to let go of me. Finally, his hands let up enough that I could choke out "Okay, okay, I will go clean the house." He looked surprised for a second and then let me up. I started to run as soon as his bodyweight lifted from my torso. I think he realized that I was intent on escape rather than cleaning because he caught up to me at the top of the staircase. As he flung my already battered body against the wall again, I promised him I was going to clean.*

By some miracle, he believed me this time. I think he had witnessed the absolute terror in my eyes and thought that I would never defy him while fearing for my life, but I did. I ran up and down the street knocking as hard as I could on the neighbor's doors, trying to alert someone, anyone that I would probably die that night. As I continued to pound on doors, my bare feet started to feel the freezing temperatures and I realized that by exposure or abuse, I didn't have much of a chance that night.

Then my children came to mind. The promise I had made that day in the hospital. I had to rescue my children. I had to make sure they were okay even if that meant sacrificing myself in the meantime.

I ran back to our house, only to discover Bruce had locked me out. It was no surprise, but the adrenaline struck my veins as I realized that my wonderful, sleeping babies were now locked in the house with a madman, and I had no access to ensure their safety.

I ran to the windows, hoping and praying that we had accidentally left one unlocked that night. But, it was not so. My responsibility was now endangering my children. I began to pound on the door, yelling, "Let me in, let me in, just let me get the kids, and I will leave you alone!!!"

No response. The lights flickered on in my daughter's bedroom. Oh God, NO!!! Please don't let him hurt her. My determination to get inside became even stronger.

I picked up a planter from the porch and attempted to slam it through the window Instead of the breaking of glass; I found my feet covered with dirt and the shattered remains of a ceramic pot.

The noise got Bruce's attention. He opened the door with my daughter in his arms and stormed outside, all the while shoving me back, back, back and over the railing to a 10-foot drop.

As I landed on the ground, I knew that I had to rescue my kids. I refused to have them grow up with a father who would beat a woman (and likely them) when things didn't go his way.

I climbed the stairs to the door once more, but this time I had recalled a brick that I confiscated from my daughter a few days before. I knew that I would be able to get in the door if I could break the glass with that brick. It took two blows to break the double-paned glass. It felt like slow motion as I watched the shards of glass fall down around my feet. I started to reach through the opening I had just created and felt him grab my hand. As he slammed my hand down against the doorframe, I could feel it fracture, but I was not about to give up.

I wanted my children safe. I set aside the pain and continued to reach for the lock. He decided to try a new tactic in shredding my arm against the broken glass that still remained. I was determined, and I was not about to let a few cuts slow me down. I think he realized my determination as the door, the porch and the floor inside became so soaked in my blood that you could no longer recognize the original color of the wood and tile.

So he opened the door again. This time he shoved me over the railing with such force that I blacked out.

I don't know how long I was unconscious, but I do recall coming to and realizing that my children were still in that house. I couldn't balance myself enough to walk, so I crawled around to the front of the steps. Slowly, I dragged my battered body up the stairs, pulling myself up with the arm that could still hold weight. I knew this was the last time. My body would never be able to take anymore. My only hope was that this time, I could get the kids out before he killed me.

As I reached the top step, I realized that I would have to use the wall to stand while I attempted one last time to get in the door. I put my weight against the wall and attempted to raise my body a little at a time, and then, my miracle came. The police pulled up next door. One of the neighbors had called, thinking that my skulking, crawling body was that of a burglar.

As the police came up to the porch, I started to cry. I couldn't believe God was going to save my babies and me. The rest of the night is a little bit hazy. The police called an ambulance, and they went upstairs and woke the children up to ride to the hospital with me.

Bruce went to jail that night. I can't imagine what might have happened if the police hadn't shown up at the exact moment that they did. When I was released from the hospital, my church had found me a room at a battered women's shelter. That was the beginning of my deliverance. All praise given to God that I have found freedom now!

Blossom's testimony was amazing! Within this chapter of our lives we both struggled with communicating our pain to people and seeking help. We thought that no one else would understand our struggles. There were times within our situations where it was hard for either of us to breathe, eat, or think. All we wanted to do was stop the pain–pain from our hearts being ripped apart by the people we loved the most or from losing a loved one. There seemed to be only one way to stop the pain in our minds, and God intervened both times in two different scenarios. Listen, when you are walking in the darkness of your struggle, please know that there is light at the end of the tunnel. What seems like a big problem today will transform into a big answer for someone else's problem tomorrow if you keep pushing ahead in life.

The devil had Blossom and I thinking that everyone would think that we were different or crazy, so we should not expose or mention our suicidal thoughts to anyone! God said in John 3:20-21, "Everyone who does evil hates the light, and will not come into the light for fear that their deeds will be exposed; but whoever lives by the truth comes into the light, so that it may be seen plainly that what they have done has been done in the sight of God." We realized that God had seen our hurt and pain, but never forgot that He created our hearts. If you are depressed or in a circle with someone that is showing signs of depression, please get them the proper help. The next step should be that you enter into a heart-to-heart prayer with God, either for them or yourself. I only mentioned a couple of signs of depression throughout this chapter, but there are a lot of them and you may be overlooking some obvious ones, so please do your research. Please contact the National Suicide Prevention Lifeline (1-800-273-8255) or seek shelter from abusive relationships. It is better to be safe now by knowing you took the proper steps and not regret it later. Earlier I mentioned that not every depressed person thinks of suicide, but every suicide victim was once depressed so please take that into consideration, also. At the time, I didn't realize that suppressing my feelings would directly lead me to depression.

I had to realize that the solution to the problem of pain that I was feeling, wasn't more pain. For example, if I were to accidently slam my finger in my car door. My first thoughts would be to scream, hold my finger, and stop the pain as quickly as possible. My solution wouldn't be to slam another finger in the door of my car in hopes of making that pain go away. If I tried that solution, I would be crying like a little baby. Now, let us take self-inflicted pain or suicide into consideration. The moment your past or future becomes unbearable and you decide to hurt yourself, you are being selfish. Yes, you would be inflicting more pain on yourself, but also others. It's like taking your child, spouse, family member's or friend's finger and closing it in the door because you want your pain to stop. Now that you're dead and gone, they are all left with hurting fingers and possibly looking at the same solution for relieving their pain.

What is considered a normal life in today's society? Life is not always fair and, yes, it seems to have its favorites. Life evolved from love and yearns for fellowship. Younger generations use the term "YOLO" meaning "You Only Live Once." I truly believe that with all of my heart, so let's not give up on life. The Creator of love during our lives will never give up on us. For those who feel as though they don't matter or no one loves them, I want to be the first to tell you that "I love you!" and our Father loves you, also. He truly loved Blossom and displayed His love multiple times throughout her story. I want to take the time and show you one area that His love proved to be true for Blossom. She was pushed from the second story balcony not once but twice. I truly think that during those falls, God had His angels catch and adjust her body as she fell to the ground in such a way that it didn't cause her severe physical harm or death.

People have previously died from falls under 10 feet or have received life-altering disabilities. His love once again proved to be just and pure. If you are in an abusive relationship and your loved ones are trying to save your life by warning you, please listen to them. Just remember that every bruise, black eye, and broken limb that you receive not only hurts you, but they also break your loved one's hearts. It's proven that a person can withstand pain because of love. When it becomes a physical altercation the only person that is doing the loving is the one that's receiving the beating. God created us for love. Love doesn't hurt in that manner. When you love someone you want to give them affection such as hugs. God may be answering your prayers by sending your loved ones into your life telling you to leave. I realize that I will be stepping out on thin ice when I say this but staying in some abusive relationships is almost like committing suicide. They will only get worst and it is only a matter of time before they beat you to death physically or mentally, simply because you never took heed to the warnings that you were sent and walked into an encounter with the unspoken killer. Now, if you are dancing with the unspoken killer and you don't want to live for yourself, please, please, please live for me!

Pause Insight before the encounter:

- We should have told someone about our inner struggles, thoughts and desires.
- We needed to realize that it didn't mean that we were crazy because we needed to see counselors, but that we were just normal, hurting people.
-

Pause insight after the encounter:

- Realize that we do not have to feel like we are alone in this world while we are facing our issues. Understand that we are loved and had either one of us followed through with suicide that we would have hurt a lot of our loved ones.
- Blossom should have listened to her own heart when she said, "I *had this nagging feeling in the pit of my stomach that something wasn't right"* *instead of ignoring it.*
-

Unwrapping the Gift

I can remember how every year throughout my childhood, starting on December 1st my excitement for Christmas would begin to build up. That was the day my family would put up our Christmas tree. We would come together as a family and talk about the gifts that we wanted while we put the tree up. That day made it official to me that in twenty-four more days I would open all of my gifts and feel as though I was in Heaven. Every day when I came in from school, I would first call my mom's name to make sure that the coast was clear. Then, I would look under the tree to see if there were any new presents under there that may have slipped past one of the many inspections that I provided daily. Finally, I would examine every nametag only focusing on the presents that belonged to me. I would carefully place the present near my right ear and give it a gentle shake in hopes of revealing its inner secrets. Then I would make sure that I placed it back in the exact spot, and I do mean exact, so my mom would never know what I had done.

In my house, the real presents, if any, would come out during the week of Christmas. My mom couldn't always afford presents for us. Therefore, when she was able to, it was the best feeling ever, and I couldn't wait to open the presents! There were times that I would take a knife and slit the clear tape on the presents to try and get a peek at it. Looking back at this situation I can see how crazy it was for these simple facts: first, the day we put up our Christmas tree, I told my mom what I wanted, so I already knew what the gifts in the boxes were. Secondly, my curiosity would still get the best of me, and I needed confirmation of what was inside of the boxes. Was it the amazing gift that I had suggested? Finally, I couldn't wait to play with the toys and share them with others to show them how special I was. On the night of December 24, it was our custom to put cookies out for Santa to show appreciation for the gifts that he came bearing. Throughout the night, I would constantly hear noises and wake up. I would sneak into the living room in hopes of getting a glimpse of Santa and his reindeer only to be saddened at the sight of my mom in the living room making a clatter as she was cleaning up the house in preparation for his arrival. Eventually, I would drift off into this amazing sleep only to be awakened by my brothers saying, "Get up! Get up! Santa came!" I would pop up and the only thing racing through my mind was to make it into the living room as fast as I could.

Once I rounded the corner out of the hallway into the living room in a full sprint, I would drop down and slide on my knees stopping a few inches in front of the tree. Then, with excitement I would grab all of my presents and rip into every one as if I were a lion tearing away at the flesh of his last meal. I would always save the best for last. There was one Christmas morning in particular where I can remember opening a box that contained my Nintendo. I was so excited! I stayed up playing that video game for days until I finally became bored with the games that came with it. My present was a gift until I opened it and realized that it was my Nintendo. Then it became my game and was no longer a mystery. The anticipation of receiving or giving a gift is one of the most exciting things in life. I never slowed down enough in life to enjoy the anticipation side of things. I always wanted to bypass that part and dive right into the presents. That's how we are with a lot of things in our life. We never slow down to look at the details on the wrapping paper, to realize that the present was wrapped with love, or to appreciate the ribbon and other minute details that were a part of the preparation for that moment.

Can you remember the color and type of paper used to wrap your last gift? How many pieces of tape were placed on that gift to conceal its love? Think about how many times that person may have moved the ribbon around on the front of that box trying to find that perfect spot to make that gift special. The next time you receive a gift, take a second to look in the gift giver's eyes and notice all of the love and anticipation that is flowing out of their expressions. It's important to realize that presents are not something that we are entitled to even if it is our birthday or Christmas. No, presents or gifts are given to us simply because someone loves us. The Gift is a very special chapter that will hopefully give insight, knowledge, and meaning to a lot of lives. Our Father has given every human multiple gifts in life. Ultimately, what we do with each gift that God has given us will determine the quality and outcomes of our life. That is why I feel led to discuss a very special gift with you in the following pages of this chapter....

The Gift

Proverbs 4:23

"Above all else, guard your heart for it is the wellspring of life."

In Genesis 1:26 God the Father was speaking to His Son, Jesus, and the Holy Spirit when he said, "Let us make mankind in our image, in our likeness..." You may wonder what this means exactly. Does it literally mean that our physical bodies were created to look like God's? Perhaps, but I believe that it's much deeper than that. I believe that God the Father was referring to the fact that we were created as multi-dimensional beings. In 1 Thessalonians 5:23-24, we find that we each consist of a body that is physical, a spirit which is our innermost part that connects with God, and a soul which is our mind, will, and emotions. These three components that make up our being reflect the image of God. He created us in His image so that we can experience intimacy with Him and with others. As you read through the Bible – both the Old and New Testaments – you will find that God is constantly reaching out to mankind and desiring for us to pursue a close personal relationship with him. The word "intimate" means that which has to do with our soul and spirit. When the Lord presented the Ten Commandments He started with 1) "Thou shall have no other gods before Me;" and 2) "You shall not make for yourself an image in the form of anything in heaven above or on the earth beneath or in the waters below. You shall not bow down to them or worship them; for I, the Lord your God, am a jealous God..."

The significant thing about these two commandments is that they show us God's steadfast desire to have an intimate and pure relationship with us. The fact that we are able to truly connect with our creator and Savior is an amazing privilege, but God didn't stop there! He also gave us the ability to connect with other human beings in emotional, spiritual and physical ways. This leads me to the gift that I am going to talk about in this chapter... It's a gift that isn't talked about enough inside of the church. It's a gift that isn't talked about enough by parents and their children. It's a gift that isn't talked about enough between single men and ladies who have yet to unwrap it. The gift I want to talk about is the gift of virginity. It's time for us to break the silence, take this "book" off the shelf, open it up, and discuss it's true worth and purpose.

In the world we live in, the enemy uses the media, peer pressure, and all other avenues possible to try to convince people that sex is purely a physical thing. However, this could not be further from the truth. God created sex as a means for humans to intimately connect. Although the act appears to solely be physical, the Lord actually designed humans so that when we engage in sexual intercourse, we are actually intimately connecting with each other on emotional and even spiritual levels as well. As a result, it is impossible for a person to engage in sexual intercourse with another person without forming bonds to them or what some refer to as "soul-ties."

Each time we engage in intercourse with another person we are allowing them to connect with us in the most intimate way possible. We are allowing them to delve into our innermost being and leave with a connection to us forever. Sex is a physical experience that connects people's emotions and spirits.

Once we engage with another person in sexual intercourse, we share a bond with them. Have you ever looked at a dating relationship where the individuals didn't treat each other right, but couldn't seem to break up? Have you ever wondered, "Why won't she leave him?" or "Why does he put up with her?" Chances are that couple may have already been sexually active together, which in turn has formed a connection between them that is now there forever. That connection will continue to keep them together in a relationship until some very purposeful and painful decisions are made to break the relationship.

Of course, this type of connection and intimacy is not bad when it is formed in God's will – in a marriage. After all, it was God who created sex as a means for us to form these intimate connections with another person. In the New Testament, we find that Christ is compared to a bridegroom, and the church or the body of believers is referred to as the bride. This is to show that Christ came as a way to connect believers to God the Father in a personal and intimate way. Outside of our relationship with God, the next most intimate relationship we should have is the relationship with our spouse. Our husband or wife should be the only other person that is allowed to know every single detail about us – physically, emotionally, and spiritually.

Now some of us unwrapped our gifts way too early; some even unwrapped them not knowing what they were doing. Unfortunately, some gifts were unwrapped unwillingly for us. Thankfully, some of us are still holding on to our gifts. Within this chapter, I am going to share with you what I did with my gift. There is also an amazing testimony later in the chapter by a special person named Audrey who has been holding onto her gift even though at times it has been a real struggle for her. To be honest, there are times that she is ashamed of her gift. As you read this chapter, hopefully you will gain a better understanding of how valuable some gifts can be – especially the gift of virginity.

Let's stop and take a minute to look at this famous example of marriage and God's faithfulness. "But after he had considered this, an angel of the Lord appeared to him in a dream and said, 'Joseph, son of David, do not be afraid to take Mary home as your wife, because what is conceived in her is from the Holy Spirit.'" – Mathew 1:20.

It's pretty amazing that an angel actually came to Joseph and told him that it was okay to take Mary as his wife. You may laugh and think that you know a lot of young men who wish an angel would show up and tell them who their wives should be! I, too, think this would be helpful! However, in this situation it was necessary because Joseph and Mary were engaged, and Mary was pregnant! This created a serious situation because in the Old Testament a girl could actually be killed for being promiscuous – having sex outside of marriage. However, Mary was a true living testament to God's promises.

Mary was a virgin who God the Father used to give birth to Jesus Christ. God searched the land for a person true at heart to be worthy of carrying His son. He found Mary holding true to His Word and worthy of the job. She was sound inside and out. God wanted someone with a pure spirit, profound love, and a heart that sought to do His will and follow His commands. Most scholars believe that Mary was between 12 and 14-years old when she was blessed with this task. Today we shudder with disapproval, disappointment, and worry when we hear about girls that age getting pregnant. However, in those days' it was common for women to become engaged and married around these ages. Nevertheless, the truth still remains that Mary was pure in mind, body, and spirit so God honored that and appointed her with the task of giving birth to Jesus our Savior. Within this chapter, I want to talk about a couple of topics that we may not all agree on but they need to be explained to our younger generations!

It was necessary for that angel to tell Joseph that Mary was pure and that God had shown His favor to Mary because in the Old Testament the rules and laws were a lot stricter. For example, in Deuteronomy 22:13-21(NIV) "it is written, If a man takes a wife and, after sleeping with her, dislikes her and slanders her and gives her a bad name, saying, 'I married this woman, but when I approached her, I did not find proof of her virginity,' then the young woman's father and mother shall bring to the town elders at the gate proof that she was a virgin. Her father will say to the elders, 'I gave my daughter in marriage to this man, but he dislikes her. Now he has slandered her and said, I did not find your daughter to be a virgin. But here is the proof of my daughter's virginity.' Then her parents shall display the cloth before the elders of the town, and the elders shall take the man and punish him.

They shall fine him a hundred shekels of silver and give them to the young woman's father, because this man has given an Israelite virgin a bad name. She shall continue to be his wife; he must not divorce her as long as he lives. If, however, the charge is true and no proof of the young woman's virginity can be found, she shall be brought to the door of her father's house and there the men of her town shall stone her to death. She has done an outrageous thing in Israel by being promiscuous while still in her father's house. You must purge the evil from among you."

Again, we thank God for finding favor in Mary and allowing Jesus to die for our sins, and forgive us from them.

However, the fact remains that many of us will still live with regret and other consequences because we unwrapped our gifts too early.

I want to do whatever I can to encourage young people to practice abstinence and pursue God's will for their lives so that they will not have to face regret and consequences in relation to their purity. No matter how uncomfortable it may seem, this is a topic we need to talk about with young people if we are ever going to help them make wise decisions with their gift of virginity. I have found that communication is the key to the success or failure of every situation in life. In my heart, I feel that if we adults want to encourage something within the younger generations, then we just need to make suggestions. If we want to prevent some of the same mistakes that happened in our lives from happening in their lives, we should make recommendations. If we want our youth to realize how special their gifts in life really are, then we just need to give them our testimony!

I have to admit that I unwrapped my gift too early. I opened it because all of my friends at that time were applying a lot of peer pressure on me to be like them. They constantly were telling me that I wouldn't be as cool as them until I lost my virginity. That was one of the biggest mistakes of my life. I can remember that day as if it was yesterday. I came home from school went into my room and closed the door behind myself. I took my book bag off and sat it on the floor next to my bed as I laid back and contemplated my next moves. As I lay there with my head on the pillow and fingers interlocked behind my head, I replayed over and over in my mind the last conversation that I had with my friends that day. I thought about how I had been lying to them for years and now they were catching on to the lies all because my answers to their questions seemed to have holes in them. I had been lying and telling them that I was not a virgin, but now it was as if they could all see right through my lies into the truth. In my mind I had already decided that I needed to stop lying to my friends, and I needed to prove myself to them. All of a sudden, I remembered a girl that was a friend of mine. She lived near me, and I knew that she had a crush on me. She was a couple years older than I was and had a hint of a promiscuous side to her.

I sat up on the bed and looked at the top right dresser drawer that was staring at me from across the room. My heart started pounding harder as I approached that drawer because I knew what was stored inside of it. I slowly pulled opened the drawer, and I could see that the condom that my brother had given me a year before was still sitting there. In his mind he knew a day like this would also come for me. He felt that it was necessary for me to have a condom so that when or if I were to enter into this level of a relationship I would be "safe." Well, this girl and I weren't really in a relationship, but I was raised in the hood and I knew what friends with benefits (FWB) were at that time. I had never explored the FWB avenue before, but from my understanding it would resolve my issue. In my mind, I foolishly reasoned, "There is no commitment so no one will get hurt, right? Of course we will still be friends and everything will remain the same, right?"

Well, I slowly reached inside of the dresser drawer, retrieved the condom and placed it inside of my pocket before I entered into my living room. Her mom just happened to be visiting at my mom's house on that day, so the opportunity presented itself, so I walked right into it. I left my house and started walking. I remember arriving at her house and knocking on her door. I was toiling with the situation in my head as I waited for her to open the door. Then it happened! The door opened and she invited me in, so there was no turning back at this moment. To be honest, she had no clue that she was about to receive the privilege of unwrapping my gift. I was trying to stay calm and cool as we walked down the hallway to her room and closed the door. It was the weirdest thing ever, because it was almost as if she could read my mind and knew why I had come over to her house. A lot of it had to do with the flirting and games that we would play to get each other's attention prior to this moment. As I sat on her bed my heart was racing out of control, and I thought about a hundred ways of getting myself out of this situation, but none of them could find their way from my brain to my lips before she kissed me.

All of a sudden, she stopped kissing me and asked, "Did you remember to lock the door when you came in the house?" I replied, "You were the one that closed the door behind me," so she jumped up and ran to the door and locked it. One thing that I have realized throughout life is that God always provides a window of time or opportunity to escape. He leaves the choice for us to use that window in our hands. I realized that was my window to get up and leave, but my curiosity and my fear of my reputation had me bound to that room. She made her way back down the hallway and into the room and once again closing the door behind her. I knew that this was going to be the biggest mistake of my life, but I needed to know the answers to all of my questions. I can remember walking out of the house regretting every moment of it. Man, was I ever wrong! I realized while in the act that we would never look at each other the same again. The feeling that I had just wasted my virginity on someone that I knew that I wasn't going to have a relationship with, let alone be married to, was overwhelming me with guilt. As I walked back through the door of my house where my mom and her mom were still sitting on the sectional couch, I felt such shame. I felt as though the moment the door opened, and I walked in their eyes fell upon me. I felt as if they could read my guilt from the look in their eyes. The feeling was as if they knew what I had done, and they were judging me! I still remember my mom stopping me in the living room to ask me a question. As her lips started to move in reference to her question my body temperature accelerated and my breathing increased. Sweat started to form on my forehead, and I became very fidgety to the point she stopped and asked me, "Are you ok?" I told her yes and that I had to use the bathroom really bad. She said, "Ok, but before you go I have to ask you a question?" I said, "Ok" with a racing heart. She proceeded to ask, "Have you seen the remote control to the television?"

With a sigh of relief I said, "Yeah mama it's on the floor next to your chair," and I darted out of the room. I can remember reaching the bathroom and closing the door behind me. I slowly walked over to the bathroom sink and turned on the water. I captured the water in the palms of my hands and submerged my face into it. I eventually raised my head up and stared guiltily into the mirror at the new guy staring back at me, and thought, "I can't believe that just happened." After making it back to school and telling my friends, they all gave me praise, but there was still something inside of me that wasn't right. Later, I would realize just how big of a mistake it was, because that became the beginning of an addictive driving force that made me only appreciate the opposite sex for one reason and one reason only!

As I was writing this chapter I had many long talks with friends, strangers, and family members, and we all had one thing in common. We all agreed that if we could go back in time when our gift was wrapped that we would leave it wrapped until we could truly cherish it. We all also agreed that we would love to relive that moment so that we could pause and save our virginity and respect the anticipation that would evolve during the process of waiting and finding our husband or wife. Those people who have waited until their wedding night to experience unwrapping their gift know what I am talking about. There are others who just keep unwrapping and rewrapping the same gift and know that it's not the same.

As I was doing research on the topic of virginity it was brought to my attention that this topic can be a really big gray area for a lot of people. It is a gift that some are quick to throw away, some are ashamed of it if they haven't unwrapped it yet, and others wish they could take back.

In "The Gray Area" I talked about walking in the gray areas in life, and how these gray areas are designed by our minds to justify our actions at that time. As I began to research the boundaries of virginity, the number of people that were confused shocked me. Some females were confused about whether or not they were still a virgin or not. They were wondering if because they had never had vaginal intercourse they were still a virgin, even though they had already engaged in other sexual activities. Also, guys were trying to validate their virginity through all kinds of reasoning such as saying they were still virgins if they had not had an orgasm or because their penis never fully entered the girl they were with. The scripture we read earlier from Deuteronomy 22:13-21(NIV) was based off of whether or not the new husband thought that the hymen was intact. The men in the Old Testament were deciding if a girl was a virgin by looking for blood to show that her hymen broke when they consummated their marriage. I thank God that our eyes have been open since that era. Elizabeth Lee, MD for The Palo Alto Medical Foundation researched the topic of the hymen and virginity, discusses on their website (http://www.pamf.org/teen/health/female-health/hymen.html) that several reasons have been found as to why a woman's hymen could break before she has had intercourse as well as several reasons why a woman's hymen may not break the first time that she has intercourse. As a result, you truly can't tell if someone is a virgin simply based on whether or not she has a hymen that is intact. Based on that evidence alone, we would have probably stoned a lot of innocent girls within this day and age had it not been for the furthering of our advancements in technology and research on the topic of women's health.

Traditionally, virginity has been described as never engaging in sexual intercourse, but this definition has become a "gray area." Today young people are bombarded with sexual images from many different sources in society and media. As a result, many are left with questions such as, "Are oral sex and anal sex considered intercourse?" "How far is too far?" In regards to the Word of God, these sexual acts are not addressed specifically; however, in Song of Solomon 8:4b the Bible says "Do not arouse or awaken love until it so desires." These acts that are physical, do create an arousal, which in turn creates emotional ties. It's important to look at the whole picture and ask ourselves, if I engage in these acts will it bond me to a person that one day I won't want to be emotionally, physically, and mentally bonded to and ultimately leave me hurt in the end? When two people in a marriage give themselves to each other sexually, they are providing fulfillment for one another's needs. Even sexual activity that is not intercourse creates the release of the chemical dopamine in the brain. This chemical releases hormones and creates the "feel good" sensation. It also is the same chemical that is involved when addictions are formed. God created this chemical to release during sexual activity so that spouses would form an "addiction-like" connection to each other- For them to continue to want each other more and more. When sexual activity outside of marriage occurs, the same type of connection takes place only like a bad addiction; once it's started, it's hard to control and even harder to stop. We usually refer to this process as "one thing leads to another."

The Lord has given us the Bible to guide our decision-making and to show us His will for our lives. I Corinthians 6:18 tells us to "Flee from sexual immorality." It actually isn't gray when you read this verse. In fact it's very black and white, the Lord is telling us that all sexual activity is considered the same outside of the bounds of marriage. God looks at the whole picture. Perhaps we should all do the same. When compromising situations arise, we should ask ourselves "what need am I trying to meet with this other person that I should be going to God to meet? It may appear to be a sexual need, but deep down is it really loneliness or the desire to connect? Will engaging in these sexual acts provide the fulfillment I am looking for long term or rather will "one thing lead to another" developing into an addictive cycle ending in the lack of control, pain, confusion, shame, and a lack of connection with God.

It's important for us to understand that God is not a God of confusion; He doesn't want us to get trapped in gray areas. Instead, God has given us His Word – the Bible – to help us understand exactly how He wants us to live and conduct ourselves.

I Thessalonians 3:3-5 (ESV) says, "For this is the will of God, your sanctification: that you abstain from sexual immorality; that each one of you know how to control his own body in holiness and honor, not in the passion of lust like the Gentiles who do not know God." I think that if we gain a better understanding of the following three key terms we can clear up a lot of this confusion: What are sin, immorality, and sexual immorality?

According to the Word of God, sin is anything that separates us from the one and true living God; sin is a direct violation of God's will for your life. Sin is the opposite of holiness.

In Psalms 51:5 David says, "Behold, I was shaped in iniquity; and in sin did my mother conceive me." We were born in sin and the world was shaped in sin after the fall of man, which began with Adam and Eve (Genesis 3). What happened in the Garden of Eden was the beginning of man's sin. Satan had come in and manipulated Eve into thinking that God was a deceiver and that God was keeping them from something that was meant to be "good" for them. Eve believed the voice of Satan over the voice of God. Adam followed his wife's lead of eating the fruit and led the world into sin. As a result, the very first act of disobedience to God's commands separated man and woman from God, when this separation (sin) took place God had to send His son Jesus to be the atonement for all mankind. The atonement was the life, crucifixion and the resurrection of Jesus Christ. The Bible says in 2 Corinthians 5:21 "For our sake He made Him [Christ] to be sin, who knew no sin, so that in and through Him we might become the righteousness of God."

Now that we know that sin is everything that separates us from God, let's look at what immorality is. Before we can begin to define what immorality is, we first have to understand what morals are. We need to understand what is immoral and where moral standards come from. The word "immoral" simply means the opposite of moral. Morals are merely the set of laws established by our heavenly Father. In the book of Exodus, Moses spent time with God, and God spoke divinely to Moses as to how the people of Israel were to conduct themselves. God entrusted Moses with the Ten Commandments. In the New Testament, Jesus' life, ministry, and teachings continue to provide us with standards to live by. Jesus' life was the perfect example of a perfectly righteous or moral life.

Again, we need to understand that when it comes to sin, there are no loopholes. It's natural for humans to try to justify their actions, but God does not see things this way. For example, the seventh commandment says, "You shall not commit adultery." Many people try to turn this commandment into a loophole by trying to reason and think, well, if he isn't married, or if she isn't married, or if I am not married then I have not committed adultery. However, in Hebrews 13:4, it is written, "Marriage should be honored by all, and the marriage bed kept pure, for God will judge the adulterer and all the sexually immoral."

Scripture says that we are the bride and Christ is the bridegroom, so when we enter into sexual immorality or sexually immoral behavior, the adultery isn't against man or woman, but it's against God.

While virginity is God's gift to you, more importantly it's God's gift to your spouse. God didn't just say that we shouldn't have sex outside of marriage, because He was trying to create impossible rules to follow. He is trying to ensure that you get to experience something even better — how He created perfect love to be. In the Bible God describes marriage as giving oneself to another person. It is sacrificial, which is the opposite of self-serving. Pure sex was created to meet the needs of your spouse not your own and in turn, your spouse for you. True love is birthed in complete sacrifice of yourself for someone else. The greatest example of this is Christ. He (bridegroom) loved His bride (His people/the church) so much that He sacrificed Himself for her and is waiting in Heaven, like a bridegroom waits for his bride, for the day that He can bring His people to be in Heaven with Him.

If we truly believe that God knows our life before it even begins, which the Bible says He does, then He has known if we will be married and to whom we will be married. In Jeremiah 29:11, it is written, "For I know the plans I have for you." In weddings we say, "What God has joined together, let no man separate" so if God knows us and created us and at the same time ultimately knows and created our spouse, then adultery simply means having sex with someone who isn't your spouse...if you're not married, then that person isn't your spouse, and it is, therefore, adultery. In fact, if that's not the person you are intended for...you are in fact having sex with someone who was meant to be for someone else. God created our lives, and He has full knowledge of our futures and our past. Just because we may not know who our spouse is, doesn't mean that He doesn't know. If you have sex with someone, and they end up getting married to someone else, that person was not intended for you, and, therefore, it's considered adultery. Perhaps that person won't ever get married, but if it's not the one who was intended for you, and you are not married (in God's definition of marriage, one man and one woman) to that person, it is adultery.

God's Word states the foundation of what sexual immorality is. In Leviticus chapter 18, God tells the people of Israel how to conduct themselves as it relates to one another sexually. In verses 19-20, God limits sexual activity to inside of marriage and prohibits it from outside of marriage. Why did God do this? Well, because we are all human and He created us to love, cohabitate, communicate, reproduce, and replenish the earth. God created man first and woman was formed from Adam's rib; this is a clear indication that God has divinely selected just the right man and just the right woman for one another to engage in intimacy with one another. God says in Genesis 25 after the woman was formed from Adam's rib, that the man and his wife were both naked and were not embarrassed or ashamed in each other's presence.

If you happen to be reading this chapter, and you have unwrapped your gift too soon, you may have feelings of embarrassment and/or shame. You may feel the embarrassment of a person not valuing your gift or the shame of the act of sexual interaction between yourself and another person. These feelings often come upon us, not necessarily during the sexual act, but sometimes after. Ever wonder why? Well, let's take a look at the scripture again. The key here is God says that the man and his wife both were naked. This is an indication that sex was never intended to be between boyfriend and girlfriend; it was only intended to be shared within the sanctity of the marriage bed. Sex has become a three-letter word that is mistaken for love, relationship, and commitment. However, sex was always, and will forever be, an intimate act that may be shared beautifully in the holy marriage bed between husband and wife, man and woman. It's a place where shame escapes us and the divine nature of who God is comes in as an aroma of love and commitment between two people divinely yoked together for the glorification of God's divine will, plan, and purpose for them in the earth. When we read Hebrews 13:4, we find that when two become one connected together through the interworking of the Holy Spirit, the marriage bed is undefiled, man and woman have no shame, and God is glorified every time. As I pointed out earlier, sex is not simply a physical act. It is all about intimacy and allowing another person to connect with your innermost being. That is also why the feelings of guilt, shame, or emptiness often accompany sex outside of marriage. I Corinthians 6:18 tells us, "Flee from sexual immorality. Every other sin a person commits is outside the body, but the sexually immoral person sins against his own body."

I have a good friend named Audrey. We met years ago when we were in college, but we were not very good friends then – probably because she was focused on serving the Lord whole-heartedly back then and I wasn't. However, after I fully surrendered my life to Christ we were reconnected. As we talked about our lives, our personal ministries, and our interpretation of the Lord's current will for us, the topic of virginity came up, and Audrey told me that she was still a virgin. I was totally amazed. I was so inspired by the fact that she had remained true to herself and to the Lord for all of these years. However, Audrey was not as inspired by herself as I was. She knew that she wanted to serve the Lord and do the right thing, but she also knew that there were times when she wondered if it was worth everything that she had to "miss out on" or give up. I've asked her to share her testimony about her purity with you.

Something that is pure is often described as un-marked, not tainted, new, or un-touched. To have the word "pure" describe you is something most people would consider an honor. In terms of sexuality it means still possessing the greatest gift one could ever have to give away. To be honest, I am not one of those people who considers it an honor. My name is Audrey, and at times I have really struggled with my gift and have at times considered it a curse. It made me different from everyone else. The average American loses their virginity at the age of 17. I remembered watching TV shows of families where parents were lamenting over the fact that it was time to discuss the dreaded "birds and the bees" with their children. During the conversation, the child would ask the parent, 'how will I know when I'm old enough or when the time is right" and the parents would jokingly reply, "When you're 30" The humor of this punch line was its implied sarcasm. After all, isn't it rather absurd in our modern "hook-up" culture to tell a person to wait that long to have sex? It's even been mistakenly thought to be bad for one's health. But in my life it's not a punch line, it is reality. While I may be still technically "pure" in the world's eyes, I am far from perfect.

That was one of my greatest fears in sharing this story. I don't feel I am the greatest example of "innocence." While I've never crossed that line, I've teetered over it more times than I would like to admit. I thought my story would be seen as unrealistic or un-relatable, but humans were created to be relational and when it comes to relationships, temptations are inevitable. Everyone faces moments in life requiring them to "pause." Perhaps only in their mind, but nevertheless, it requires a decision to give in or abstain, whether it's your first time, the 100th time, or there have been so many times that you've lost count. This is a story about a time I was faced with that very decision. You will hear my internal struggles as I wrestle with my morals and my flesh.

Bradley was one of the most popular guys in the junior class. He had caught my eye many times in passing. He was usually with a girl from my class that he was steadily dating for most of the year, but word had gotten around that they had broken up. She was what I would consider a fairly normal "girl next door type" as was I. Still, I never imagined he would be interested in someone like me. I was pretty certain he didn't even know that I existed. I later found out that was not the case at all. I'll never forget the first day he talked to me. It was the last day of my sophomore year of high school. Everyone was signing yearbooks with things like "don't ever change" or "have a great summer," and saying their good-byes for the summer. Even though summer was only two months long, and we would all be seeing each other again very soon, for a high school student, so much could change over one summer: new friendships could form, old friendships could grow distant, and although unlikely to happen–at least for me–one could never rule out the prospect of romance. Those kinds of things happened for my friends, never me. The only chance I even had to meet boys was at my church camp and even then the relationship usually only lasted that week until everyone went home to various parts of the state.

Little did I know that this summer, I wouldn't have to look any further than just down the street! "You're Jason's sister, right?" asked a male voice from behind me as I was putting my yearbook into my backpack. I turned around very surprised to see Bradley standing there. I looked to the left and to the right. Perhaps he was talking to someone else, but there was nobody else around and I definitely fit the description. Jason was my brother. He was a junior, soon-to-be senior like Bradley. Although the two were in the same grade, they were not part of the same social circle. Bradley was loud, out-going, and popular. My brother was a "nice guy," kind of quiet, played football, but was by no means a "jock." Jason mostly hung around with his girl-friend. I knew quite a few guys in their grade, but most of them knew me as "Jason's sister." This was not the first encounter I had with Bradley. In fact, all week I seemed to be the object of his "middle school" flirtation. I would be at my locker and felt a tap on my shoulder only to find him quickly fleeing the scene. Up until that point I had shrugged it off. I figured perhaps he had gotten the wrong girl. After all, I wasn't a girl who often got noticed by boys. I was a fairly modest, good girl from a good Christian home who often had a lot of guy friends. I never really had "boy-friends" that I singled off with for a long period of time like my older two siblings had. In fact my mom always prided me in that (possibly to my detriment later on in life now that I'm finding myself 31 and still single).

He asked if he could sign my yearbook and I gladly obliged still not sure why he would want to. Then, he started to tell me that his birthday was in a few days and he would be having a party. He said that I should come. He handed back the yearbook and there were the words every girl dreamed of having her crush write in her book. This is what it came down to. Where all the mysterious flirta-tions that had played a back and forth game in a girls mind all year "does he like me? Doesn't he like me?" were all made clear in two little words and there they were in my book. The words "call me" with his phone number next to it. I squealed with delight–after he walked away of course! Yet I was still unsure if this was all happening or if it was just a dream. I snapped back into reality, trying to come up with some justifiable reason for what had just taken place. He was probably just teasing me like he had been all week. I'm sure he probably wrote that in a lot of girls' yearbooks and there would be many of them at his party. The night of the party finally arrived. He had called earlier that day just to make sure that I was still coming. My heart was pounding loudly as I made my way down the street to his house not knowing what to expect. How did I never realize how close he lived before? He must have ridden the same bus to school, although he drove his Dodge Omni now. It didn't look impressive, but he was older and could drive. To my surprise, there were only a few guests at his house that night. It was mainly his close friends who I didn't really know. We played video games and he made sure I sat next to him and even offered to give me a ride home since it had gotten dark. When we got to my house, my brother was home, and he and Bradley exchanged menacing glances before Bradley squealed his tires and sped off. My dad peaked out of the door to see what all the noise was, but thankfully Bradley was long gone by that time. My brother and my dad did not seem too pleased, but I was filled with glee and anticipation of the next time he would call. It came a few days later. Bradley was going out to get a Father's Day card and called to ask if I wanted to come along. It seemed harmless, but the first response from my parents was "No, you know you're not allowed to date until you're 16." I did know this, but it seemed a little ridiculous considering that my birthday was a mere three weeks away. Was I suddenly going to become magically more mature *after blowing the candles out on my cake? It also seemed rather obscured in my mind because unknown to them was the fact that even though I had not technically "dated," I wasn't exactly as inexperienced when it came to boys as they may have thought. I had my first kiss when I was 14 with a boy I had randomly met at a youth club. We made out for a while at a friend's house whose parents pretty much let her and her friends hang out in their basement doing whatever they wanted unsupervised. I found out later he made out with my friend a few hours after I had left. I had also "dated" a guy name Dave without my parent's knowledge. He went to my school and had been introduced to me by this same friend. He was 16, but still a freshman. That should be a little indication right there of what kind of guy he was.*

He was nice and had even met my mom when she gave him a ride home from school. He also lived near us, and I would often ride my bike to his house. His parents were the "hands off type" and by that I don't mean telling us to keep our hands off each other; they also let their children do whatever they wanted. Hence, it wasn't much of a surprise when his sister, who was a senior, announced that she was pregnant by her seemed to be "live in" boyfriend. Dave had been sexually active and although we weren't, it didn't keep us from exploring and being physically affectionate in the school hallways. We acted as if we were in our own little world as if nobody were watching. However, I later found out that everyone was watching, including my brother and Bradley.

Apparently, we became a common locker room joke in the junior boys' locker room. My brother and I are only 17 months apart in age and as a result were nearly inseparable as kids. We did everything together, but that began to fade as we got older. In high school it got to the point where we somehow seem to have developed a "don't ask don't tell" policy. He gave me a ride to school every day and blared the music the entire way there at which point we said our good-byes and walked on to our separate lives. His girlfriend was pretty much his life at that time. She was very much estranged from our family. I didn't know that much about her and never asked in accordance with the "understood policy." I'm pretty sure he had his secrets too. I would usually take different routes in the hallway to avoid them, however if that were not possible I would awkwardly pretend to not notice them.

Jason and Bradley never got along. They were in the same grade, but apparently not the same social circle–at least that's what I attributed it to. Unfortunately I would find out the real reason a little too late. Perhaps my brother's verbalized disdain for Bradley was also a cause for my parents' hesitation with allowing me to spend time with him. Nevertheless, they finally consented for me to go shopping with him. We did go shopping, at first, but took a detour to the kids play equipment at the park. It was dusk and there were a few children there. Bradley playfully chased them around. They seemed to enjoy it, and I wondered how everyone could have such a negative view of this fun loving guy. Suddenly, the sky turned dark and large drops of rain fell from the sky.

It quickly turned to a full on storm. With our car far away, we sought shelter in a plastic crawl tube. It was probably not the safest place to be as lightening lit up the sky, but it was quite romantic at the same time; although, I still wasn't even sure if that's what he was going for. Any uncertainty was cleared in a moment when I felt his hand slide over mine. I sat still, nervously gazing at the opposite end of the tube. After a few minutes we decided to make a break for it. Bradley jumped out of the tube, grabbed my hand, and we took off in the pouring rain towards his car. It was so romantic. That was the beginning of one of the best and worst summers of my life. A few weeks later was my sixteenth birthday, and I was finally "officially" allowed to date him. Since we lived so close we usually hung out at each other's houses, rode bikes, or went to the park. We did seem to spend more time hanging out at his house since his parents weren't as strict as mine. As our friendship progressed, so did our physical relationship. We would find time when his parents were occupied downstairs to go up to his room and fool around for a bit. We also began spending quite a bit of time at Bradley grandparents' house since they lived right on the lake and boating happened to be one of his favorite pastimes. His grandpa actually had a boathouse where he kept his own personal yacht along with several speed boats he was fixing up, one of them being Bradley. I would go there and spend time with Bradley as he worked on the repairs. One night it was finally ready to try out and we headed out on the lake. I was a little nervous. I had been on a boat before, but never one this small, and that had just been refurbished by a 17-year-old. The motor ended up turning off while we were out on our joyride. Bradley turned the key and the motor sputtered to start, and eventually kicked in for a few minutes before shutting down completely.

Thankfully, we had oars and weren't too far from shore. I ended up rowing while Bradley held the flashlight and fixed the motor. I'm generally not a big risk taker and was hesitant to even go along for this test drive. This seemed like the kind of situation you saw on the news or read about in the paper. "Teens Go Missing After Becoming Stranded In the Lake." Needless to say, I was very happy to be back on the shore and was thankful my lack of better judgment didn't result in anything worse. I thought to myself, "I'm never going to make that mistake again." However, it was only a week or so later that I found myself in that same predicament, only this time the stakes would be a lot higher.

Bradley had asked me to join him at his grandpa's house as usual. Only it wasn't until we arrived that I realized this time they were not home. After following Bradley outside, it seemed that he was well aware of this in advance and already had a plan for the evening. We went into the boathouse, but this time instead of Bradley fishing boat, he began preparing the yacht. Bradley grandpa was a very easy-going kind of guy, but I had a feeling he would not approve of this. That seemed to also cross Bradley mind, but it wasn't stopping him. Not wanting to seem like a chicken, I reluctantly got in the boat and off we headed towards the middle of the lake. The lake was very large. We had never ventured this far and certainly never in a yacht that Bradley had no experience operating. We finally came to a stop. I'm not sure how many miles out we had gone, but the shoreline was no longer visible. Bradley dropped the anchor and we ventured to the back of the boat where there was a cushioned bench on the back deck large enough for two people to lay on, which we did.

For a few moments my nerves subsided as I enjoyed the feeling of the water gently rocking the boat, the view of the clear sky above us and the arms of my man wrapped around me. We talked and playfully flirted while caressing one another until the conversation took a serious turn. "Babe, there's something we need to talk about," Bradley said. "What's that?" I playfully responded as the butterflies returned to my stomach. "You know what it is," he said. I honestly had a pretty good idea, but wasn't assertive enough to be the first one to say it so I continued playing my game of naivety. We went back and forth until he finally had the guts to say it. "We need to talk about how far we are going to go." "Oh, uh…." were the only words I could stammer out even though there were about a billion things going through my mind. Being raised in church and a very conservative family, I knew what my answer was supposed to be and even though I was pretty sure it's what I wanted my answer to be, I wasn't so sure why. I had always been told that God created sex for marriage. This principle had been drilled into me my whole life, yet I found myself very confused. Didn't God also create feelings, emotions, and hormones all of which seemed to be creating an excitement and curiosity in me that were beginning to cloud a judgment call that seemed so crystal clear before? Suddenly, I found myself in optimum conditions on a secluded boat with only water around us, lying next to my crush, "Mr. Popular," who I thought never knew that I existed. It was amazing how my wishful thinking had become a reality in just a matter of weeks. It seemed so unbelievable. Almost like it was too good to be true. I began to wonder if it really was.

Why did he even like me to begin with? How could it be that someone who didn't even seem to know me a few weeks ago be at a position to be asking me to give him the most precious gift that I could only ever give one person? Did he really even care about me? I wasn't sure. He definitely never said he loved me. So why was I feeling so compelled to go all the way with him so that he would like me? Perhaps it was because I didn't completely trust him or his motives. I had recalled a conversation we had prior to a make-out session a few weeks earlier. He mentioned how one of his classmates had disappointedly joked that he had it rough because his girlfriend, who was a classmate of mine, wouldn't even let him get to second base, which to him meant touching underneath her top. I sensed a tone of jocular sympathy coming from Bradley for his friend almost as if to say "too bad for him" considering that we had already rounded that "base." I remember the instant feeling of regret and somewhat of cheapness that I felt in that moment. I remember thinking that I was impressed with my fellow classmate's determination to uphold standards that I had not realized she had, and being a little ashamed that I had not done the same and now my boyfriend was bragging about it to her boyfriend. This conversation came back to me while on the boat because here was my second chance to let the outcome be different this time. Instead of feeling ashamed and lowering my standards, I could voice them and walk away feeling confident, or would I? Perhaps Bradley would break up with me if I didn't go all the way with him and then I would feel sad, worthless, and alone. Things had just started getting good. I finally was old enough to date and had a cool, popular, senior boyfriend.

School would be starting soon and I couldn't wait to show him off to all of my friends. They would never believe it. I had already begun to make plans of how we would ride to school together and go to the homecoming dance. Did I really want to risk all of that? I heard how the boys made fun of my classmate who didn't go to second base, would that soon be me if I didn't go all the way? But there remained a pit in my stomach that I believe God planted there the day that Bradley had recalled that story. Now it was more of a "red flag"–a feeling that was in the back of my mind that I just couldn't shake. One that made me question Bradley motives. Did he really like me, or was he simply trying to "round the bases." Was I just an object to him, a means to an end? He must really have cared though, most of the time he was so genuine and just the fact that he had wanted to discuss it had to count for something. Yet, there had been other "red flags" I had noticed over the previous weeks. Situations that made me uncomfortable and pushed my boundaries seemed to be comical to him. He had confessed to me one time that I was wearing his favorite jeans. I was caught off guard, surprised that he knew my wardrobe so well. It was then that he confessed to me that he knew me well before I knew him. He had been behind me in the hallway one time and noticed me in front *of him…well he noticed "the jeans" rather. He asked his friends with him who I was and they told him I was Jason's sister. He had remembered those jeans ever since then, or at least how I looked in them. I guess I should have felt good about it, after all, it was a compliment right? But all I felt was self-conscious and objectified.*

On another occasion while riding in his car he would put his hand on my leg and slowly inch it higher and higher to a point that he knew I was uncomfortable with, but that just seemed to motivate his charade even more. While stopped at a red light he chuckled as he pushed my head down near his lap to see if other motorists would be intrigued by the perception of what was going on. Was this just another one of those situations? Despite all of these thoughts that were going through my head, none of them could actually make it to my lips. The smell of his cologne, the feel of his strong biceps, the look of his baby blue eyes and his adorable dimples, my sense of curiosity, and most of all, the longing I had to feel accepted and not to disappoint him took over as I found myself instead saying, "Let's go and I'll say stop." I tried to sound confident in my response still it was hard to mask my uneasiness even once I gave it. We started gently kissing, and then making out.

My heart started racing with a mixture of excitement and still fear and worry. There were a million thoughts still flooding my mind. It was beginning to all start feeling very planned out, the boat, he had to have known when his grandpa would be gone so he could take the boat, and what exactly was his plan? Take me out to the middle of the lake and have sex with me? Why did he think I would so easily give into this plan? Was he prepared if I did? I certainly wasn't on birth control. Did he bring any protection? If my parents knew where I was they would be extremely disappointed. Was my brother right about Bradley all along? My family had their suspicions about him, but I defended him.

The whole time his hands found their way from my waist up to my breasts then slowly began to trace the shape of my body lower and lower. WE had NEVER gone this far before. How far was I willing to let it go? If I said stop, would he actually listen or would he simply laugh it off as he had done before, only this time it was different. This time we were miles from anyone else intervening or hearing cries of rape if he didn't listen. He could pretty much do anything he wanted.

How had I let it get this far? I should have known better. Was it too late to turn back? Would I be considered a tease? I mean, heading out on the boat alone, I should have known. Was I suddenly obligated since I was compliant thus far? Did I really want it to stop? How could something that felt so good, feel so uncomfortable at the same time? What started as an innocent boat ride could change my life forever in so many ways and with that thought I summoned all of my courage and let out a firm, STOP! Thankfully, he stopped. We lay there for a bit. He tried to convince me to at least go skinny-dipping, but at that point all I wanted to do was go home, which, after seeing his attempts were fruitless, he reluctantly started the motor and headed for home. He tried to lighten the tension on the way back by asking me if I wanted to drive, but I sat huddled in my seat not wanting to look him in the eyes.

Things were never really the same after that with Bradley. I guess you could say that was the beginning of the end. We did hang out a few more times after that day, but I seemed to only be around for his personal amusement and to be the butt of his jokes. It's hard to say why I didn't just break-up with him, especially considering the way he was treating me, but I was attached. Even though we didn't technically have sex, a bond was starting to form due to the intimate physical things we did do, and I didn't want to let go of the plans I had made for us in my mind when

Bradley had first started showing interest in me. As summer was coming to a close, I found myself calling him to get together, but he always seemed busy. I even caught him at home when he said he was at his grandpa's. His family had no idea what was going on so they invited me in for dinner. Bradley barely said two words to me the entire night, still I had hope that once school started things would change. It didn't.

All of my dreams of having a senior boyfriend, a ride to school, a date for homecoming were all gone on the first day when we both walked into the building at the same time, and he didn't even mutter one word to me. Prior to school starting I had bragged to several friends about our summer romance, and now I felt like a fool. I was beginning to see him for his true colors. Days passed and more information was revealed. A conversation that had apparently taken place in the locker room between some boys and my brother had come to my attention. The boys, including Bradley, had dared my brother to take photos of me in the shower. No wonder my brother had so much disdain for him. In the end, Bradley never planned on saying anything to me. That might have been acceptable for him, but it wasn't for me. After days of being ignored, I summoned my courage once more and confronted him at his house. He never really said why he wanted to break up, but as the pieces started to come together, I began to realize that I was a pawn piece in his game of chess. He was strategically planning his moves in such a way that would have allowed him to checkmate me and the game would have immediately been over. I thank God for giving me the wisdom to see what his moves were and allowing this game to end with a stalemate so no one won. A stalemate in the sense that he never unwrapped my gift, and his true intent was revealed. I don't know how I became the target, whether it was the "jeans" incident, or if he had it out for my brother, or perhaps he had seen me be rather openly affectionate in the hallways in the past and therefore assumed I was "easy," but as soon as he found out that the pieces were not going to create the perfect picture he had planned, he was done. That is what probably hurt me the most. He had a way about him that made me feel really special when he never really cared about me at all.

What I realized the hard way is that God doesn't just tell us not to do something for no reason. He is our creator. He knows what will hurt us and what will give us PURE joy and fulfillment. I hesitate to tell this story because I was ashamed that I even allowed things to go as far as they did. I potentially put myself in danger because I was curious. My parents had told me not to do it so naturally, I wanted to, but what I realized later was that in telling me "NO", my Earthly parents, just like my Heavenly Father, were trying to protect my heart. They knew from God's Word, that sex is an intimate bonding experience that is meant to join a man and woman who have committed their lives to each other in marriage. Anything outside of that is a compromise of the very best that God has for us. It may feel good at the time, but comes from a place that is self-serving and will ultimately be less fulfilling than God's plan. Satan is a distorter of truth. By his very nature, Satan CANNOT tell the truth. Satan attempts to get us to second-guess God's Word by asking us, "Did God REALLY say you couldn't have that? In terms of sex it may sound something like this, "Did God really say to wait?" "You want to be closer to this person, don't you? Just one time, what can it hurt?" "The Bible is so old and outdated, it's not relevant to today, and things have changed"

All of these lies swirled in my head, and still do, when I am tempted. As duped as I felt after Bradley broke up with me, I couldn't have imagined how much worse it would have felt if I would have had sex and subsequently given my virginity to him. In the end, there was no guarantee the outcome would have been any different other than it would have felt even worse and the consequences more permanent than just a temporary broken heart. I am thankful that even though I was disobedient, God still protected me. He helped me overcome those lies in my head by allowing me to "pause" and think about the potential consequences of my actions and ultimately make the right decision. Doing the right thing can be difficult at times and it can make you feel like you're different when it seems like you're the only one, but I want to encourage you that the right decision pays off better in the long run than meeting immediate desires.

Throughout life, I am thankful that God helps me to pause and remember what I've been taught by my parents and through His word. Even when I have made bad decisions, God forgives me and protects me as I wait in anticipation for the one day that I will meet the man He has for me to marry and will be able to give my gift to him completely and unashamedly.

Wow! Now that was a true test of inner strength. I want to thank Audrey for sharing this testimony of one of her personal trials. The amazing thing about this testimony is that Audrey is walking in the grace of God. She is now 31 years old, and her gift is still wrapped. Over the last several years God used Audrey in one of His very special ministries. Her assignment was to go out and witness to, save, and bring lost sex trafficking victims and prostitutes back to Him. God would send her out into places where most people wouldn't have the strength of mind, body, or spirit to go. She was no stranger to the streets or brothels in Las Vegas when it came down to saving the souls of lost female victims.

This was not an easy task. It came at a great cost. She had a constant inner battle brewing as she walked within God's grace, completing His missions. Audrey would think that she wasn't worthy of preaching to these girls about the value of their gift, when she has never even opened her gift to understand its true value. I truly believe that her purity and obedience to God make her more qualified for the job. God doesn't want her to relate to the trafficking victim's and prostitutes during the rescues. He wants her to lead by example under His grace and mercy and allow this story to be told like a lantern leading the way through the darkness.

I don't want you walking away from this chapter thinking that because you have un-wrapped your gift that it has lost its value and is no longer worth saving. If you are inside of a relationship where you are sexually active but outside of marriage, it's not too late. You can always rewrap your gift, and it will regain its lost anticipation. Yes, there will still be some scars or regrets, but the Lord will honor your commitment to now do the right thing. When you think about it in the terms of another sin, it would make perfect sense. For example, if you ever made a bad decision and stole something; then it is obvious that you should now do the right thing and not choose to become a professional thief. The same is true when it comes to sex. It is important for those of us who have given away our virginity, or even lived promiscuously, to choose to rewrap our gift and ask the Lord to honor this choice. Practicing abstinence once you have already been sexually active is difficult, but it's important to hold onto this decision because we don't want the gift of our intimacy to become like a white elephant gift that we keep rewrapping with high hopes that the next person will place a higher value on it than the previous recipient. You may have already lost your virginity, but you can always recapture your respect, self-value, and purity. The blood of Jesus covers a multitude of sins, and it wipes our slates clean. We may not be able to recapture our virginity, but I once heard that, "A person may experience a lot of first-time experiences in life." With that in mind you can rewrap your gift and wait it out until God brings you your soul mate and spouse. This allows you to unwrap your intimacy with that person and make it the first time you experience love in the form for which it was created. I felt so inadequate to write this section of the book because of the lack of respect that I displayed towards my gift.

I would constantly tell Audrey how she really needs to give this testimony. Audrey would constantly remind me that I needed to tell my story so that it would remind her, and others like her, why she should keep her gift! There were times throughout her life that her mind was just as curious about her gift as my mind was on the day that I gave mine away. The way I see it, it is almost as if Audrey is a version of Adam and Eve before they ate the forbidden fruit. Her eyes are closed to a lot of the sin or ways that I have viewed the world. Satan is whispering in her ear, "Eat the fruit!"

I am the version of Adam and Eve after they ate the fruit. My curiosity got the best of me and my eyes were opened to a lot of things at a really early age that I should not have experienced. The moment that I allowed that version of sin to enter into my life, my eyes were wide-awake, and I experienced what Adam and Eve felt when they were in the presence of God. The only difference was I felt it from my mom when I walked into the living room even though she never had a clue, because I never told her. I now realize that was the Holy Spirit convicting me for my actions. Like so many others, I now wish that I could take it back, but I am thankful the blood of Jesus has redeemed me, and I am able to tell you today that, I am striving to live a life of abstinence from things displeasing to God, so that I may live in accordance with His will.

If you are like Audrey, and you have practiced abstinence your whole life, then there is no need to be ashamed of the fact that you are a virgin. In fact, you should be proud and know that you will be the greatest gift that your future spouse will ever receive.

Unfortunately, I caved to the peer pressure around me that was like the serpent's voice, and I experimented with the idea of FWB's, giving sex a meaningless tone and taking God out of the equation to be more like the world. All those years ago, I thought I was in a gray area, but I now know it's very black and white. We need to step out of our gray areas and realize that the boundary lines are clearly laid out in the Word of God. We need to face the facts that sex outside of marriage is a sin, and we need to commit to not allowing others to lure us into their gray areas. Instead let's focus on what the scriptures teach and practice walking in God's will and preserving the value of our gift – the true intimacy that we will someday share with the person we will marry. I'm not telling you that it will be easy – in fact I can guarantee you that it won't be. However, in 1 Corinthians 10:13 it is written, "No temptation has overtaken you that is not common to man. God is faithful, and he will not let you be tempted beyond your ability, but with the temptation he will also provide the way of escape, that you may be able to endure it." In both my and Aubrey's stories, it was clear that there was a moment for us to escape the situation; we just had to make the choice. On that note, I'd like to be very blunt and leave you with this thought: there are a lot of wrongs or "bases" between holding hands and having sex. Some people call them gray, but God clearly sees them in black and white as sexual immorality; so stay off the playing field until you have said, "I do" and signed your (marriage) license to play on field. Also, there are a lot of opportunities to make the right choice, so draw your boundaries conservatively so that you don't speed right by your "way of escape."

Pause insight before the encounter:

- Audrey's brother, Jason, knew his personality and what kind of things Bradley talked about in the locker room and tried to warn her.

- When going over to Bradley grandfather's house and nobody was home Audrey should have immediately suggested that they go somewhere else – perhaps out to eat.

-

Pause insight after the encounter:

- When Bradley and Audrey were on the deck and he asked how far she wanted to go, she was reminded of the multiple times in the past where he had teased her while they were in the car, and he ran his hand up her leg making her feel uncomfortable. He asked her if it made her feel uncomfortable and laughed when she said that it did.

- One instance was when they were on the deck and Bradley said there was something that they needed to talk about and asked how far she wanted to go.

-

Finding Borrowed Time

This next chapter was the hardest chapter for me to write. I can remember sitting at my computer staring at the blank screen, and then a soft inner voice came to me saying, "Write about life from your mom's point of view." It took me sitting there and staring at the computer screen for about thirty minutes before the Holy Spirit started guiding me in the direction that was needed. I then made a couple of phone calls to a few key family members to research my mother's life. To be honest, I was blown away with the information that was shared with me. I had lived with my mom for my entire life up until she died and never truly knew her. Well, I knew a part of her, but I never realized how little until this chapter. She was such a strong woman that she tried to carry her yoke, family burdens, and pain on her shoulders all by herself. As my protector and provider, she had an image to uphold, and she did it very well. It puts me in mind of Moses in Exodus 17:8-13, "The Amalekites came and attacked the Israelites at Rephidim. Moses said to Joshua, Choose some of our men and go out to fight the Amalekites. Tomorrow I will stand on top of the hill with the staff of God in my hands."

Joshua fought the Amalekites as Moses had ordered, and Moses, Aaron and Hur went to the top of the hill. As long as Moses held up his hands, the Israelites were winning, but whenever he lowered his hands, the Amalekites were winning. When Moses' hands grew tired, they took a stone and put it under him, and he sat on it. Aaron and Hur held his hands up—one on one side, one on the other—so that his hands remained steady till sunset, so Joshua overcame the Amalekite army with the sword." Just like with Moses, some burdens may seem too impossible to carry, and we may need the help of the Hurs and Aarons of this world. I thank God for my mom's support system when things may have gotten too heavy for her to bear. I thank God for them picking her back up and helping her win all of the battles that she couldn't face alone and remaining steady until her sunset.

Borrowed Time

James 4:14 (NKJV)

"Whereas you do not know what will happen tomorrow. For what is your life? It is even a vapor that appears for a little time and then vanishes away."

As I lay in this hospital bed and my life passes before my eyes, I can't help but question some of the choices that I have made in my life. I have to tussle with the reality and theory of death being the ending or beginning of my life. I have seen this road from a distance, but God's blessings have always detoured me back to the highway of life. Lord knows that I am so afraid right now, and I would give anything to be in a healthy state of mind, body, and soul. I have heard that from the moment that a person is born into this sinful world they are destined to die. It is what you do in between those two moments that really matter. I think that I have coped with life the best way that I knew how. Ultimately, I know that it's up to me to decide whether I go to Heaven or Hell. In John 14: 1-5 it states, "Do not let your hearts be troubled. You believe in God; believe also in me. My Father's house has many rooms; if that were not so, would I have told you that I am going there to prepare a place for you? And if I go and prepare a place for you, I will come back and take you to be with me that you also may be where I am. You know the way to the place where I am going."

I know that Jesus was trying to comfort His disciples, clear up any questions that they had and ease any fears that would emerge. Maybe it worked for them, but it's not working for me! I am full of questions! I am full of fear! It's easy to believe when your reality is not standing face to face with death. Now my whole life boils down to one question, "Do I believe that Jesus died for my sins?" To be honest, I am not sure what I believe now that I am in my final hour. Here is what I know…I know that life has been hard for me, I have made a lot of mistakes in life and because of those choices I may end up in hell. I know that it is written in Ephesians 2:8-9 (NIV) "For it is by grace you have been saved, through faith—and this is not from yourselves, it is the gift of God, not by works, so that no one can boast." Yes, but what does that truly mean? If that is true, why are there people still going to Hell? Maybe I should have spent more time in church! Lord, please help me!! I don't want to die just yet, and I really don't want to go to Hell!

My parents have always pressed God in my heart, but just like the prodigal son I had to experience life for myself. I know that my faith and how much of what I believe in His Word is the key to unlock the gates to Heaven. I have to be honest here that my mother's faith was strong and my faith was weak throughout life. Life has given me enough wisdom to understand the difference between the young and old souls in life. Most young people rely on themselves to make it through life and use very little faith. As you become older your body starts to fail, and your faith grows as the world alters your concept of life. So, through your aging, wear, and tear, and your trials and tribulations evolves your spectrum of faith. At the young age of forty-six, I am not sure that my faith is where it should be. My adolescent, pure, uneventful faith grew into a wavering faith that usually ended with the question, "Why?" Yes, why was I dealt this hand in life? Why does my faith have to be tested the older I grow? Why am I so afraid to die?

I have stood beside death and at times showed affection and love towards it. I have been running from it my whole life, and now I am just plain tired. I am tired of running, fighting, breathing, and living. I am tired of all the physical hurts, mental pains, and all of the spiritual losses. I think that the souls that we have encountered in life that preceded us in death make it a warm and welcoming place within our heart. I am Ida Mae Weaver, and this is my legacy. My son Tarrance is going to shed some light on my story from my point of view.

I made a couple of bad choices in my life that I wouldn't necessarily call mistakes. My family has always stood beside me throughout my encounters. I can remember the first time that I became pregnant with my oldest son Cornell Lashaun Hall. Although he was conceived out of puppy love, he was my first child and the first grandchild introduced to our family. My second child was a blessing to me also. His name was Paul, and I knew that he was a special child from the moment I gave birth to him. I can recall my midwife coaching me through the birthing process. With a grin on her face from ear to ear, she looked into my eyes and said, "Ida, we have us another fine little baby boy!" as she held him up to the light so I could see him. As I laid my head back and closed my eyes to catch my breath, my midwife laid Paul on his back so that she could clean him up. I will never forget the next words that came out of her mouth! She exclaimed, "Oh my, that is a bad sign!" As I opened my eyes, I asked her, "What is a bad sign?"

I was told that the moment she placed Paul on his back he flipped over on his stomach all by himself. The midwife said that is a sign that a baby will not live long. Well, as days faded into months my family's love for Paul grew. There was truly something very different about Paul that we all sensed. He seemed to have the intelligence and the strength of a one-year-old from the moment he was born. I had never seen anything like it in my whole life. My midwife's words were starting to fade off into my mind like a sunset in the sky. Plus, I was constantly reminded that this baby was a gift from Heaven. One day I can remember sitting on the couch in the living room with my sister. We heard a knock at the door and neither one of us had on clothes that strangers could see us in, so we both ran to our separate rooms to put on more appropriate attire. The moment that I walked into the room, I could tell something was wrong. I walked through the threshold of my room at the end of the hall, and something pulled me over to my baby. I touched him in hopes of calming this intuition inside of me, but he did not respond! It was then that I KNEW! Slowly, I reached down as I held my breath, and my heart started rapidly pounding to see if he was ok. I could feel that his body was lifeless. His little arms fell and were suspended in the air between my hands as I held his head in my left hand and his diapered butt in my right hand. The questions filled my head as emotions started to overflow from my body. Did the midwife curse my baby? What did I do wrong for my baby to deserve this? Is it because Paul was made outside of wedlock? Suddenly, I turned and ran back into the living room screaming, "My Baby, My Baby!"

The insurance man that was knocking at the door was now standing in the living room. He could see that I was in a state of panic, so he took my baby and called the paramedics, but it was already too late. Paul died at seven months from crib death or what is known as Sudden Infant Death Syndrome (SIDS). According to the free dictionary by Farlex–SIDS is considered death from cessation of breathing in a seemingly healthy infant, almost always during sleep. I can't help but think that if I had been in the room with him, maybe I could have saved him! Did I overlook the warning signs that he was sick? LORD, why did you let my baby DIE! As I held Paul, kissed Paul, and laid Paul to rest, that was my first encounter with death.

Well, a couple of months went by, and I can recall that at times my teenage friends and I would walk around and pick up cigarette butts off the ground and smoke what little remained of them. Smoking was a nervous habit that I developed over the years to help cope with my nerves. I didn't have a job at the time, so I couldn't afford my own packs. To be honest, I wasn't old enough to purchase them either. I can recall the first time that my dad confronted me about my habit and where I was getting my supply of smokes. In my family, honesty was a key to survival in our household. Since my father was a military man, our household was run by a different code. My loving parents would never ask a question that they didn't already know the answer to, so the truth was the only avenue to freedom.

My mom's favorite line was, "Girl, don't you lie to me, I brought you in this world, and I WILL TAKE YOU OUT OF IT!" So, of course, the fear of my mom's wrath made me gravitate closer to my dad. I knew he wouldn't like it, but I told my dad the truth. My dad made a deal with me, because he knew that I would still smoke and I was his little angel. He made me a promise that if I would stop smoking the cigarettes off the ground, he would buy me a pack every time he received a paycheck. The only rule to this agreement was that I was never to be caught smoking any cigarettes by either him or my mom. It was a sign of respect, but hey, out of sight and out of mind was a phrase that I would learn to love. I respected my father's wishes, and he honored his deal. I had the best father in the world. It was like I was the son that he never had since they produced six children, and we were all girls. We had a really special relationship, and I have to admit that I can't help but smile when I think about the fact that my sisters had to have been a little jealous of our relationship, but they just had to get over it.

During my healing process, I met the love of my life Wallace Weaver. Within a year of my son dying, I was married and working on starting a new family. Things were making a turn towards the good in my life now. We loved each other as much as a teenage couple could love. Within our first year of being married, I gave birth to Wallace Weaver Jr. (WJ). The first year of his life was the scariest for me. I was so afraid that this would be a repeat of what happened to Paul.

At the age of seventeen, my dad let me drive everywhere for him. He would always sit in the back so that I would feel like I was in control and was the only one in the car. That is until I would look in the rear view mirror and see a grin on his face and his hat tilted slightly to the right as I drove with confidence. A couple of months passed by and dad and I were on our way home from visiting my uncles and cousins on his side of the family. As I made a left turn off of red oak drive and pulled into our drive way, I remember hearing this tapping or shaking noise behind me. As I looked in my rear view mirror, I noticed that he was shaking and foaming from the mouth. As I screamed, "Dad, Stop it, Stop it," but he didn't respond. I threw the car in park and exited the driver door and ran inside of the house screaming for help. My mom came running out hollering, "Lent, Lent are you ok?"

When she opened the right side passenger's door, she noticed his eyes as they rolled in the back of his head! She screamed, "No, No!" I wasn't sure what was happening, but she turned and screamed at me to get in the car and drive! "Drive to the hospital as fast as you can!" As I ran around to the car to the driver's side and opened the door, my heart was racing. I can recall trying to get the key in the ignition, but my hands were shaking too bad. My nerves were shot and only getting worse as the seconds passed. My mom yelled, "Baby calm down and just drive," in-between her pleading with my dad to stay with her. I took a deep breath and did just that. So, I pulled out of the driveway with the desire for high speeds and fear of what was happening. I glanced in my rear view mirror, and I could see the panic on my mother's face as she cradled my father's head and the tears were streaming down her face. She kept saying, "Baby, stay here, don't leave me. Stay here!" She then took her hand and started wiping the foam away from his mouth. We were only about a mile away from our house and still had about seven miles before we would make it to the hospital, when I heard a sound that I will never forget and know that I will someday make! It was a sound that I had heard over a million times throughout my life time, and never gave two thoughts about it. It was a sound that collectively changed our crying into weeping! Genesis 2:7(NIV) says, "Then the Lord God formed a man from the dust of the ground and breathed into his nostrils the breath of life, and the man became a living being." I never thought about how that would sound as the breath of life entered into Adam's nostrils, but I will never forget how it sounded as it exited my dad's mouth.

He took one last breath and silence filtered through the car as his body movements ceased, and we could hear it leave his body. Immediately, my mom's prayers turned into screams! I felt as if I was punched in the gut! I watched in the mirror as the back seat of the car where my dad once sat as a proud chauffeured father turned into an ambulance as my mother tried to revive him, finally transforming into a coroner's car. Once we arrived at the hospital, they only confirmed what we had already known by giving it a label. The label was called, "Stroke at the brain!" This was a hard pill for me to swallow to know that when I looked in my rear view mirror his grin would not be staring back at me. I have to admit that my dad used to keep a bottle of bootleg, moonshine, or gin on stash for himself whenever he wanted to indulge. When he would finish the bottle and walk away, I would always search for the little corner of alcohol left in the bottle to drink. He was my world, and the influence of a parent carries a lot of weight. So, now I find myself here without my father and such hurt and pain in my heart. Months passed by, and I received a job working at the local mill here in town. I found myself surrounded by women that were older than me and who were experts at drinking. I noticed that when I was with them, my hurts and sorrows went away. I now know that it wasn't because of their company that I felt at ease but the comforts from the spirits that I was drinking.

As a family we would learn to live together without our dad. On the first couple of holidays there was always an empty seat at the end of the table that would honor our love for him. Our bond as sisters grew into a substance consistent to that of super glue. I love my sisters with all of my heart. No one or nothing will ever come between us, and we will always be together, so I thought. I can remember my supervisor walking up to me one hot summer day while I was working at the mill. I was told that I needed to go home because there was a family emergency. As I pulled into the yard there were people everywhere. I parked the car and proceeded to walk up towards the group of trailers on my mother's property where all of us sisters lived. I could see my sisters screaming and crying. Emotions started to rise up in my body as I searched the crowd and started mentally checking off the people that I saw. It was a process of elimination so that I could determine who the commotion was about. It seems that everyone was staring at my sister Edna's trailer. Edna is the second to the oldest sister. So now, I am about twenty feet away from her front door. As I made my way through the crowd, people were beginning to whisper, but I couldn't make out what they were saying. My eyes were now fixed on my sisters and my mom as they consoled one another. Just from their demeanors as they displayed love for one another and a reflection of their tears, I started to cry, also. Puzzled by the fact that I could see Edna in that circle, I wondered why we were standing in front of her trailer. Step after step narrowed the distance between their knowledge and my curiosity. With about five steps remaining my husband grabbed me from the side and just hugged me as he whispered in my ear something that made my knees buckle from beneath me. Wallace told me that Mary, my third to the youngest sister, was stabbed to death over forty times by the husband (Stanly) of another one of my sister's (Emma)! Due to the jealousy in his heart, Stanly went to question Mary about Emma's whereabouts and if she was truly at school.

Of course with that being Mary's sister, she did what any sister would have done, and she stood her ground as she stated the facts: Emma was in school. She respected the love for her sister. Edna and my mom later told me the details of them discovering Mary's body. When they walked inside of the trailer, they saw Mary standing with her back to them slumped over the kitchen sink. They were devastated by the amount of blood that was present throughout the kitchen, which created an eerie dark environment since the curtains were closed, and the smell of blood was in the air. They continued walking slowly towards the kitchen as a team, since Mary wasn't responding to their questions our mom slowly reached out her hands to touch Mary on the arm to see if she was ok. It was our mom's touch that unlocked Mary's love in her legs as they gave way, and she fell to the floor with wounds all over her body. Even though Stanly stabbed her over forty times – which included stab wounds to her face, neck, and chest areas – Mary still had the courage, power, and love to stand back up on her feet after he left her to die as a symbol of her love for Emma! She held true to the bond that we all made as sisters to one another!

I am so thankful for my husband paying close attention to the details as the killer returned to the crime scene inquiring about what all of the commotion was about. Stanly was acting really surprised to hear the details of the murder scene as Wallace explained it to him. It was then that Wallace looked down and said, "Hey man, you have blood on your shoes." Stanly then disappeared into their trailer that was on the same lot, where he attempted to clean the blood off. Wallace reported the information to the detectives. Once they approached the trailer to inquire about the evidence Stanly decided to just admit to the crime. We were all family, so how could he commit such a crime? He was our brother-in-law and one of our closest friends! We were all just sitting at the same table together earlier this week!

I never sat down and talked to anyone about how I felt after losing three very important people in my life in a short amount of time. I really felt as if I needed to talk to someone about this, maybe even a counselor, but I didn't want my sisters to think that I was crazy. I mean no one else talked about getting help, so I just learned to live with the hurt and pain. I felt as if each one of those deaths took a fourth of my heart. Now, how was I supposed to divide up the last fourth among my marriage, kids, and family? I was mentally tired. This life seems so unfair. Years have passed by, and I feel as though I'm just running through the motions of life. The stress of my losses and the trials of my marriage drove my husband and me apart. How was I supposed to give love to a family when I don't have enough love inside of me to supply? Plus, I just found out from my doctor that I was pregnant again–with another baby! I can remember walking into the doctor's office for the second visit without my husband and talking to the doctor about possibly getting rid of this baby or possibly putting him up for adoption. My doctor told me that I would be making a big mistake and that he had a feeling about this baby boy. He told me, "This one will be your momma's boy!" and "He will stand by you until the end!" With a renewed outlook on life, I stood up and looked in the mirror with thoughts of walking into this pregnancy with a failing marriage, two sons, and a future momma's boy. The time arrived for me to endure this pregnancy and face my worst fears again. I gave birth to my fourth child, James Tarrance Weaver. For the first year, I was terrified and would not leave Tarrance alone in the room. It took a while for my fears to fade, but I learned to manage. A couple of years after our new addition to the family, our marriage took a turn for the worst. We decided to separate and go our own ways. Now, I had three kids that I was supposed to take care of until they are old enough to make it on their own. I vowed to scrape up what little love I could and spread it among my kids, even though it was only coming from one-fourth of my heart and it would be spread really thin. Nothing in my life was going as planned, and I felt like I was the black sheep of the family. I would soon find myself working two to three jobs trying to make ends meet. When I would get off of work, at times I would need a drink to relax my nerves and help me make it from day to day. Trust me, my mom constantly told me to stop drinking, but she had no clue how I felt inside. It's not affecting my family or job so I don't see the big deal.

Well, as the years passed by, I found myself facing another tragedy in my life. As you have already read, "WJ" was shot and killed at a young age. In my mind, I am constantly haunted by my son's last words, "Remember to take care of my kids if I do not make it back." I could have saved my son's life had I just stopped him from leaving! So there went the final one-fourth of my heart. All of my kids were out of my house except Tarrance who was a freshman in high school now. I felt that I couldn't go on. The pain on the inside hurt so badly that my soul was longing to be on the other side with the familiar souls. I never took a gun and placed it to my head, but I frequently had a glass to my lips.

Almost four years have passed by, and the hurt and pain have now intensified to unbearable levels. The alcohol does not numb the pain anymore. When I look at my own reflection, I see a woman who is dying. On the inside, I can feel death as it is taking over within. I can feel it within every breath that I take. I know that my body is losing the battle as the poison is being pumped through my heart into my veins to defile my other organs. I can feel my organs throughout my body start to struggle as they fight a losing battle. I can feel frequent muscle spasms in my stomach and chest areas as my muscle tissue weakens. Every step reminds me that I am getting closer and closer to my demise as they become fewer from the lack of oxygen in my lungs. There is this constant smell that only I can smell that lets me know that I am rotting from the inside out as my once white eyes start to take on a yellowish tint.

The decisions that I have made in life have lead me to my final hour in life. The irony in this situation is that I spent my whole life running from death just to have life pick me up and turn me around and convince me to run towards death with an open heart. As I lie here in this hospital bed where I began earlier in the chapter, I lie in the bed with my eyes closed and the ventilator pinning me to this world. I can hear my son's voice as he kneels on both knees beside my bed and prays for my life and pleads for my soul. I would do anything to feel his touch, but my sense of touch has already left me. With only minutes of my life left on this earth, my son's prayers soothe my soul as he starts by saying, "Father, please save my mother because I don't know how to live without her. I know that I am young, but I will truly be in debt to you for the rest of my life. Do as you will with my life, Father, just spare hers. Father, do you hear me? I will give my life over to You so that she may keep hers! Take my life, Father and allow her to live. Was not the blood of my brother enough to cover our sins? She didn't deserve the hurt and pain that she has had to suffer. Please allow her to hear my prayers Father. Please, turn Thy ears towards my lips, Father!"

Deep down inside of his heart, Tarrance seemed to think that I didn't love him enough to live for him. I wish that I could console his tears as he opens his heart up over a lifeless body to our loving Father. I am screaming from within this body, but my lips aren't moving, "Tarrance I love you more than life itself!" "I swear, baby, that our destinies will cross again! On that day I will tell you and show you what I no longer have the strength and desire to tell you at this moment. Please, baby, don't turn your back on our Father and think that He didn't answer your prayers, because this is my prayer that He is granting. I will be heading to a better place where there will be no more hurt and pain."

"Lord, I know that my only wish was to see him graduate from high school. Now since that doesn't seem possible because it's January, and I will not survive the next five months, please grant me this last request. Let me use my last breath to tell him that I love him one last time!"

I can hear Tarrance get up from his knees as the doctor walks over to his side and begins to talk to him. The doctor begins to tell him that "...!" Wait! Wait! Doctor please don't leave that burden on this son! You have no clue what a decision of this magnitude will do to his life!! Father, please stop them! Please give me the strength to say something or take my life before this has to take place!

My Father never granted me my last request before Tarrance was faced with the decision to unplug my ventilator to end my life. I could hear Tarrance say, "Do what needs to be done!" as he walked out of the hospital room with a half of a heart and out of my life forever! Shortly after that the rest of my family members approached the side of my hospital bed one by one and said their goodbyes before the doctors pulled the plug. I can remember my life flashing before me as my family started to cry off in the distance to my right. As I gave my life back to God, I would soon join my loved ones as calmness fell over my body...

Ida Mae Weaver died at 46 years young on Thursday, January 22, 1998. Another day that will be etched in my brain forever. I received a different perspective of my mom after walking in her shoes as I wrote this chapter. Towards the end of this chapter as my emotions and tears got the best of me, I felt such guilt and shame for not considering what life must have been like for her. It is true that I was only a teenager at the time, and to me parents were still invincible at that age. All I wanted her to do was to stop drinking, but now I understand her encounters in life. I only looked at her from one point of view — her role of being my mother — I never took into consideration that she was a grieving mother, wounded daughter, hurting sister, and a suffering ex-wife. I finally realized that drinking was the milder road of avenues that she could have taken.

My mom was right about me exiting the room with half of a heart. One fourth of my heart left with WJ and the other fourth left with her. From the start of this book until now, God has allowed my journey of writing this book to be a healing process for my soul. God has poured His wisdom into my soul and given me a new outlook on life. I now know that my mom only had a fourth of her heart. That there was a void that took up three fourths of her heart and she was trying to use gin to refill that void. Wisdom has shown me that I should learn from her mistakes and look to God to replenish my heart. I will admit that at one time I was very broken and now I am still broken on the inside. I was following the only pattern that I knew at that time which was called tradition. Now that I have stepped out on faith and allowed my eyes to fall upon the Lord, a restoration process has started taking place in my life. My heart is no longer half-full but has grown to three-fourths of its full potential. I know that this part took place because God's unchanging love started to overflow into my heart.

It's weird how families can walk through the same life but have such different views on it. It is at that moment in time that each of them will make decisions that will alter the DNA of their family tree. A blessing, tradition, or what seems to be a curse will evolve based off of one choice in life. People are so quick to judge a person's habits without searching for that life altering truth. I would love how Bishop Jones would walk up to a stranger and say, "Tell me your story..." because everyone has a story to tell regarding their endeavors in life.

In my family each member has chosen a path based on the choices that they have made in life. Each choice made has affected the paths of everyone in their close circle: My parents' paths evolved into a divided family, WJ's choice to leave our house on his final night, Mom's choice to drown her sorrows, and my choice to understand and respect their choices as I share their legacies in hopes of saving more lives.

Pause insight before the encounter:

- Ida could have opened up and suggested that she and her sisters seek counseling instead of harboring all of that pain inside for years.
- Ida could have lived for her family.
-

Pause insight after the encounter:

- Ida probably wishes she would have stopped WJ from leaving the house on the night that he was killed.
- Ida probably wishes she found another way to deal with her pain in life.
-

Entering His Ultimate Love

There is no way a person can talk about the ultimate love without talking about how our Father allowed His Son to be born into this sinful world. He allowed His son to walk the earth and live by example for future generations. *He allowed Him to be* nailed to the cross for my lustful acts, suicidal thoughts, and hatred towards others. I would always watch, "The Passion of Christ" and think to myself, "What horrible people!" Why didn't they believe that Jesus was the Son of God? If they only knew then what I know now, that He was truly the Christ, then they probably would not have crucified or have been that mean to Him. I would always think that if I was alive during that time, I would have most likely helped Jesus. I could have taken some of the lashes for Him. I would have done something or anything within my power to assist in helping the Son of God. I know that Jesus had God the Father backing Him, angels beside Him, and our salvation standing before Him. I realized that He had all of the support or help that He needed. As a servant and a follower, I would have felt obligated to help my Lord in some way, shape, or form. In my heart, I know that this is a mission that needed to be completed for our sins, but my human nature that He has given me wouldn't have allowed it to happen.

As my thirst and hunger grew for His Word and I developed a deeper understanding about the people who crucified Jesus Christ, my heart became filled with anger. I realized they were selfish people that wanted power and were easily persuaded by the multitude. All of them had already heard of the miracles that where performed throughout the regions, but they were afraid to be different. They were afraid to think and walk on their own opinion, so instead they agreed with the multitudes. The truth is that none of them could have taken the type of beating that they administered on

Him. They were bullies, cowards, and evil people. I never sat down and thought about the souls of the council that decided Jesus fate. I never pondered until now about if their souls went to Heaven or Hell. These were the very people that committed the ultimate sin against the Creator Himself! If anyone should go to hell it would be that group of people.

Later in life as I developed into a more seasoned Christian and continued to develop a deeper understanding within my studies for Jesus, I realized that the very people that committed those crimes against Jesus were human and faced a lot of trials and tribulations in life. They were of and from a hurting generation and probably were frequently asking the question, "Why GOD?" It seemed as though they were walking in their gray areas a lot during those times.

All of a sudden a soft voice said to me from within, "Your generation is no different than that of the past! Peter thought that he wouldn't deny Me either and would stand firm and help Me, but instead he denied Me three times. Wasn't it you that grew angry with Me and turned your back on Me when your mom and brother died? You didn't stop there, but you sinned against Me on a number of occasions, thus performing the very same act of my crucifixion against Me that the others did. Tarrance, no one killed Me. I chose to die for your adulterous acts, acts of theft, and your love for hatred. Every act that you performed against Me was a hammer strike against the nail that pinned Me to the cross. Every act of sin after I have revealed myself to you, as I did to your forefathers, was like a lash from the whip tearing at My flesh on My body. You are no different than the people that performed those very same acts against Me."

It was then that I stopped playing church and started seeking a relationship with GOD!

Now within this next chapter, you will hear the heart-beat of a young girl evolving into a woman. You will see how she dealt with and is still dealing with her one-on-one encounters with obstacles in her life that resulted in some hurt and pain. While reading this chapter you will be reminded that ultimately, we tend to blame the one for this hurt and pain who is truly blameless; we forget that God is love even when death and life are sometimes unexplainable.

The Ultimate Love

Exodus 34:5-7 (NIV)

Then the Lord came down in the cloud and stood there with him and proclaimed his name, the Lord. And he passed in front of Moses, proclaiming, "The Lord, the Lord, the compassionate and gracious God, slow to anger, abounding in love and faithfulness, maintaining love to thousands, and forgiving wickedness, rebellion and sin. Yet He does not leave the guilty unpunished; He punishes the children and their children for the sin of the parents to the third and fourth generation."

For some of us, I know that life just doesn't seem fair. Love seems to only exist in cheesy movies that usually have a fairytale ending. Earlier in the book, I shared with you that I figured that it was easier to quit love than to have it drop me again, and that was true. I can remember my first thoughts on the first day I arrived at college. To be honest, I came from an area where the ratio of black and white people was relatively equal in numbers. For college I moved to Springfield, Missouri, where the percentage of blacks at that time was in the single digits. I can remember sitting in this really big chapel that would sit about 2,100 people. I sat in the very back of the chapel so that I would not be noticed. The room was filled with silence and everyone was staring at the person standing on the stage in front of us. I could see that his lips were moving, but I ignored the words coming out of his mouth because something else had my attention. Behind the guest speaker, above his head, off to the right there were what seemed like an infinite number of organ pipes attached to the wall. I was trying to imagine what type of horrible sound would come out of those pipes. As I scanned the room looking from right to left, I was searching for kids who were just like me, lost, hurt, and had experienced the pits of life. On the inside my heart was racing because I knew all of the sin, hurt, and pain that existed in my body. As I was scanning the chapel, everyone was smiling and whispering to one another. They all looked as if they were all angels and had not experienced any hurt and pain in their lives. I knew that I was at my breaking point, and since my heart was angry at God, I felt like the devil. I had never been in an environment like this before. First, this was the first day for me attending a Christian institution of higher learning. Second, there were only a handful of black kids there. Finally, the majority of the black kids that were there seemed preppy. I can recall thinking, "This environment will not work for me!"

It was at that point I started to worry about what people would think about me. I felt like everyone could see my sins covering me and would judge me. I felt like my past was written on my forehead. The Lord would later start speaking to me through His word. I would later understand that before Paul received his name change he was Saul, the man who persecuted Christians and was well known for it, even so much that after he became Paul, people were still afraid of him. Yet he didn't go around trying to clear his past. Christ gave him a mission and he went forward, worked, and changed the world through the power of Christ. Don't worry about what people say or think about you. When God gives you a PATH, He handles your PAST! I would not realize it until later that it was at Evangel University that the seed was planted in my heart that would later grow, giving me a better understanding about who He is.

Now, as I travel around the United States with Bishop Spencer Jones giving my testimony in all of these churches, I continue getting asked the same question over and over, "How did you find it in your heart to forgive your brother's killer?" My answer is always the same. I would always say that it's easy because I have a set of role models leading me by example. If my nephews and my niece can forgive their grandfather for killing their dad and love him, then I can do the same. The older generations tend to get caught up in educating the younger generations, and often fail to examine what they are taking the time to do with that information. It is when we take a step back and truly look at our students that we become the students again. We have so much to learn from our youth and this was one of my biggest lessons in life, "The Art of Forgiveness."

Throughout this book, you have heard me discuss a couple of little key nuggets that may be helpful in your life such as choosing the top three people in your life and filling them in your top slots so they will inspire you to make better decisions in life. I have also hinted around the fact that I truly believe that every decision that you make in life will affect at least two to three people in your life. Finally I want you to take notice and reflect on the last item that may not have been as obvious throughout this book. Within the chapter "Borrowed Time" you were able to capture a glimpse of what my mother's life may have been like. You were able to see the forces that drove her to make some of the decisions and choices that she made. Also, throughout this book you were able to walk with me in my thoughts and emotions and examine my decision-making skills. You were able to see me progress from a boy to a man shifting through my mom's unfailing love, losses, and pain due to the hand that she was dealt in life. Now each choice that she made in her eyes was to better her and her children's lives in some way, shape, or form even if some of those decisions seemed a little selfish at times. We all are guilty of that at some point in life.

Through family tradition I developed a similar way of dealing with my hurt and pain by adopting the method of sweeping it under the rug. I never sought counseling or help in hopes of developing new tools or methods of breaking the family curse or spirit of depression until later in life, but by that point it was almost too late. So my decision making skill at times wasn't the best answer to my problems that were staring me directly in my face.

Once I applied the method of sweeping my problems under the rug to my situations, they eventually resurfaced years later staring me in my face again. Then I felt as if my problems demanded my attention because they came with such authority and power that I had never experienced in life before. I found myself alone and secluded, in an apartment, during my darkest hour, with a gun to my head.

So there you have two generations that shared different lives but similar events. With her permission I am going to add a third generation to this equation. You have heard how these events effected my mom (first generation), myself (second generation), and now you will see how they affected my niece Britania (third generation).

When my Uncle Tarrance asked me to share my portion of life within this book, at first I was excited. He explained God's vision that was filtered through him, and the fact that he wanted to stand up and be a vessel for God. He wanted to speak for the unspoken, hurt, and afraid. So when he asked me to stand beside him in hopes of saving lives, I was honored. He promised me that neither God nor he would ever leave my side as we walked on this endeavor together. As I took a couple of days to pray on it, my fears of reopening my scabs and wounds started to get the best of me. This is no easy task but if it is God's WILL than it has already been written.

I pray that one day I will wake up out of this nightmare and realize what beauty this world possesses. I can't help but think that I am sleep walking as I tread throughout my life. I can only imagine life from an orphan's point of view. How life is not really all that it's cracked up to be. How they could build up hatred and anger throughout life as families may take them in or put them out. After a while all of your hopes and dreams become stagnant and cold. Your dream of becoming a doctor when you grow up has been minimized into hopeful thoughts of just being loved, taken in, and cherished for the jewel that you are. My heart has been in constant turmoil ever since that night when my father, WJ, was killed.

Never in my life did I imagine my life would have turned out the way that it did. The many trials and tribulations I have endured have affected my life greatly. There were times when I thought I couldn't go on. It was at my weakest moment when God turned my life around.

Losing my dad at the age of four was a devastating thing for me. My dad was my world. I didn't understand why my father had to be taken away from me or why God would allow it. While growing up, I went over and over in my head the many different possibilities that I could have taken to prevent my dad's death. I blamed myself for the longest time. You see, I lived with my Dad, Uncle Tarrance, and Grandmother Ida. My mom and dad were going through a transitional phase in life and were in the process of regrouping to get a new place. My mom would ask me all the time if I wanted to come spend the night with her and my brothers. I loved my dad so I wasn't going anywhere without him. I asked my father to come with me that night, and he did as I asked him to do. After we arrived over there, as usual I was in my dad's lap in the recliner, and my brothers were on the couch with my mom since there wasn't enough room in the chair. My daddy loved reading books so he decided to read one as we waited to fall asleep. I drifted off to sleep at some point during the turning of the pages and was awakened by a familiar sound. It was my Granddad walking in the door. I heard him say, "Wallace didn't I tell you not to come over here to my house!" as he walked to the back room. My dad lifted me up and placed me on the floor as he put his shoes on and tied them. Then he picked me back up in his arms and said, "Joe, I don't want to fight," and started heading for the door that was about four feet to the left of the recliner that we were previously sitting in. As we started our journey to the door, I looked at my mom and brothers laying asleep on the couch. I slowly turned around and faced the direction that we were heading when I heard a loud bang! My ears started ringing as I heard my daddy make this grunting noise. I looked at him and could see the pain in his face as we traveled towards the floor. The moment that he sat me down I looked over at my Granddad scared and confused, and I can only imagine the smoke still coming out of the barrel of the shotgun. My dad fell on his stomach as he was reaching behind him to feel the spot that was causing him so much pain.

I can still hear my dad's last words, "I love you and always respect your mom! I am going to go to sleep for a long time," but I had no clue what he meant at that moment. I ran over to my mom with such fear and confusion inside of my mind, body, and soul. I can remember crying and screaming as my mom got up and took us into the back bedroom of my grandfather's house so that we didn't have to see the horror that had already taken place. My brothers and I stayed inside of that room for what seemed like an eternity. Finally, I remember a police officer coming through the bedroom door and carrying us out of the room one by one. First Raheem, then TJ, and lastly, myself. I can remember hearing the officer telling me to close my eyes and place my hand over my eyes so that I would not have to see what was going on. Well, my eyes had already witnessed it, and my mind needed to understand what took place so I looked! As the officer carried me in his arms with my head on his shoulder my surroundings slowed down. I tried to keep them close but I was worried about my Daddy. When I opened my eyes, I could see him sprawled out on the floor a couple of feet from the door. He was lying in a pool of blood, but he wasn't moving. As we exited the house that was the last time that I saw him before they walked me over to my Grandma Ida's arms who was standing outside of the trailer waiting.

I have to admit that I had only been back inside of that trailer once since my father died and it was a month after the incident took place. My mom had to go get all of my Grandfather's belongings out of the trailer since no one was paying the bills for it. I can still remember thinking that nothing had changed from the night that it all took place. Everything was in the same exact spot as we left it on that night. There was one thing that caught my eye, and I can still envision it at times when I close my eyes. Although they cleaned up the blood, there was still a big red spot on the light colored vinyl flooring that outlined the spot where my Daddy's blood once laid. I struggled and still struggle with the point where my life meets its reality. It still feels like a dream. How can one incident take away two very important people in my life? I lost my daddy and my granddad in that one night. At such a young age, I didn't really hate my granddad because I was too young to understand the full picture. I have never really opened this part of my heart and some of these secrets have been tucked away in those chambers to never be spoken about until now.

Five months after my father's death, my mom remarried and my life took a turn for the worse. We moved into a light bluish-gray colored three-bedroom house. If you were to enter into our living room and walk towards the back of the room to your left would be a hallway. Walking down that hallway, the first door on your left was our den and the door directly across the hall from it was the bathroom door. Now if you continued down the hallway the next door on your left was my room and directly at the end of the hall was my brothers' room which they shared. Now upon entering the living room and walking to the back right corner you would see the door to my mom's room. My stepfather was secretly a drunk and a big time alcoholic and would spend a lot of his time in the living room. He would always demean me in many different ways. I can remember this one incident when I was about 6 years old. My mom went to work that afternoon. He took us to go see his mom, and we stayed there for a couple of hours. Once we left there then we stopped by one of his friend's house. I'm guessing his friend was having a party because there were cars and people everywhere. Some people were outside smoking God knows what, and others were on the porch drinking and playing card games. My stepfather told us that he would be right back and that he wouldn't be long. He walked inside the house and didn't come back for hours. My brothers (TJ – 4 years old and Raheem – 3 years old) at that time had fallen asleep, but I refused to go to sleep in such a place. The house looked similar to a crack house. He finally came out of the house hours later, and I told him that we were hungry. He said he would stop and get us something to eat. I could tell he wasn't himself at this point. On the way to get food he started speeding and driving recklessly. I was so afraid that I jumped in the backseat with my brothers and we all threw on our seat belts. My actions didn't seem to faze him at all as we made it to the destination to retrieve our food. Before we could finish eating our food, we had pulled into the driveway, and he told us that we all had to go right to bed once we entered the house. As we passed through the living room and entered the hall, my protective instincts would not allow me to sleep in my room. I decided right then that I would pass my room and sleep in my brothers' room that night to make sure they were safe. The only sound filling the house that night was him sitting upfront in the living room yelling to himself.

As I sat up with my back against the wall and my two brothers laid next to me in bed. I decided to extend my arms out to hold them and pull them in closer to my body as we waited. I felt like an eagle sitting in the nest with her wings extended over her young to shield them from the world. I stayed up all night staring at the door wondering if tonight was going to be another hurtful night! If he was going to bust through the door just like he had countless times before and release a rage that would cause more hatred and anger to build up inside of me. Well, God kept protected us on that night, but He deserted us all of the other nights. I was so glad to see my mom the next morning.

I experienced ***every type*** *of abuse you could possibly think of from him. I was cooking and cleaning at a very young age just because I had to keep him happy. There are a lot of things that my mind, body, and spirit won't allow me to talk about to this day. There were even nights where he would get so drunk that he would whoop my brothers and me for no reason. I can recall hearing him start in on my brothers, and I would try to keep him off of them, but he would overpower me. I hated that man with a passion. Many nights I would run down the hallway and lock myself in my room and hide under my bed in fear that he would hurt* *me. I could hear his intoxicated voice traveling throughout the house as his anger would reach its boiling point. As I sat trembling under my bed, I would cry and cry and talk to my dad in a whispering voice. I would say, "Daddy why did you have to leave me? I NEED you! Please help me!"*

I never told my mom about the abuse that I endured because he would threaten to beat her. I tried to protect her in that way, but regardless if I told her or not, he would beat her anyways. There were many times I would try jumping on him to get him off my mom. I would hear them in the other room arguing and at times I could hear the abuse knowing that I was too small to make a difference, but that didn't stop my attempts. I would run up the hallway across the living room and into their room to help her.

My hatred towards him grew so deep; I had very visual thoughts of how I was going to take him out of this world. I needed to stop all of the abuse, hurt, and pain that he was causing my family. Then one night he was very drunk, maybe even high, and he decided he wanted to tell me how much of a sad excuse of a man my dad was. He called my dad so many things that night something in me just snapped. I made his dinner that night very special. I became very afraid the next morning when he didn't wake up. I would walk by the doorway of his room staring at his motionless body. I would look for any signs of life, sounds, or movements but there were none. I just knew that he was dead. Well, a couple hours after my reconnaissance had ended, he ended up waking up! I heard him in the bathroom throwing up from his massive hangover and he survived.

The only way I was able to escape the madness at times was to go visit my Grandma Ida's house. That was always a treat, because she was one of the closest things that I had left to remind me of my dad. That is until January 22, 1998. When Grandma died, I felt like the world was coming to an end. I knew she was sick, but not sick to where she would be leaving me. I kind of felt disappointed in God as well. I didn't understand how He could keep taking people from me. At her funeral, I was so hurt that I never even went to the casket to view her body one last time.

It seemed so unreal to me. It didn't dawn on me that she was really gone until I saw them lowering her casket into the ground. I can still hear the voices of my loved ones whispering in my ears that day, "Sorry for your loss." Some even told me, "Girl, if you don't look just like Ida." I do resemble my grandma down to the bone, and I could practically be her twin. That's a gift God gave me though. My grandma still lives through me, and I see her every time I look in the mirror. I now realized she never left me, because she has always been with me in spirit. Not long after my grandma died, my mom finally got tired of taking the mental and physical abuse from my stepfather. We decided it would be safer to move while he was at work one night. I have to admit that I was much happier in my new home, and I felt much safer. I finally was able to escape the living hell that I had endured for nearly five years.

While experiencing middle school, I wasn't very popular at all. All I wanted to do was fit in with everyone. I wanted guys to like me, I wanted to wear make-up, and I wanted to go to parties like normal kids. None of this mattered to anyone though. I felt like I was alone and I had no one. Guys taunted me and made me feel like the ugliest girl in the world. They would call me a toad or goose bumps. Middle school definitely was not a good experience for me. Not only was middle school a bad experience for me, my mom also moved my grandfather in with us. I can remember when I saw my grandpa for the first time in nine years, and I was about thirteen at the time. I felt a bit overwhelmed. It totally blindsided me to see him sitting in my living room when I got off the bus from school that afternoon. I truly did not feel angry or vengeful thankfully. I had talked to him a couple of times on the phone over the years, and God had dealt with my heart. That's how I knew I was a strong person to be able to come face to face with him. After I got over my shock, I gave him a hug and told him welcome home.

Over the years I had a lot of mixed emotions running through my body, but I still took on the role to take care of him. I cared for him like he was my child. I fed him, bathed him, changed his diapers when situations required me to, emptied out his toilet when it needed to be and so on. My mom worked a lot to keep bills paid in the house and to pay off my grandfather's medical bills that his insurance wouldn't cover.

During the summer before I started high school, I felt the need to transform myself. I decided to cut my hair and wore clothes that I would not normally wear in hopes of fitting in with everyone else, and I started wearing make-up. I felt as if I could be someone different, and I could erase my past.

The changes that I had made to my appearance made the difference, because I finally was able to fit in with this one particular group that I had my eyes set on. I felt good about myself and the guys that I once wanted to like me finally started to notice me. I met new friends and stopped hanging out with the friends that were true to me. My new friends introduced me to alcohol and that became my main focus. I felt like I could drink my problems away. In high school, I was a great student taking a couple of college prep classes and advance placement classes, but I was still making a lot of dumb choices. I didn't care though. I felt like I was at my end.

My relationship with my mom sucked because there seemed to be a space that existed between us. She was trying to get her life back on track, and I was trying to discover one. The only people that I felt like I had in my *corner, were my brothers. On top of that I was trying to make sure my grades stayed up as I was taking care of my grandfather full-time for my mom. I know that I said, "God had dealt with my heart," earlier in the chapter, but the devil always wants you to test that theory! My love for God was being tested. I tried to obey Him and show my love for my mother by following these rules and by not killing my granddad, but my love for all of them and my patience was really being tested. My grandfather would taunt me and call my dad all sorts of names, or he would say your dad didn't amount to a pile of beans (putting it in a nice manner). So here I was caring for my father's killer and making sure he stayed healthy while he made my life more pathetic than it already was.*

My father's killer doesn't understand that within my nightmares my boogie man has a familiar smile, sound, and touch. When I wake-up screaming at the top of my lungs that the people who are running to my rescue can't save me, my mom will never understand because she still has her father. My brothers were too young to share the same bond that I had with our dad, and my granddad... well let's just say that I don't think that my granddad truly understands the level of pain that he caused in my life from that night on. I can't look at or hear a shotgun and not think of what took place.

He doesn't realize that the proudest moment in my life will now be my saddest. On the day that I choose to get married that as the music starts to play, and I start my walk down the aisle in my all white dress, that my smile will never be complete. On that day I will never hear my father tell me how beautiful I look! My tears of joy will actually be tears of sadness. That with every step that I take and the closer I make it to the man that I am supposed to love and spend the rest of my life with the more I will doubt him. Will he hurt me or leave me just like every other man in my life has? Will he, at some point, start lying during our marriage, by saying, that he will never hurt me! Or that he will never leave me? That's a lie because all men do and will at some point in time! My Granddad will never fully understand that I will never have the honor of having my last dance with my daddy. I can never wrap my arms around him and whisper in his ears saying, "Daddy, I am afraid as I start a new life." For him to answer me back saying, "Pokey, it's ok because I will always be here for you!" As I lay my head on his shoulder to get comfort from the smell of his cologne as we dance my fears away! I often wonder how life would have been if my dad was still alive and my Granddad had died on that night. Would I feel better? More secure? Would I feel complete? Would my nightmares turn into dreams or remain the same?

Just the pain alone from these thoughts is too much to handle at times. The consistency of these mental debts drove me to start popping pills to make some of the pain go away. Sometimes I would look to the heavens and say, "Dad I will get revenge for you!" So one day I told my grandfather, "You have some nerve talking that mess to me about my father, knowing that I'm the one that feeds you, and I'm the one that gives you your medicine!" I told him, "If I really wanted to I could overdose you and think nothing of it!" Soon after those words I paused, and I realized that my dad would have disapproved of my behavior!

Upon my 16th birthday, I got a job working at Burger King. So, not only was I keeping my grades up, taking care of my grandfather, and taking care of my brothers, I now had a job as well. It was crazy stress at first, but I balanced it. My mom gave me a car to get back and forth from work and school, but I had to pay for gas and the maintenance for it.

I ended up meeting a guy while working there, and he turned my life around and gave me purpose. I fell madly in love with him, and I spent all of my time with him. My mom didn't approve of him because he was 19. She told him that he was too old to be dating her sixteen-year old daughter. I didn't care because at the time I was feeling the need to be very rebellious. He was a way for me to escape my reality and he became my safe haven. However, the day came when I found out that I loved him more than he loved me. Once again the sores on my heart were torn open again as the news reached my ears. I found out that he was sleeping with my so-called best friend. It was then that I realized that I needed to get away. I need to escape all of the hurt and the pain. So I decided to join the Marine Corps and try to change my life into something positive.

I needed to separate myself from all the negative energy in my life, but through all of my trials, I grew and learned and became a better person. At first I felt bad for running off because I felt like I abandoned my granddad. I still to this day love my granddad to death despite what he did. He is, and forever will be, a part of me. My granddad was and still to this day is a very sickly man.

While in boot camp, I would constantly send letters home checking on my granddad's health and making sure he was adapting to the new environment without me. I got some scares while I was there about family members in general but none of them were about him. After graduating from boot camp, I took a leave of absence briefly before going to my next training, and I picked up where I left off with my granddad.

It was sad visiting home, because my granddad had felt as if I had abandoned him. While I was home, I spent as much time with him as possible so he would know that I would be back to visit him soon. When I went to combat training and school to learn my job in the Marine Corps, I learned that I was getting stationed in Japan. I cried for three whole days and revealed the news to my family. I took leave again to spend time with them before being shipped off to Japan.

Before leaving, my granddad told me, "I am very proud of you and it is time for you to live your life and stop worrying about me." He also said, "I have lived a long life and you have your whole life ahead of you." I cherished those words and moved forward with my life.

I decided to follow my granddad's instructions. I began to take a lot of pride in myself as a Marine. Also, I began dating a guy who I very quickly began to fall in love with. I had felt empty inside for so long, that I now became consumed with this feeling of love. In December 2010, I became pregnant with my first child. I was very excited and so was my boyfriend, especially because we were trying so hard to have a family.

In January of 2011, I lost my child due to the baby being stuck in my fallopian tubes. At 5:12 AM on January 27, 2011, I woke up from a sharp pain jolting through my abdomen. All I could do was clench up in a fetal position. That's when I felt moisture all in my bed. I took my phone and turned the flash on to see what it was. I then realized I was lying in a pool of blood. I immediately panicked. I got out of bed trembling and panting while holding my stomach as I eased across the room to wake my roommate up, and then suddenly the sharp pains hit me again. So I started screaming and yelled my roommate's name, and she finally jumped up. She turned the light on and freaked out when she saw the condition I was in. I managed to change my clothes, and I headed down the catwalk to go notify my boyfriend of my condition. When he saw me, he freaked out. He and my roommate ran to the duty hut to notify the duty.

My boyfriend was in restriction for some trouble that he was in prior, so he couldn't come to the hospital with me. My roommate came in his place. When I got to the ER, I was told I had an ectopic pregnancy and had to be rushed into town for an emergency C-section because I was dying. They loaded me up in the ambulance. I was in so much pain and losing so much blood that the EMT gave me a dose of morphine to stop the pain. I passed out before getting to the hospital, and when I awakened, my section leaders were at my bedside. I had already had the surgery, and I had to get one of my tubes taken out. The doctors said they weren't able to save it. The doctors told me that there was a point in that procedure where I had died and had to be revived due to the severe blood loss. I spent two weeks in the hospital barely eating or sleeping because I was emotionally depressed.

Upon leaving the hospital, I was told I couldn't bear children anymore because my other tube was damaged. This news ruined my life and at that moment I had nothing to live for anymore. For the next month that I had to recover, I locked myself in my room to be away from everyone including my boyfriend. This tore our relationship apart, and it made it hard for us to be together. He was hurting like I was, but I couldn't stand to see him knowing he was the father of my child. Eventually, I accepted that I wasn't going to have children of my own. Due to me accepting this, I focused on my career and making myself better.

In April of 2012, I found out I was pregnant again. I was so excited, but I couldn't get attached to the child because the doctors told me I had such a great chance of losing him. When I reached three months into my pregnancy, I knew my son was here to fight and stay. I felt complete again. On January 4, 2013, my son was born, and I have loved every moment of being a parent. I live and breathe for him. I have a new sense of living, and I know that I am on my way to being okay.

No matter what I go through, it's not about me anymore because my son is the star of my world. Please don't be confused and think that I am telling you that I feel that all of my decisions up to this point have been the right ones. I have overcome a lot, but I am still human, and I have still made some decisions of my own that were not necessarily God's will for me. I am definitely not suggesting that young women who are hurting and living with hearts that are broken try to get pregnant outside of marriage. This is definitely not the solution to a broken heart. However, I am eternally thankful for the fact that God is merciful and loving, and that He accepts me as I am and meets me where I'm at.

I am a mother now, but my heart has not been completely healed. It would not even be fair for me to put that burden on a baby. I now understand that God is the only source of healing, and because I have a son who I love so much, I am now determined more than ever to press my faith into the Lord, lay my brokenness at his feet, and accept his healing and grace.

To any children or adults that have faced the tragic event of having to witness a parent's death, I say to you, keep a positive mindset and never give up. You keep living life as if they were still here. They didn't leave you just because their bodies have left this earth. You carry them in your heart to push you through the bad times and the rough times. They are watching down over you in heaven protecting you. God has a plan and everything happens for a reason. If my dad was still living, my life would have shaped out differently than what it is now. I have grown into a strong young woman who can endure things most people can't. Each decision you make from this point on is your choice, and you will have to live with it, but ask yourself, do you want them to die in vain? I know it may hurt to see them go, but we will see them again one day in Heaven. This is just temporary.

I can understand why Britania compared herself to an orphan. We may feel like orphans sometimes once the perfect image of a family is ruined. We tend to try to recreate that very same family atmosphere using different pawns.

I believe that God did create us out of love. He showed love through the ultimate sacrifice which was allowing His son to walk in love and establish the standards of love. God created us with the full intentions of us loving each other like we have never loved before. Unfortunately, if that powerful love that we feel for someone is ever tainted or lost, that version of it is gone forever. As we walk through life, we try to establish that similar version of love for that feeling we are so used to having. For example, in Britania's life, her mom tried to establish a family atmosphere that would reflect the love that was lost by quickly remarrying, but it created more pain. In my life, I had to learn the hard way, through several failed relationships, that when love is lost we don't need to create love, we need to only embrace the love that surrounds us.

The moment that Joe was free from jail, Britania was faced with the decisions of supporting her mom's love and loving the very person that redefined love for her. The other option was to turn away from her mother's love and walk outside of God's grace and the true definition of love. In the Bible it is written that you should honor your mother and father and your days shall be long. To me a true display of love is respecting, loving, and serving against all odds. When the chips are stacked against a person, often we tend to turn our anger towards God, since He created love and could have saved or preserved your version of that love during that time.

Well, Britania walked inside of God's grace and those actions truly opened my eyes and touched my heart. We have to realize that God separates Himself from sin and is the author of love. Throughout Britania's testimony, you see how she was in search of love because it was altered in the beginning of her life. While in search of love, you can also see how God's hand, which is full of love, was and is currently covering her life. As family we all tried to display love the best way we knew how as we all struggled with defining our own newly defined definitions of what love was.

I know that at times, in some of our lives, we may create love (a child) in hopes of filling the void where love was lost. We figure that we can just focus on our version of love and the underlying pain will go away. Well, that is true but only for a little while until it comes full circle and is staring you in the face once more. Again, as we walk throughout these stages of love some of us may feel like orphans walking in and out of the presence God's love. What we fail to realize is that God's love is infallible, unchanging, and is the cornerstone of our foundations. He never changed His version of love, and it has been and always will be encompassing our lives. His love allows us to make our own choices in life and to somehow love us throughout our mistakes or sin.

I pray that this section touches your heart as it did my heart. I hope that you were able to see God's hand in all of this pain. If a little girl can set aside the pain in her life to truly embrace, love, and care for her father's killer, then we can learn a lesson from that. I know that Joe is her granddad, but that is what makes this story so complex. You don't have to take my definition or standard of what love means throughout this book. Just listen to the heart of a little girl that grew up to become a loving mother, who set the human version of love down and picked up the Master's version throughout her journey.

Pause Insight before the encounter:

- Britania should have realized that she is beautiful. Sometimes in life we tend to focus on the negative things in our life and forget the positive things. At times we feel that people can see our sins and shortcomings.

-

Pause insight after the encounter:

- *Never give up, no matter how hard life may seem. Better days are approaching.*

-

Understanding Hindsight

There are so many times in life that I have looked back over my life and wished that I could have done things differently. If I could go back in time, I would try and eliminate all the decisions that I would call mistakes. I would try to prevent all of the heartache and pain that I have caused or received throughout my life. I would give love a true chance to be a friend within my life instead of shunning it. I would have greeted my mornings with high hopes and expectations instead of expected failure and disappointments. It seems that every moment counts in life, and it's impossible to relive every moment in time. Over time I have learned to accept my past, adapt to my present circumstances, and embrace my future. Within this next chapter you will understand and relive a couple of memories with me and my cousin Tim as you walk through our lives.

Hindsight

Ezekiel 37:12-13

Therefore prophesy and say to them: "This is what the Sovereign LORD says: My people, I am going to open your graves and bring you up from them; I will bring you back to the land of Israel. Then you, my people, will know that I am the LORD, when I open your graves and bring you up from them."

I can remember one particular time while I was in high school, and I came home one night from football practice. As I walked through the door of our single-wide trailer, I could hear my mom and her friend talking in the kitchen to my left. As I walked through the living room into the kitchen, I could see that there was a bottle of gin sitting on the counter to my immediate left. It dawned on me that they were drowning their hurts and sorrows again. As I turned my head towards my right where they were sitting at the table laughing and reminiscing on happier times, part of me was happy to see my mom smiling and enjoying herself. The other part of me envisioned the countless times that I had been sitting in the hospital room this year from the side effects of the infinite bottles of gin. I can recall thinking that the side effects should be listed on the side of every bottle of alcohol just like the pharmacy companies have to list them on their pill bottles. They should read as follows, "Warning!! Side effects for your **Kids:** May cause lonely night, tears, disappointment, fear of abuse, shattered dreams, and resentment. **Spouses**: Divorce, arguments, cussing, and minor to severe fights. **Drinker:** Slow and painful death, cheating, contagious spirits on your family, and more problems. Suddenly, I immediately walked over to the bottle and picked it up and was headed to the sink to pour it out. My mom leaped out of her seat and yelled at me saying, "YOU BETTER NOT or I will whoop your ...!" I knew that it was just a figure of speech since she had not disciplined me in eleven years. Out of respect I placed the bottle back on the counter. In Deuteronomy 5:16 it is written, "Honor your father and your mother, as the Lord your God has commanded you, so that you may live long and that it may go well with you in the land the Lord your God is giving you." Even though I did not approve of her decisions, I had to respect her out of love. As I found myself standing face to face with her in the kitchen, my heart felt like it was in a million pieces. I decided that this was the time to express my feelings to her. I told her that I loved her and that she shouldn't drink, and if she didn't stop I would pack my bags in my car and leave.

On that night in that moment she said, "You don't love me!" As I stared into her eyes, tears started to run down my face. In my mind I was thinking, "How could she say that when she is my source of life, my smile, and hope. I mean if there is one woman that I will love my whole life and never divorce it will be my mother, right? Pride had no room to stand in between our love!" With a defeated heart filled with confusion, I slowly turned and walked out of the kitchen as her best friend at that time started laughing and mocking me. So, I pleaded again and her friend spoke up and repeated what my mom had said, "You don't love her!", because she was my mom's ego. She called my bluff and said that I wouldn't leave, so I packed my bags and went to my dad's house and stayed for a couple of days. My dad and I sat up late that night talking about what took place in my mom's kitchen. He reminded me that it wasn't her and that it was the alcohol talking through her. Since I had never drank alcohol before, that concept was far from my reality. Well, I ended up staying at my dad's house for about five days, and a series of events took place during that time to test our mother and son relationship. I refused to call her because she needed to understand that she meant more to me alive than dead, and that my worst fear in life was that she may die and leave me here alone. She had to understand that she meant more to me than life itself. I decided on the fifth day that I needed to move back in with my mom, because I was missing her and I had not talked to her in almost a week.

I had never lived with my dad before, and I realized this wasn't going to work. When I walked into the trailer there was a feeling in the air that no one had been there in days and the house was empty. She had nowhere to go so I assumed that she must have been visiting one of her girlfriend's houses for a couple of hours. I waited and eventually went to bed only to awake the next morning to a motherless house. Panic started to set in. I called all of her friends and none of them claimed to have seen her. I went over to my mom's cousin Cookie's house because I figured she would know where my mom was if anyone would. I knocked on Cookie's door and she invited me inside. I asked, "Have you seen my mom?" and she said, "Yes, she packed her stuff and left with a man a couple of days ago." Well, I knew that my mom didn't have a boyfriend and that was out of her character. I automatically knew that she was lying because she had this contradicting grin on her face. I decided to walk closer into her space and ask again, "Where is my mom?!" Now granted, Cookie was my mom's age and her son was bigger than me, but none of that mattered at this moment! To me that Bible verse about honoring your parents didn't apply here as she said, "Go to Hell, and I will not tell you where she is!" The only thoughts running through my head were of my mom being hurt or dying somewhere alone. Is she in the hospital again connected to the tubes and machines as her life passes her by? This can't be how it ends between us can it? She needs my help, and Cookie thinks this is a joke!

I have to admit that I lost it on that day. I took a step back away from Cookie and kind of allowed myself to enter a place that was foreign to me. When that rage came over me, I could not control my emotions. When the dust settled and my senses came back, the damage was already done. There was a hole in her wall the size of my fist and some items knocked over. How could I have been so disrespectful and lost control to the point of regretting it? As the tingling feeling in my right arm increased, the sound of Cookie yelling at me calmed me. Her exact words were, "If you get out of my house then I will tell you where she is, and I am going to tell my son to kick your butt!" I returned to my car and drove home and within an hour my mom was back home. I later found out that she was hiding out at her best friend's house. Although that was the very first house that I went to apparently they weren't ready to reveal their playful secret, until I hurried the process along. I wasn't angry at her, but I was sure glad to see her walk through that door.

Now when I look back over that situation, we both handled it wrong. I was a scared teenager that was afraid of losing his mother. I figured that if she stopped drinking she would be around until she was 90 years old. I was thinking that if I prayed and she listened to the doctor, then everything would work itself out. I now realize that I never took the time to try to understand why she drank the way she did. I am now familiar with the hurt and pain of losing someone that shared her womb to give me life. The pain I feel from losing my mother has made me able to begin to understand that if I take that feeling and multiply it times one hundred and reverse the roles in this situation, then, and only then, can I imagine how broken emotionally, mentally, spiritually and physically she must have been. Through her eyes she was trying to fill the void of losing her son with alcohol. It is written in Job 6:11, "What strength do I have, that I should still hope? What prospects, that I should be patient?" I am sure this is how she felt from the physical wear and tear on her body and related to Job 14:22 when he said, "They feel but the pain of their own bodies and mourn only for themselves." I am sure that the doctors had already given her an expiration date as she tussled with the inevitable. She faced the loss of her son, the truth about losing the fight of her life, and leaving her baby son here in this world alone. Now when I look back, I realize how selfish I had been the whole time. I think about how if I could rewind the hands of time and receive a second chance, I would make sure those things would be very different. I would hold her and tell her how much I loved her. I would take full advantage of the five days that I gave away and pushed her out of. I would not have argued with her and tried to make her see my point of view. I would have tried to be her fortress during her storm!

Let me be clear about my mom again; this is not who she was, but only who she became during the time she was intoxicated. The side effects listed above were not all side effects that I experienced as a kid, but maybe someone somewhere may have felt them. Every decision that is made in life will affect at least two or three people in your life. The moment that you make any decision–or if life circumstances make them for you–the waters are disturbed and the ripple effect is in motion. Growing up, whenever I would focus on my hurts and sorrows in life, my mom would always tell me, "Toughen up! There is someone, somewhere that has it worse than you." I know that it sounds bad that I am able to rise up from my defeat because of the failures of someone else. Just know that as a Christian my goal when I stand to my feet is to turn around and extend my hand to those that are sitting or possibly lying down due to life's encounters.

Throughout my personal faith journey, as well as throughout the process of writing this book, I have learned that it is difficult to learn to have hindsight that focuses on the positive. It is not always easy to reflect on the trials and tribulations in your past with the intent to learn from them and to find God's presence in them. However, I have found that learning to do so will change your life.

I asked my cousin Tim to take a journey down the road of reflection and share his hindsight with you. Tim is not only my cousin, but he is like a brother to me. He is truly one of my best friends in this world. This is because we understand each other in a way that others cannot. We have shared some of the same tribulations and trials. We come from the same place, and we share the same family. I know you will find his story inspiring when you see what he has overcome and what he has learned from it.

It's been said that hindsight is 20/20. I don't feel that is necessarily true for me, because that would mean that I could look back at the events in my life and have perfect clarity as to why each of the things that I went through happened. For me hindsight is more like 20/40. I can now look back at a decade in my life that seemed so hopeless and so lonely, and I can see that I was never truly alone. God was there. He was answering prayers – mostly my mother's – He just wasn't always giving me the answers I was looking for. Although looking back I can see that God was present, I am still left with many unanswered questions? I still wonder "Why" a lot.

My name is Tim and this is my story. In one decade – the span of 10 years – I lost every one of the people in my life that loved me or took care of me. You may think to yourself that we all experience loss. If you are in the later decades of your life, you may even think that you have recently lost everyone that matters to you. Unfortunately, for me this decade encompassed what should have been the most carefree years of my life – my childhood. You see, this decade started when I was eleven-years-old and came to a crashing end when I was twenty-one.

I was born in Aiken, a small town in South Carolina, where southern hospitality is the creed that everyone lives by. Where you can take a stroll down South Boundary Avenue where the tall oak trees intertwine over the road for about two miles creating a tunnel that will pierce your heart forever. Only allowing enough sun light through to highlight every leaf giving you the full effect of God's beauty. I lived there within what is known as "Thoroughbred Country" with my parents and my three older siblings. Our life was pretty simple, but we were happy. My parents were both fairly young–in their mid-thirties. Both of my parents worked hard to support our family, so I spent many long wonderful days at my great-grandma's house. Her name was Rosa Carter and she treated me like I was the most important person in the world. My great grandma was a special woman to everyone. My mother, Rosa Bell Kennedy, was named after her. Her house was always filled with the sounds of love. That would range from her faith-filled hymnal worships as she hummed her way throughout life, to family surrounding her 24/7. There was always the smell of fresh homemade biscuits, and there was always a meal to accompany the smell. I loved spending my days with her, but I looked even more forward to spending time with my dad watching wrestling and rough housing.

My dad was a family man who stood 5'11' tall and weighed about 160 lbs. Most people would describe him as a loving and feisty man. He would talk to anyone! His kids were his life when we were smaller. I was fortunate to have had both of my parents in the household. A lot of my friends only had their mom taking care of them. I can recall one particular visit from a relative that would start the change of events in my life. I was about 11 years old at my great grandma Rosa's house. My older sister Tasha, who was about 13 years old at the time, and my grandma Mamie were also there. We were all sitting around watching Wheel of Fortune on the television, when suddenly my cousin Missy came rushing through the door panting and screaming one-word sentences as she bent over placing her hands on her knees. My grandma Mamie told her in a calm voice, "Child, calm down, catch your breath and tell me what's wrong!" Missy took her hands off her knees and stood up straight as she took a deep breath. As she begun to talk, her words streamed in my head in slow motion, because her information was shocking.

Missy informed us that she had heard that my house was on fire! My mind had not processed what my ears had heard as I replied, "My house?" Missy turned and looked at me and screamed, "Yes!" I was scared and hopeful that it wasn't true all at the same time. Mamie, Tasha, and I all piled in Missy's two-door white Toyota and headed towards the small country community on the outskirts of town where we lived. As we approached our community, which was called "Nicholson Village," I frantically gazed out the window in hopes of seeing something that would prove Missy's clams wrong. My mind was racing with endless possibilities. I noticed that the skyline was mildly dark *with a pinkish tint to it as the sun retired behind the trees. Suddenly, my senses were awakened to the smell of the fire. I searched the tree line aimlessly trying to see other evidence of this eye-opener. As we exited off of Main Street onto Community Drive, we could see smoke barreling into the sky and the glow of fire through the trees. I couldn't believe it. I thought to myself, "Maybe it isn't our house!" However, as we got closer and closer I could see the fire trucks around my house and the glow of the fire engulfing it. When we exited the car, I could feel the intense heat pressing against my body. The ashes were floating through the air like little gray snowflakes. I immediately felt sad and empty. It was a scary feeling to think that everything we owned was about to be gone. I could hear the crackling and popping sounds from the fire consuming my house and surrounding trees. This would have been traumatic enough for any eleven-year-old boy, but then it got worse – I followed my grandma Mamie closely, and we walked over towards the fireman. The captain of the crew came towards us.*

I watched him as he took his hat off and held it in his hands and begin to speak to her. I noticed that sweat was pouring off of his forehead. I could smell the burning evidence all over his fire suit. My ears began to burn and ring as I listened to him tell her, "I am sorry to inform you of this tragic news, but we have a found a deceased male in the bathroom." My chest immediately began to throb as my heart began to break because I immediately knew that my dad was the only person there tonight! I thought to myself, "What! This can't be!" My eyes immediately focused on the backside of the house. I anticipated seeing fireman breaking through the windows and bringing my dad to safety, but that would not become a reality. All I could see was smoke pouring out of the window as the evidence of the water defeating the fire that was escaping the house. How could this be? They said he had made his way up the hallway before collapsing, due to the lack of oxygen in his lungs. They found him in the bath tub which was below the window where he was trying to escape this fate, but was trapped. Ultimately he had died from smoke inhalation. My grandma then said, "Oh Lord!" and began crying and praying. She told the fireman that my mother was on her way from work and would be here shortly, and they should not tell anyone else of the bad news before she arrived. Well, my mom arrived about fifteen minutes late as they had already extinguished the fire. I can remember her stepping out of her car shaking her head in disbelief then franticly searching the crowd for her family. My grandma walked up to her and hugged her and gave her the terrible, life-altering news. My mom started screaming and crying as she asked, "Why, God, why?" before she began weeping uncontrollably. I remember that part of my world crumbled in that moment. I was hurt and very afraid. Prior to that day, my mom would always say that my hugs made her day feel better. On that day as I hugged them as they hugged each other, I realized that this pain and hurt made my hug nonexistent. As I hugged my mom, I knew deep down inside that I was afraid because my daddy was my hero. Without him how would we make it in this world! I wish I could say that was the worst night of my life... but it was only the beginning.

After losing my dad, my house, and my belongings, I didn't know how to feel. I was angry and I was lonely. We all moved in with my grandma Mamie, but she still worked and now my mom seemed to be working all of the time too. As a result, my sister and I spent more and more time at my great grandma's house. My two older brothers were not around much for me to enjoy. They were six years older than me, so they were working and trying to buy cars and others things for themselves. They also tried to help my mom take care of us. I loved my great grandma and the time I spent with her. She kept me busy, and I played outside for hours on end as well. However, I longed to spend more time with my mother and brothers, too. I never really talked to anyone about the way I felt inside, so as the pain that I felt continued to get worse I began to isolate myself from others. I didn't feel like putting much effort forward in school, and the friends I did find were quite troublesome. During the week I would stay with my great grandma, and life seemed pretty good, but on the weekends I would go back out to the village, and I seemed to fall right in step with the trouble that was easily found out there. I felt as though I needed to help pull the weight around the house. Now that my dad was gone, the income intake was suffering. Well, the boys in the village told me that I could make my own money, so I started selling drugs with them, hanging out at the recreational center more, participating in street violence and getting into all kinds of trouble. I would go back out to my great grandma's house and escape all of this, but with-in two years after my dad's death, she died as well. Losing my great grandma seemed to break another large piece of my heart. As a result, I fell deeper and deeper into the life I found on the streets.

Within two more years, my grandma Mamie passed away from breast cancer. Again I felt alone. I felt abandoned. I wondered how there could be a God who supposedly loved me. How could He care for me when He continued to take away the people on this earth who took care of me? As if I hadn't experienced enough hardships thus far, a year after my grandma died from breast cancer, my mom was diagnosed with breast cancer. I was completely blown away by this. My mom had been a rock for the rest of us as we had gone through the loss of each of our loved ones. All these years she had worked her fingers to the bone to take care of us. We had struggled through real poverty, but it was not because of any lack of effort on my mom's part. She just couldn't get a break. It didn't seem like it was possible to believe that God loved me. In my heart, I felt pain, anger, bitterness, and loneliness. However, I also felt an overwhelming love for my mother, and she continued to faithfully love God and tell me that I should too. This actually almost made me love Him less because I could not believe He would let my mother get cancer when she loved him so much! After all, each loss I went through was also a loss she went through. I lost my dad, my great grandma, and my grandma, but my mom lost her husband, her grandmother, her mother and her own health! This realization made me very angry with God.

By age fifteen, I was fully initiated into a gang and living a very dangerous life. However, there were still two things in my life that constantly pulled me in the other direction. The first was my love for my mother. She had become my reason for living. She was my mom, my best friend, and my stability. The second thing was football. My mom had signed me up for football when I was very small, and it had gradually become my passion. Football was the one outlet I had where I could let my anger out and not get into trouble. I had a lot of talent; as a result, I always had coaches who were investing in me and trying to guide me.

My mom battled that breast cancer courageously. I was there with her whenever I wasn't in school or at football. She underwent chemotherapy for about eight months before they finally decided that she would need a mastectomy. With the chemotherapy I can remember how it would make her lose her appetite. How she would feel nauseous and struggle to keep food in her stomach. Most of the time that was an impossible task. I would listen about how her taste buds felt numb and the only things she could really enjoy were foods that had a salty taste. I remember how sad my mom was. My mom pondered on the thought of people judging her body and possibly laughing at the fact of her losing her hair. Eventually it broke my heart to watch her transition throughout the different stages of her life. I knew that the wig and stuffed bra would hide the truth on the outside, but nothing could fix the hurt and pain on the inside. The hardest critic that she knew was herself. She was so self-conscious about being bald during the chemo and she felt devastated when she had to have the mastectomy. I was always telling her how beautiful she was to me. When her hair started to grow back, it was silky and wavy. She was completely overjoyed when her hair was coming back. I'll never forget the way she laughed and told me, "I don't have to wear this stupid wig anymore!" By this point I truly knew that life is NOT fair, but I still could not believe that my mom had to go through this battle. After her mastectomy, the cancer did go into remission. It was a really joyful time in our lives.

I was glad that my mom had won this battle. I was throwing myself into football and excelling on the field. I was constantly in the highlight videos on the news. You have to have passing grades to play, hence I was doing ok in school as well. However, being a star athlete can come with trouble, too, such as parties and girls. I loved new shoes, and looking good, so there was one other thing I had become a really good at and that was making money by selling dope. I knew this would break my mom's heart, so I went to great lengths to keep this lifestyle hidden from her. I even kept lots of my new shoes in my locker at school so that she wouldn't see them all. At this point in my life, I was an emotional wreck. I was happy that my mom had beaten the cancer and that I was a stand-out athlete, but the hurt and pain from all of the experiences in my past were still there. As far as God – I wasn't thinking about Him.

At this point in life, I was smoking pot, drinking, playing lots of craps, running the streets and involved in a lot of fighting and violence. I was not living my life the way I knew I should have been, nor the way that my mom wanted me too. You might think that I would have been walking on cloud nine because of the fact that we had come through this battle and beat the cancer, but this was actually a point in life when I was very angry and bitter inside. I had never faced all of my past, learned how to grieve, or dealt with my feelings from all of the tragedies I had endured. As a result, I was becoming increasingly depressed, angry, and bitter. I began to isolate myself from people even more.

My mom couldn't work full-time, so money was tight around the house. I was involved in sports year round, so I didn't have time to constantly sit out of the block selling dope, but I did manage to keep selling enough to always have money in my pocket. I continued to try to hide this life from my mom. Although, as I look back I know she had to know what I was up to. After all, she grew up in the same streets that I did. However, I was her baby and she was wise enough to know that if she confronted me head on I might have walked away and then she couldn't have tried to protect me at all. Instead, she was waging a war against the enemy for my soul with her unwavering faith and prayers. As a result, I was still excelling as an athlete, and I was beginning to get a lot of attention from college recruiters even as a sophomore. All of this continued to be the story of my life through my junior year as well.

It was the summer before my senior year that my life took another turn. This was the beginning of what felt like the end to me. One morning, my mama got up and was going to cook us breakfast, but she said she didn't feel right. She left the kitchen and headed down the hallway for her bedroom, but she fell to the floor in the hallway. At first I thought she was joking with me, but she told me she couldn't move and that the pain was so bad. I remember rushing to her side and sitting with her in the hallway. She sat there for about fifteen minutes before we were able to get her into the car *and we drove to the hospital. I remember that I was literally panicked. I didn't want the worst to happen. I wondered if she was going to die right then and there. They kept her in the hospital for a couple of days running tests on her and giving her medication to make her feel better. On the day she was released the doctors said that there were some traces of the same cancers cells and she needed to schedule some more chemotherapy. I remember that she was immediately upset and said, "I can't do this; I don't want my hair to fall out again!" The doctor told her not to worry because this would be a different kind of chemo and she would not lose her hair. I remember being extremely sick inside. I was actually panicky feeling and screaming inside, "No God! No! Here we go again! How could you let this happen again?"*

Over the next five months, my mom went through a few rounds of chemo and they changed her medications a couple of different times. She had to have a port placed in her chest so that they could easily administer the chemo therapies. That port was a constant reminder of the battle going on inside of her body. The port was a direct line to her bloodstream, and I can remember her telling me that the moment they connected that port to the chemo line she would instantly feel overwhelmingly sick. I would tell her that was a sign that there was a war going on inside of her body between the medicine and the cancer and that the medicine is winning. All of the treatments seemed to have worked well and the doctors believed that my mom had indeed beaten the cancer again. However, what they didn't know was that the cells were still changing and spreading.

Halfway through my senior year I was getting all kinds of offers for college scholarships, I was being nominated for different athletic awards at the school, city, and state level, and I was focusing on graduating and moving on towards college ball with big dreams of eventually going all the way to pro-ball. I knew that I would someday get there, and the money I would make playing football would change my life and my mom's life forever! My plan was to make sure that my mom would never have to work again, worry about getting the best medical care, or worry about paying medical bills. I was focusing all of my energy and everything that I had on trying to make this dream come true. On about my fourth recruit visit, my plans got side-swiped. I found out about this crazy rule called proposition 48. This rule said that I had to have two years of the same foreign language to play in the division one schools that were recruiting me. I had two years of foreign language, but I had one year of French and one year of Spanish.

As a result, my only options would be to either go to the larger school and sit out a year of football or go to a junior college and fulfill my language requirement. I was so disappointed and let down. I could not believe that my high school advisors and teachers had let this slip by them. However, I actually still felt determined to keep pursing my dream. I discussed it with my mom, and we felt that sitting out a year was not the best choice. I decided that I was going to go to a junior college close to home so that I felt comfortable that I could still be close enough to help her if she needed me, I could keep playing and working on football, and then go to the University of South Carolina the following year. That fall after graduation, I started school at Middle Georgia College in Cochran, Georgia. I was only two-and-a-half hours from home and from my mom.

I had a great year in football. I enjoyed college life, and of course, college parties. That winter when school let out I headed back to Aiken a week earlier than what my mom was expecting me. I had a plan. I was going to go hide out at my best friend's place for the week and sell some dope so I could make some money. Then I would go to my mom's house and have a good Christmas. However, this plan did not go so well. I had been in town two days and already made a lot of money, so my homeboys and I decided to go out to the club that night. Before that night was over, I was involved in a major fight. I was confronted by a guy that was older than me. He was upset about the fact that some of my homeboys had apparently been selling drugs on his turf. I told him that I had nothing to do with that, but I would talk to them.

That's when he put his finger in my face and made some threats. My hot-temper did not handle that so well, and we ended up brawling and fist-fighting. When we got to the parking lot, it turned into a huge fight, and before you know it I could hear "pop- pop – pop," and again "pop- pop-pop!" The guy and his friends had pulled a gun and begun shooting. Before I knew it they had all backed up and run off. I was standing there with my homeboys when one of them said, "Hey bro, he shot you!" After that things got fuzzy. My best friend took me to the hospital and stayed with me until I was released. I was already of age, so I refused to let them call my mom. After a few days, I headed back to Cochran and stayed there for a few more days until I knew my mom would be expecting me home. I had been shot in the side, so I was babying it and moving a little slowly. My mom was concerned and asked me what was wrong, but I assured her that I was sore from a recent tackle in a football game. I told her that I would be fine. I never did tell her about that night, but after being shot I tried to stay as low key as possible. I tried to stay away from any place where there was going to be a large crowd – especially a crowd of people from the streets.

After that school year was done, I was moving forward with my plan. I attended a summer football workout at the University of South Carolina, and moved on to the campus that fall. Before I left, my mom said she wasn't feeling well, but I kind of shrugged it off and told her that she was going to be fine, and I would not be that much farther from home. Of course, football players move onto campus and start working out before school starts, so I headed to Columbia, got settled into my dorm and started working out with the team. After only my first two weeks on campus, I called my Uncle one morning, and he told me that my mom's cancer was back. I could not believe it. I was in shock, but I remember sitting in my dorm room looking around and thinking, "I have to be there for her." I packed my things up that same day and withdrew from school before classes had even begun.

I moved back to Aiken and got a job at a textile mill. I could make enough money out there so that I could help my mom and have money for myself, too. When I was at junior college the year before, I had met a girl named Brandy, and we started dating. Since I was leaving USC to go back to Aiken and take care of my mom, Brandy decided to transfer to a school in Augusta, and she and I got a place together in Aiken. I remember that I felt really happy that she came to be there with me and my mom. Brandy was really funny and made my mom laugh a lot. The more she laughed the less she thought about the cancer. Brandy kept my mom really busy, too. Her presence really made our life feel a lot lighter than it had been the past few times that my mom had been sick. In only a few short months we found out that we were going to be having a baby! This was something else that my mom looked forward to. She was very excited. The next nine months for me were a mixture of excitement about the baby coming, and worry and fear about my mother's health. I also had a lot of responsibility on me now, but my mom was enjoying life and seemed to be doing really well.

My son Anterious O'Ryan was born in June! I called him AO. This was the happiest I had been in years – maybe even since I was a small child. However, now my mom was beginning to show more severe signs of the cancer. By the end of July Brandy, AO, and I moved in with my mom to help take care of her. In August, Brandy took AO to Georgia to stay with her mom. My mom's symptoms were becoming worse on a weekly and even daily basis. She ended up being diagnosed with bone cancer as well as breast cancer. I remember telling her that they could test me to see if I could be a bone marrow donor for her, but she would not let me do it. One day she showed me the scar on her hip from where they took her marrow and I remember that it hurt me so badly to see scars like that on her. As the weeks passed she began to feel excruciating amounts of pain. It was so intense that she would sweat and moan in her sleep. She would toss and turn and could not get comfortable.

Through all of this pain and suffering, my mom still held tightly to her faith in God. She continued to read her Bible, pray, and go to church. I can remember that she was always singing Gospel songs even when I'd be like, "Come on, Mom." I know that she not only prayed for herself and her pain, but she prayed for me, too. She had been talking to the Reverend Jessie at church about me. He was the new head pastor and my mom had been telling him how worried she was about me. When she was talking to him about me, he said that he had played football at a Christian college out in the Mid-West, and he felt like that would be a good place for me. My mom told him that we didn't have money for a private Christian school, but Reverend Jessie told her that the Lord could use football to get me there. He told her that he had been following me in the news and knew how extremely talented I was. My mom started talking to me about how much she would like me to go to this Christian college to play football. I thought she was really losing it! I told her, "I ain't going to no Christian school." "I want to go back to USC when the time is right." My mama just kept telling me that she didn't think that was what was going to be best for me anymore. She really wanted me to consider going to this school named Evangel. My Great Aunt Christine had also been talking to the Reverend Jessie about my cousin Scottie going to this school.

The Reverend had started making phone calls and talking with the head football coach at Evangel. He really wanted to get me out there to play. I really didn't want to go! I will never forget how this unfolded. The Reverend was having his first revival week at church. My mom brought my cousin Tarrance with her, and he ended up wanting to go to school at Evangel, too. Mom and Reverend Jessie had been working on me trying to get me to go, and now they were putting pressure on me because the coach at Evangel had agreed to give me a full-ride scholarship and to extend scholarship money to my cousins as well if I agreed to go. I decided that I would agree to go to make everyone happy. I knew it really meant a lot to my mom, and for the first time in a long time, I could see where God might have been involved in this scenario, because I would not have gone alone, but now my cousins would be coming with me. It was settled! We would all go to Missouri in January for the spring semester at Evangel. I was nervous.

Meanwhile, I will never forget that there was going to be a T. D. Jakes event in Augusta in September. My mom was so excited. She began telling everyone that she was going to go and that she was going to get healed there. I didn't understand after all of the hurt, pain, and suffering she had experienced how she was still holding on to her faith. I hadn't had a relationship with God in years. I felt He had let me down one too many times and that He didn't care for me, so I didn't care for Him. Yet hearing the faith that my mom had that she was going to be healed from this cancer made me want to believe, too. I wished that the event could come sooner so that I could see this miracle. In the weeks that led up to that event, my mom continued to suffer more and more. All the while, it was tearing me apart *watching my mom suffer and listening to her moaning and crying out to Jesus every night.*

There would be nights where she would be sweating until the bed seemed to be soaking wet. She would shiver and cough until what seemed like the point that her fragile body couldn't take it anymore. Then she would fall asleep praying for strength and healing and wake up moaning in pain and praying for mercy. Some nights I would lay in the bed next to her with my arms around her trying to comfort her and let her know that everything would be okay and to make her day. It seemed to be short-lived before the pain would hit her again! She felt like God would perform a miracle through T. D. Jakes. I felt helpless because there was nothing that I could do to ease the pain for her except take her to this upcoming event.

The night before the T. D. Jakes event my mom was in a lot of pain. I will never forget that night. I prayed with every ounce of faith that I could muster. I walked into our bathroom and shut the door so that I wouldn't disturb my mom. To be honest she probably couldn't hear me over her moans from the excruciating pain she was experiencing. I got down on my knees facing the sink next to the toilet, and I opened up my heart. I said, "I know that I have my doubts, God, but make me a believer if that's what it takes to save my mama. Please, Please, Please take the pain away from her. She is full of faith, and her faith has never wavered. Her prayers aren't being answered, so here am I, Lord! Please take the pain away and help my mama. I will do anything just take it away!" As her moans and groans became louder, I prayed harder.

"Please don't let her suffer anymore. I will stop selling drugs, gang banging, and go to school. Just please don't let my love, my heart, my world, suffer anymore and make her better!" Once I finished praying, I got up and exited the bathroom. While passing through her room, she asked

with a quivering voice, "Baby, can you turn the air conditioner in the room on high for me please?" While granting her wish, I said," It's not good for you to sleep with that frigid air blowing! I will come back and turn it down in a while." She made me pull her bedroom door closed so that the air would all stay in there with her. I kept checking on her every hour or so, I cracked the door so that if she needed me she could just call my name. She seemed to find some relief and some sleep. It was the wee hours of the morning when I finally drifted off to sleep in my room down the hall. A few hours later my mom's uncle knocked on the front door. He was coming by to borrow my Jeep to go out of town for the day. I greeted him at the door and let him in. He told me to tell my mom that he was here.

The next few minutes of my life are burned into my memory forever. I was still a little groggy as made my way from the living room to her room. I slowly opened her bedroom door and as I stood in the door way, I could see the head of her bed a short distance off to my right facing away from me. Her bed ran parallel with the wall directly in front of me with minimal space between the two. I immediately felt that the presence in the room was different. It was almost as if a spirit was hovering above the room. There was a chill that embraced the room, not from the air conditioning, but my intuition giving me the sense that something was wrong. The blinds were slightly open in the room so I could see that she was resting, while laying on her right side with her back facing me. There was about five feet from the doorway where I was standing to the bed.

As I started to take the steps towards the right side of my mom's bed, I noticed there was an eerie silence shadowing the sounds of the air condition! As I called, "Mama, Mama", I decided to reach over and turn the air conditioner off that was slightly to my left. Then, I turned my attention back to my mom. I walked about three feet back towards the foot of her bed, and I decided to sit down on the bed next to her feet. I grabbed her left foot and stroked her feet and ankles a couple of times still whispering in a soft voice, "Mama, Mama, wake up! We have company." Figuring that she was still really tired, I decided to walk around to the left side of her bed so that I could see her face. With my eyes focused intensely on her during my short walk to my destination. I decided to gently ease on the bed and nudge her left arm. The moment that my warm hand made contact with her cold skin it all hit me at once. I could see that her eyes were still closed as I started shaking her harder and harder while calling her name saying, "Mama, get up!" "Get up please Mama!" I did this about three times and then I immediately knew that the worst had happened. In complete shock I walked back into the living room where my uncle was and said, "My mama's dead!" He said, "What?" and then headed into the room and looked for himself. Within seconds my world went black. I couldn't breathe. I couldn't think. I went outside and sat on the porch steps and started screaming at the top of my lungs, "Why God? Why would you take the person that loves me most? I opened up my heart in a prayer to you, and she still died!" With tears streaming down my face, my great uncle walked out on the porch and hugged me. He then called 911 and my family members to inform them of what had happened. Within minutes cars started pulling up and family members were rushing into the house to see my mama one last time in her rarest form. As the house filled with sounds of whispers and screams, I retreated to behind the house where I proceeded to weep and curse God. I wondered if my prayer had caused this. This was not the answer I had prayed for.

I really can't remember a lot of the next few days. They went so fast and felt so unreal that I just couldn't even cry anymore. The day of the funeral I remember getting in the limo thinking that this is all a bad dream, and I'm going to wake up soon and everything is going to be all right. I can remember sitting in the pew at the church trying to think of anything that I could have done to change the situation. What could I have done differently? How could I have saved my mama? Maybe I shouldn't have asked God to end her suffering. The time came to say my last good bye, and I walked up to the casket. As I started walking up to the casket, I remember looking at her thinking how peaceful she looked. She had the same peaceful look that she had when I found her laying on her bed and that is when it really hit me that I would never see my mama again. I can recall sitting in front of the church looking in the direction of her casket and noticing all of the beautiful flowers that surrounded her. As she laid in her casket with her hands crossing each other on her mid-section. I slowly I kissed her cheek, took a half a step back, said, "Mama, please get up!" and fainted right there. The world seemed very cold to me after that. There was no silver lining to my cloud; no sun shining in my sky. I was twenty-one-years old, parentless, alone, filled with rage, bitterness, anger and resentment. I was feeling like I had been betrayed by God.

From September to December, I was so depressed that I tried to commit suicide three times. First, I thought I'd shoot myself, but every time I pulled the trigger the gun would not fire. A few days later I tried to poison myself with a bottle of pills, but immediately I vomited them all up! After that I tried to starve myself over the next four-to-six-weeks. I didn't eat; I didn't sleep. I laid on the couch and let myself dwindle from about 198 pounds to 152 pounds. I never even went back to work after my mom died. I quit paying the bills and everything. I ended up sleeping on a park bench for a few nights, but then the landlord told me that he didn't feel right putting me out because my mama wouldn't have liked that. He had heard I was going to play football at a Christian college after Christmas, so he told me to feel free to go back and stay in the house until I left. He said I didn't have to pay him any rent, but I would have to find a way to pay the utility bills. One morning before the sun came up I was half awake and half asleep drifting in and out and I could hear my mama's soft faint voice say, "Get up, Baby. This ain't it for you." That's when I got up off the couch and slowly began to live my life again.

One evening right before Christmas, I was sitting in the house. It was cold and dark because I had no electricity, no water, and no food. I was all balled up under blankets on the couch. I was extremely depressed again thinking about the fact that my mom and I would not be spending Christmas together. Randomly memories were flooding my brain. Like the time she was standing in the kitchen next to the stove preparing our Christmas meal. She would constantly have talks with our Father in heaven, but on this particular time her favorite song came on the radio. I would love to hear and watch her sing when her favorite Christmas song, "Merry Christmas" by the Temptations was playing. The wooden spoon would instantly transform into a microphone and the kitchen became her stage. She would sing as if the world was watching and no one could hear her. In that moment all of her hurts and fears would vanish. By no means did she sound like a Patty LaBelle, but her voice would always soothe my spirit. My memories started to fade when suddenly there was an unexpected knock on my door. I hesitantly, got up and answered the door. There stood a lady who I had never seen before. She was about 5 feet 4 inches tall dressed in a flowery blue dress with a sweater cap on her head. She said to me, "I don't know if you need this or not, but God told me to give it to you. She handed me $100 cash, a sub-zero winter coat and some boxes of food full of items that would not spoil. Then she said, "God wants you to know that you are doing the right thing, and He loves you." For me this was conformation about the fact that I was getting ready to go to Evangel. I knew I would need the winter coat there for sure.

When I first got to Evangel, I played football, went to practice and class, but spent the rest of my time hiding away in my dorm room. I still wasn't really ready to move on with my life. I didn't know it when I first got there, but my mama was right – going to Evangel really did change my whole life.

As I stated at the beginning of this reflection, I don't feel that my hindsight is 20/20. I cannot reflect on my life story with perfect clarity and tell you that I know why I have experienced each of the things that I have gone through. I cannot tell you that it is perfectly clear to me why God would allow me and my family to experience so much loss and pain.

In spite of this, I can reflect on my life and tell you that I wasn't alone. God was there. I can see that although there were really tough times, my mom never let go of her faith, and God never let go of her. I know that her prayers saved me on more than one occasion. I am convinced that my mom's prayers are what kept me alive the night I was shot. She may not have known where I was that night or what was happening, but she knew I wasn't where I needed to be in life, and I know she was praying for me. I am also convinced that Lord answered my mom's prayers by letting her live as long as she did after her first initial diagnosis with breast cancer. I was my mom's baby, and I was only in the eighth grade when that first diagnosis was made. However, my mom lived to see me graduate from high school, go to college, have my son and commit to going to Evangel where she knew the Lord would continue to work in me. I know without a shadow of a doubt that the first time she was diagnosed with breast cancer the Lord could have taken her home, but that she prayed to see these things and He allowed her to. Realizing this has helped me to realize *that sometimes the Lord is not answering your prayers because he is answering the prayers of someone else who is involved. I have come to understand that not getting the answers that I wanted didn't mean He was absent.*

I know that the Lord orchestrated the conversations that my mom had with the Reverend Jessie and the conversations that he had with the football coach at Evangel. The Lord honored my mother's prayers and brought me to that Christian college. God knew I would be too scared to go alone, so he sent my cousins with me, and to this day Tarrance, Scottie, and I share a special bond. We are each other's strength, voice of reason, and best friends. Really – we are brothers. I can honestly say that attending Evangel was the turning point in my life. My whole life changed after that. I slowly but surely began to open my heart back up to the Lord while I was at Evangel. I felt like an orphan when I got to Evangel, but looking back I can see that the Lord brought me there so that he could surround me with a family – His family – the body of Christ. Even when I was still very angry, depressed, and reserved, God brought classmates, dorm mates, professors and coaches into my life who consistently reached out to me.

I was not completely ready to accept all of the friendships and love that were being poured out to me; yet through it, the Lord was planting seeds in my heart and watering them. Growing up in my family meant that Sunday dinners were always a big gathering. I thought that this would never be a part of my life again. I did not look forward to eating Sunday dinners in a school cafeteria. The Lord knew this and connected me with a Miss Sherry. Miss Sherry had been a faculty member at the college for a long time, and she and her husband loved to invest in students. Many Sunday afternoons they would host a Sunday lunch for several student athletes. I was one of them. I will never forget how much I appreciated the fact that I could eat a home-cooked Sunday meal and sit in a living room watching Sunday football. This was just one of the many ways that God's love was shown to me while I was at Evangel. Perhaps my mother had the intuition to know that this small college would offer me a family atmosphere that I would not find if I had gone to a huge Division One college.

During my fourth semester at Evangel, I met my wife Kim. I was attracted to her because she was different. She had the same strong faith in the Lord that my mother had. Being around her made me want to be the man my mom saw in me – the man she had prayed and believed that I would turn into. Five years after I met her, we traveled back to Springfield, Missouri, and were married in a chapel not far from Evangel. During our first year of marriage, Anterious moved in with us on his eighth birthday. I could not have asked for more! I could hardly believe that I went from being that guy who was alone, bitter, and angry to being married and having a family. Five years later we became pregnant with a little girl. I will never forget the joy I felt in my heart when Kim looked at me and said, "I have the perfect name! Let's name her Rosabell Ann" I was speechless, but she was right – it was perfect! Two years later Ella Ruth was born. Today, my wife and I own a home in Georgia, and I have the privilege of raising my three incredible kids every day. I never could have predicted this future for myself.

I cannot say that every day since I left Evangel or since I married Kim has been easy. I have still had to deal with the pain that follows me from my past. I have still had to deal with sadness and depression. I have still awakened many days and asked God, "Why?"

When I left Evangel I was working with a sports agent and getting ready to hopefully go to the NFL draft. We had a team that was already planning to pick me up. However, right before my dream finally became a reality; I was in a car accident that changed it all. I was not permanently injured for the rest of my life, but my back was injured quite badly. It took months and months of healing to simply get rid of the pain from the injury and to regain my full range of motion. It was very hard for me to understand why God had given me so much talent in football and allowed it to be one of the positive things in my life if He wasn't going to allow my dreams of going pro to become a reality.

I cannot tell you that I know 100 percent what my calling is right now, but I know that He spared my life many times, and brought me through this difficult life's journey for a reason. I have heard people say that you cannot truly relate to people unless you have experienced what they have experienced.

I hope that means that I can touch the lives of people who are hurting, grieving the loss of loved ones, or feeling angry and depressed. I understand these things in a very real way, so I hope I can let others know that they are not alone; they can make it. I truly hope that I am given opportunities to help the hopeless find hope. I know that without a Savior this would not be possible, so as I continue to try to press deeper into him I will try to bring others into his loving arms as well.

I pray that as you read through my story and my Cousin Tim's story you were able to see that although as we battle the trials and tribulations of this life we may feel beaten down, alone and afraid – truly God's presence is there. Joyce Meyer says, "God is working more than you think! So many little things in life that we think are coincidences are actually God ordained." This understanding may be the true key to having hindsight.

Pause insight before the encounter:

- Tim wishes he could have asked his father more questions about being a man instead of figuring them out the hard way in life.
-

Pause insight after the encounter:

- Instead of living in a state of depression and anger Tim could try to understand that although his prayers for his mother were not answered, her prayers were answered – she lived to see her baby graduate from high school, she met his first born, she convinced him to commit to going to a Christian college, and her pain and suffering was ended. Best of all she is with her Savior.
-

Midst of your pain

Life seems to be unexplainable at times. We know that the past is behind us, we live in the present, and to look forward to our futures. When our past, present, or future has beaten us down to the ground, it's in our human nature to want to throw in the towel. The great thing about our God is that He doesn't care where you are in life or the condition you are in when He finds you. God will meet you in the front, middle, or end of your storm. God is omnipotent (all powerful), omniscient (all knowing), and omnipresent (present everywhere) so He knows, understands and is waiting for you to arrive in every phase of your life. You just have to be willing to let Him take control or walk with you. Allowing God to take control over the storms in our lives can be one of the hardest things for a person to do. When I was depressed, down and out, and feeling left behind I threw one of the biggest self-pity parties. I alienated myself from everyone, started slacking on my chores at home, and just didn't care about life anymore.

Friends would want to pray for me, and at times would, but in my mind there was no room for God in my mess. I only allowed them to pray so that they would leave me alone. The devil had convinced my heart that I just needed to be alone. During this time, I would attend church on Sundays physically but was mentally somewhere else. There were times that I would walk into church with the full intentions of staying the whole service, but my depression had full control of me, and I would leave after five minutes.

Once you let God take control, you will start seeing things a little differently. Just like in the midst of a tornado, God has the power to make it miss two or three houses on the right side of a street or two or three houses on the left side of the street. Even though it seems like there is nothing peaceful about a tornado, if you are in the center of it there is a calmness that at times can be unexplainable to humans. There is such peace! The type of peace that will at times set your heart at ease and let you know that God is in the mist of your pain! Within this next chapter, you will hear me discuss some topics of pain and the remnants that were left behind after the storms. Please keep an open mind as we walk into this next chapter of the book.

The Pain after the Storm

Psalm 69:29(NIV)

But as for me, afflicted and in pain—
may your salvation, God, protect me.

For years now I have been experiencing something that I can't put my finger on. It always happens around the holidays. Normally around the end of September or beginning of November my days start to take on a blah state of mind. It seems to happen right around the time that we have to push our clocks back an hour. I am not sure if that has something to do with my state of mind and somehow it offsets my inner emotions. I know that my brother died in December and my mother died in January, so is this miserable fog associated with those events? Through some research I have discovered that a lot of other people experience this same cycle. Some of those people lost close family members during the middle of the year and they still experience this. Other people experience it and they never lost anyone, but like everyone else, they have experienced some trials and tribulations within their lives.

Yes, the holidays are filled with laughter and holiday cheers, so you would think that I would grow out of this cycle instead of growing content with it. However, it has become a norm in my life and I have learned to accept it as a part of who I am, yet I continue to ask the Lord to help me overcome this. I consciously don't have anything running through my mind, but subconsciously my mind is a wreck. I always tend to shy away from festive gatherings and crawl into a hole. I don't want to be around people, and I don't want people really inviting me places to spend time with their families. I have noticed that when I do accept invitations to other's family gatherings, it starts off as a fun ordeal. However, my reality quickly starts sinking in and instead of seeing the joy that is staring me in my face I am constantly reminded of what I am missing. At that point seeing a cheerful family gathered around the table as they give praise for what they are thankful for during the holidays almost breaks my heart in half. Seeing people exchanging gifts on Christmas is a constant reminder of what my family should look like. Hearing the last of the count down from three, two, and one, is the start of another year that I will have to look forward to repeating the same gloomy feeling all over again. It's hard for others to understand why I haven't been able to break free from this cycle, and why they cannot seem to conquer it for me. For those who have tried they don't understand. They think that to have a loved one stare you in your face with hopes of cheering you up and making this year better than the last year is all a person should ever want in life – right?

I know that for others, it is easy to see and hear what I have gone through in that year and realize that I am in a better place than the previous year, and assume that I should be joyful for that. However, they cannot see the pain from the past that is still deep within my heart. If you have experienced the loss of a loved one then you may understand. As people shower you with gifts you may open each one of them with a smile on your face, or you may kiss the

New Year in to existence, while still experiencing pain and sorrow on the inside.

This sorrow sneaks into your life and chokes the joy out of it. One day you are having the time of your life and then the next day and throughout the holidays you are partially putting on a fake smile, because you don't want to ruin it for the rest of your loved ones. This is one of the hardest situations to explain to people simply because they figure that their love, or your new family, or any newly developed happiness should eliminate any sadness that exists in your life. They feel that because they are present this feeling should not exist. I wish it was that easy.

In the beginning of the book I had a gun to my head, and I realized that I was at a really bad place in my life. After seeking some Christian counseling, I began to pray and ask God to open my eyes to my true calling in life. He showed me that my "problem" was in reality a gift. My mission became clearer, and I know that I must use my gift for the good of all of those souls who have experienced loss and pain.

When I look at the movie, *A Christmas Carol,* my heart goes out to Ebenezer Scrooge. I don't see a bitter old man that hates the world. I see a hurting man that is yearning for love and affection. I see a man that had life handed to him with hurt from his father's neglect, sister dying, and fiancé leaving him. This feeling was proclaimed as a Christmas ordeal, but it's much more than that if you take a deeper look into his life. Most people would agree that he hated the Christmas spirit. I would argue and say that he disliked the holiday spirit ranging from November, 1st until after the New Year. Some may view this story from the perspective of Scrooge having a counselor to walk him through his past, present, and future. Personally, I see the Holy Spirit pouring out His blessing upon Scrooge's life making him a changed man!

I have also experienced giving all of my worldly possessions away in hopes of making other lives better. I experienced a level of happiness that surpassed any other time in my life because I have a giving spirit. The fact still remains that this dark cloud always surfaces during a time in the season where most families are complete, and I feel incomplete.

Depending on the level of the relationship that you have lost, you may experience different levels of darkness and solitude. If you are single then you may try to avoid everyone and lock yourself in your house. If you are married and you have lost your parents, you may only want to be around your immediate family or the family you created out of love. There are situations where you could also be married and distance yourself away from anything dealing with family at all. These are just a few scenarios but they could all be anyone's reality on any given day.

In the authors preface, I mentioned that the process of writing this book was like giving birth to a new life and that is honestly how I feel about this process. I know that it has opened up new dimensions in my heart and mind. It has taught me that I should not be ashamed of my past and not to keep it hidden behind me. I have learned to walk boldly behind my past as I push it a few steps out in front of me embracing it as my testimony and allowing others to examine it, in hopes of giving them a brighter future.

If life alters one or two degrees to the right or left in a person's life, it can throw everything off of its axis. This next story is an example of that life-altering movement. God allows our paths to cross with other lives on a daily basis. What we do with that time is an even bigger issue. The point is that April and I decided to share our testimonies with each other. As shocking as my testimony was to April, hers was just as shocking to me. April is going to give you her story from her perspective.

I have always had a feeling that my life was and is supposed to be very special. Even before I was born into this world, I was given the name April. When you look that name up according to my birthstone you will find out that it is tied to the diamond–one of the most precious stones in the world. It can hold no loyalty to man, but requires that every man and woman envy it. Love is defined by how big it is, and danger can be found lurking around its value. It is seen moving from country to country, store to store, and from generation to generation. It is said about the diamond that, "Its true value and worth lies deep within the eye of its beholder."

Growing up like most little girls in life, I dreamt a dream of having a loving husband, lots of kids, and a fairytale ending. I can remember when the love of my life proposed to me making me one of the happiest women in the world. The diamond that sat on top of my ring, the very ring that echoed my vow and love for him to the world had endless value. God had truly blessed me with a bright future at a very young age. I was twenty-four when I was married to my husband and shortly after that we found out that we were expecting a baby–the first addition to our rapidly growing happiness. As seconds turned into minutes, my days evolved into endless baby talk. I ventured over to my parents' house on a warm summer day to be surrounded by my loved ones. My husband was off working, and I needed someone to feed my dreams of what's to come. As we sat in the family room of their house reminiscing about my past and planning for my future, a sudden pain hit my stomach. As I held my breath and placed my right hand over the area of pain, it happened again. Soon it was followed a series of high and low level pain contractions. I had done my research prior to being pregnant, and I knew this wasn't a good sign, especially being so early in the pregnancy. So I bolted off the couch and ran down the hall directly into the bathroom. I started mumbling a soft prayer, but it was too late. I was about to discover that there was blood, and my first pregnancy had turned into a miscarriage. That day turned into an unanswered sadness that still follows me to this day. It seemed as if I had just found out I was pregnant, and then it was over. My husband just told me not to worry about it and that we would try again. Some of my closest friends and family members told me that it wasn't meant to be or as they put it, "It wasn't God's will, and He doesn't make mistakes." These words didn't heal the pain I felt, but I assumed time would.

Well, my husband was right. A couple of months after my miscarriage, I found myself pregnant again. This pregnancy would be different for me simply because I had gotten my hopes up before and was let down, so I wanted to wait until I got past the miscarriage threshold before I would let myself get to excited. It seemed like it took forever, but finally I passed through my first trimester. I finally uncrossed my fingers and looked towards a brighter future! I would lie in bed with my head on my husband's chest and we would argue over names that would be suitable for our baby. I knew that it was still early since it had been only thirteen weeks, but I had been waiting on this moment my whole life. I can still remember giving up everything and anything that may cause this pregnancy to go wrong. I lied around in my pajama pants at every opportunity, gave up drinking soda, and even exercising. Well, with the past behind me and a doctor's visit approaching in the next two days, I was excited. I attended the scheduled doctor's visit and just as planned, everything was developing and my baby was healthy. Two days later, I was sitting on the couch and got a really eerie feeling. I felt like something was wrong. I couldn't remember feeling any movements at all in my stomach. I knew that it was still early, but my intuition told me to make another doctor's appointment.

This time, however, it was the 14th week of my pregnancy when I went to the doctor and he used the Doppler machine to listen for the heartbeat in the office. He couldn't find a heartbeat, and at this stage in the pregnancy you should be able to hear it quite clearly. The doctor sent me right away for an ultrasound to find out what was going on. I remember praying again and also asking, "Why does this keep happening?"

Before this appointment, I had a feeling something was wrong, but my husband thought I was being ridiculous and paranoid because of the previous miscarriage, so I went alone to the hospital for the ultrasound. As they rolled me down the hallway in the wheel chair, I began to cry. It reminded me of my very first visit right after my miscarriage. I knew that positive thoughts create positive energy, and I needed to have a state of mind that involved a lot of wishful thoughts. However, once your hopes and thoughts have been beaten up past recognition, you almost have a feeling of shame when those hopes present themselves again. I had prayed every day since the miscarriage. PLEASE GOD let that count for something! This baby is innocent please let everything be ok! What have I done Father to deserve this?

The ultrasound tech walked inside the room staring at the floor as she approached me. She handed me a phone and told me that the doctor was on the phone and wanted to speak with me. At this point, I was already in tears. My heart started racing, and I didn't want to answer the phone. I knew that my worst fears were awaiting me on the other end of this phone. I was expecting to hear the worst possible news, but deep down inside praying for a miracle. As I grabbed the phone in my right hand and placed it to my right ear, I took my trembling left hand and covered my mouth in hopes of muffling any screams that might manifested out of pain. I said with a hopeful but faint voice,

"Hello?" The voice on the other end told me the baby was still in my stomach, and the tech approached me and handed me two ultrasound pictures of the baby. The doctor proceeded to tell me, "However, the heart is no longer beating." A surge of adrenaline hit my heart as his last few words echoed in my head. I started feeling sick to my stomach, while uncontrollably falling apart. My right hand gave way to the phone as it fell to the floor. I pulled my knees close to my chest taking on the fetal position as I had been hit with one of the hardest blows of my life. Here I just received the worst news of my life, and the only person to console me was the tech that is trained to hold back her emotions. She handed me the phone again, and the doctor then explained to me that I had to "go home and wait for my body to reject the baby!" My body just transformed from the carrier of a precious item into a walking tomb! I franticly called my mother and asked her to come and pick me up from the hospital due to my nerves, tears, and state of mind. Once she arrived she embraced me, and I can remember thinking that I needed to get this baby out of me.

I wanted to get as far away from it as possible, because it was a constant reminder that I was cursed by GOD. I was full of mixed emotions, and they continued to interchange back and forth over the next couple of days. The first day or two was the worst for me. I prayed that Jesus could perform another miracle and speak life in my womb to my baby just as He had spoken into Lazarus' tomb. I know that Jesus rose on the third day out of his tomb and is still the living GOD and nothing is impossible for Him. Why won't He perform just one miracle in my life! I couldn't do anything for myself the next couple of days so I stayed with my parents. I was an emotional wreck the whole time. I finally mustered the energy to wash my body on the third day, and felt as though I was still disgusting. I didn't want anyone to touch me, because I felt unworthy of love. To carry your baby in your body knowing it is dead is one of the worst feelings a person can experience in life. I had to endure this emotional pain for five straight days with each day becoming longer than the previous one. By the fifth day, my emotions were obviously out of control. I can remember the first wave of contractions hitting my body and realizing that I had gone into labor. I made my way out of the guest room down the hall into the bathroom. Do to the level of pain emotionally, physically, and psychologically, I passed out in the bathroom and began hemorrhaging. I am not sure how long I was lying on the floor, but the next thing I remember was yelling! I was screaming from the bathroom floor because I couldn't get up. I was screaming out "Help!" in between screams of pain. Finally, my family rushed in the bathroom and took me to the hospital. When I arrived at the hospital, my doctor was not in town at the time so one of his colleagues performed the procedure. What should have been a time of joy turned into one of the darkest moments of my life! I eventually had the baby. The doctor took the baby and sent it for an autopsy.

As he wrapped the baby up and took it away, my husband wanted to see the baby, but I could not bear to. My husband said the baby was fully formed at 14 weeks, and it was a boy. When the autopsy results came back it showed that the baby's spinal cord had not closed. If somehow the baby would have survived the pregnancy, it would have had spina bifida. After all this was when the anger set in. I cried out, "God, here I am 26 and married, and I can't have one healthy baby!" "You allow millions of people to get pregnant and have abortions, but I can't have one healthy baby!" I repented of all of my sins and yet what seemed like a curse settled on top of my life. I became very numb and bitter on the inside. Well, after I delivered the baby they sent me home empty- handed along with some details of following up with the doctor. The next day, I went to my doctor's office since he had made it back into town. He wanted to check up on me since I was his patient, plus I was still in a lot of pain. I was informed that I was hemorrhaging and that my body was full of infection. He sent me back to the hospital and I had to have an emergency D & C (dilation and curettage) to fix everything and remove the infection.

It was hard to keep my connection with my husband because he just didn't understand. He wanted me to get over it as if it never happened. He didn't understand that I couldn't walk in a store, drive by a house, or even pass a park without thinking about my son! Without having some sort of anger take over my body. I would have nightmares, and visions that would leave me in cold sweats. It consumed my every thought, and my very life. I isolated myself from everyone. I was very angry with my husband, family, and friends or anyone that seemed happy or that had kids solely because they were a constant reminder of what I should have had. I was especially mad at God! Why would he allow something like this to happen to me? I sobbed, "God why are You teasing me with life and then punishing me with death?" You truly never realize how many kids you pass within a day until you lose one. It's kind of like when you buy a new car. You truly don't realize how many cars look exactly like your car until it becomes your new obsession.

The doctors recommended DNA testing to see if there were any other reasons why I couldn't have a healthy baby. The results came back and nothing was physically wrong with my husband or me. Well, as time passed by I was later blessed with the birth of two beautiful, healthy baby girls. I had no faith and very little hope throughout these pregnancies. I only expected the worst since that's all I had experienced. My pregnancy with my first daughter was luckily very routine. I just wish I could have relaxed enough to enjoy it. However, when I was pregnant with the second one, I started having problems at about 13 weeks, and I went to the doctor right away. He put me on bed rest, and I was checked every week for a month after that and there was still a heartbeat. When she was born, the nurse made the discovery that there were two placentas. The doctor sent the placenta off for biopsy and found that I had indeed been pregnant with twins, but one did not live past approximately 13 weeks and then was absorbed into the placenta.

I have to admit that I took a lot of my anger and misplaced it towards God. I had been in church most of my life, but I found myself feeling very far from God now. It took me a while before I could become close to God again. All of my friends were trying to get me to attend church services just months after the death and birth of my son, but I stayed away from God for a really long time. I have to admit that it was probably near the very end of my pregnancy with my first daughter before I went back to church because I was in a really bad place in my life and my mind. Eventually, I started to realize that even though I had endured these difficult loses there were still blessings in my life and this pregnancy was one.

I started to make my walk with Him a little more personal. I realized as our relationship grew stronger that God truly loves me and would do anything and everything for me. In the book of James 1:2-8 it is written, "Consider it pure joy, my brothers and sisters, whenever you face trials of many kinds, because you know that the testing of your faith produces perseverance. Let perseverance finish its work so that you may be mature and complete, not lacking anything. If any of you lacks wisdom, you should ask God, who gives generously to all without finding fault, and it will be given to you. But when you ask, you must believe and not doubt, because the one who doubts is like a wave of the sea, blown and tossed by the wind. That person should not expect to receive anything from the Lord. Such a person is double-minded and unstable in all they do." I have to admit that while I was being tossed back and forth by the wind that I developed spiritual motion sickness and decided to place my anchor firmly in the Lord. Although I felt incomplete in my life, I now realized that I was complete in the Lord. I had to endure this process to develop my faith in God. He had to equip me with the correct tools and trials in life so that I can now be a blessing to those entering the fire that I had once passed through.

April is correct about enduring a process in order to develop faith. If you were to look in your Bible and read the sections where Jesus performed the miracles you would commonly see a strong presence of faith. In fact, Jesus said on a number of occasions, "Your faith has healed you." Once in Matthew 9:22 and in Matthew 9:29 he says to the blind man, "According to your faith let it be done to you." We all have some level of faith stored within us. I think that just like the men in the parable with the bags of gold in the book of Matthew 25:14-28 (NIV) when the opportunity presents itself we need to invest in the stock of exercising our faith. No one wants to miss out on their blessings in life or purpose because they held onto their faith and didn't exercise it or invest it because of anger or resentment.

Pause Insight before the encounter:

- April would have realized that God loved her and wouldn't have placed so much anger towards Him.
-

Pause insight after the encounter:

- April now realizes how much God loves her and how blessed she is in life.
-

The Endless Journey within our Faith

Genesis 24:27 (NIV)

"Praise be to the Lord, the God of my master Abraham, who has not abandoned His kindness and faithfulness to my master. As for me, the Lord has led me on the journey to the house of my master's relatives."

I have often heard these words spoken, "If you have never been hurt or experienced heartache or pain, then just keep living." I have learned that our souls are made up of our minds, our will, and our emotions. When emotions are out of whack, most times it will throw our entire day off course; if we are not careful it can throw our entire life off course. Satan looks for any avenue that he can use to steal our destiny and purpose for which God has created us. Often times when our emotions are bruised through loss, heartache, or disappointment, our first reaction is to blame God. "God how could you let this happen?" is what I have heard many people ask. Why do we blame God for the bad things that we experience in life, but often never acknowledge him for the good things that happen in our lives? Many people turn away from God and many will never turn to God because they have blamed God for a negative experience whether from their past or from a current situation or circumstance.

By now you have read many testimonies of how men and women have overcome hurt and pain which was manifested in many forms. Maybe you have read a chapter or two where you can relate to what the person was feeling and the pain he or she went through. You could be reading this book and thinking there is no hope for you, and that life is supposed to hurt. I have great news for you! God never created or designed us to be buried in the brokenness of life. Jesus says in John 10:10 "The thief (Satan) comes to steal, and to kill, and to destroy: I come that they might have life and that they might have it more abundantly." God intended that we would have an abundant life of joy, peace, love, goodness, gentleness, and kindness.

I can remember waking up around 6:00 a.m.one morning to start my morning exercise routine. It was a warm summer morning and the weather was perfect. Once I finished my stretching routine, I placed my ear buds in my ear so I could listen to one of my favorite Christian Rap artists Lecrae. As I was running on the side-walk next to a busy road, I can remember praying. I was praying for guidance, wisdom, and to find my purpose in life just as I had many times before. I ran for about three miles that morning. I was staring at the ground as I pushed myself to run harder during the last one hundred yards before I started my cool down session. It was at that moment that I received a word from God. It was the weirdest thing ever. I was in the process of crossing the street when God gave me the vision for this book cover. I came to a complete stop in the middle of the road. Still intently gazing at the ground as I took my ear buds out of my ears and read the book cover as God had shown it to me. It read, "Face to Face Where

Life Meets Reality." I saw that Jesus was on the front page and I had an understanding of what it meant.

As my look of confusion turned into a smile and praise, I still had no clue of how I would write this book or what God wanted to do with it. Throughout the making of this book, every time I figured that I knew what the vision and scope of this book looked like, God would change it. He eventually transformed it from a book about my life into a book about lives encompassed by Him. It grew from a book about changing a life into a life-changing book. I would get frustrated while trying to write the chapters the way I wanted to write them, but the moment that I would give up, God would take over again. I watched a group of hurt individuals open closet doors into their darkest moments. I watched as they dragged these items out of their closets into the light. The change within them and healing process that took place because of their willingness to step out on faith was phenomenal.

There were times when I would be surrounded by writers block, and I would just get on my knees and pray. Within an hour my phone would ring, and it would be a person that I hadn't talked to within a year or even years. At first, I thought that they just wanted a listening ear as they vented, but quickly I realized that it was God answering my prayers. There were a lot of tears shed as we all walked through the fire again to relive the pain. However, as we did, it was evident that God had been present in each situation. We felt just as amazed looking back and seeing God's faithfulness to each of us as King Nebuchadnezzar did when he witnessed God's faithfulness to the three Hebrew boys in the fire. In Daniel 3:25 (NIV) it is written that he leaped to his feet in amazement and said, "Look! I see four men walking around in the fire, unbound and unharmed, and the fourth looks like a son of the gods." I now know that is when we re-enter the fire that our chains are broken.

We are set free from the spirits that bound and harmed us. When we allow God to walk us through the fires in our life, He picks us up and takes us through a total transformation. It's like the transformation of a caterpillar into a beautiful butterfly. Our job as His beautiful creations is to flutter throughout life in hopes of touching everyone with the testimonies that are written on our wings to show the beauty of the new creation that He has restored inside of us! In Colossians 3:12-14 it states, "Therefore, as God's chosen people, holy and dearly loved, clothe yourselves with compassion, kindness, humility, gentleness and patience. Bear with each other and forgive one another if any of you has a grievance against someone. Forgive as the Lord forgave you. And over all these virtues put on love, which binds them all together in perfect unity."

Just like Harmony stated in the Gray Area, "I have heard that life evolves from love. To be honest, if life is love then I can't wait to live!" A lot of us have forgotten that life was given to us out of love from our Heavenly Father and we shouldn't waste it, give up on it, or hate it. We should embrace it, love it, and share the goodness of it. My mom used to say, "What doesn't kill us will make us stronger," and she was right! I have learned to lean on the Lord, and He has given me endless strength like that of Samson!

From my heart to your heart flowed my life experiences and prayers. I was once asked by a young lady, "How did you make the change from the hurt and angry Tarrance into who you are today?" I have to be honest here. I told her that it was nothing that I physically, mentally, or spiritually did to change me into who I am today. It was all God! He heard my heart as it skipped a beat every time it was broken as my life started to crumble beneath my feet. He understood the rhythm of my heart and knew that something was wrong, but understood that this was a song that had to be played.

God knew that it needed to be played with such bass and treble that it would sync all of the other irregular heart-beats to one rhythm. God's plan was to allow me to suffer through my lyrics so that you may one day relate, under-stand, and dance to my song. So that the world may one day pause and make decisions that will impact lives instead of taking value away from them. When making a tough deci-sion in your life, remember to ask yourself what the three most important people in your life would want you to do, to help you think outside of your box. Then you can hopefully see past the wall or obstacle that is causing stress in your life to show you that there are other choices, a fork in the road, and a better life beyond that wall.

Approaching the mirror

God is an amazing God who holds the master plan to our lives within His hands. The future is where I would allow my hopes and dreams to live. As a kid I was always curious about what my future held. I would often daydream that I was inside of a time capsule. I wanted to travel into the future and make a few changes in hopes of making my life perfect. The invention of time machines had not come to pass at that moment in my childhood. Instead of waiting, I decided to create a list of goals in my life that I wanted to accomplish to give me the happiness that I envisioned. The inner voice inside of me was convinced that happiness was surrounded by money and self-accomplishments. I was always working to have a better future. I was so busy preparing and rushing into my future that I ignored what was happening around me. I now realize that I was always running from my past. I never really appreciated what God had done for me. I was too busy trying to escape from the hurt and pain that engulfed my every thought and embraced my every step, so I overlooked the here and now in my life.

Over the last couple of weeks, God has been telling me to live in and appreciate the present times. Just like in Joseph's life, God tends to give us a vision and withhold the details from us. Life would be so much easier if we had step-by-step plans of our lives. Instead, we have to walk into the unknown and have faith that HE is with us during our daily walk. God is showing me that I have a mission in life and even though I feel so alone at times I need to keep walking. I never understood that my shortcomings and pains in life would serve as a mirror to most and a window for all. I am now humbled to know that when people approach this book and start to turn the pages it may serve as a reflection of God and a soft voice from the Holy Spirit saying, "You are not alone." I know that it may also serve as a window for everyone to view into the hearts of those that are broken, so that people who have never experienced such trials and tribulations may have an opportunity to develop some tools to share empathy and encouragement as they listen to the broken hearted. God doesn't like it when we have to endure pain in our lives. God is love. In John 3:16 it says, "For God so loved the world that he gave His one and only Son, that whoever believes in Him shall not perish but have eternal life." He gave Jesus life so that He would endure the ultimate walk within pain.

The devil tries to divide households, relationships and friendships, but God encourages them. In Matthew 18:20 Christ proclaimed "For wherever two or three people have come together in my name, I am there, right among them!" This is Christ encouraging us to join together and fellowship with one another in His name. God created each of us with an important role to play in the lives of one another. Paul paints this picture clearly when he compares the body of believers to the human body in 1 Corinthians 12:24-27, "God has put the body together, giving greater honor to the parts that lacked it, so that there should be no division in the body, but that its parts should have equal concern for each other. If one part suffers, every part suffers with it; if one part is honored, every part rejoices with it. Now you are the body of Christ and each one of you is a part of it." Paul also painted a similar word picture in Romans 12:5, "In Christ we, though many, form one body, and each member belongs to all the others."

Later in verse 15 Paul encourages our fellowship with one another saying, "Rejoice with those who rejoice, and mourn with those who mourn." It is God's will for us to have a support system as we go through the storms in life. It is also His will for us to support our brothers and sisters and point them towards him as they go through storms in life.

Throughout this book I have given you examples of God's love during different circumstances in my life. It was a learning process and at times hard for me to see it, but God was with me every step of the way. Within the chapter of God's Forewarning it seemed to me that God was revealing His presence to me. He defined a moment that would serve to be my anchor in life, by revealing His vision to me, prophesying though WJ's life, and confirming His presence with my mother's back pain. All of this was taking place before the facts surrounding this incident punched me in the gut. While creating this book, I was able to look back over my life and develop some hindsight. I realized that there are a million and one things that I would go back and change if I could. As a kid growing up I thought that I had it bad at times. Now I realize that those are the times in my life that I miss the most (around the kerosene heater). Lastly, I want to give you some insight from my life and hopefully it travels into your life. In this next chapter I will talk about who I am today and why such a dramatic change took place.

Insight

Proverbs 7:4

Say to wisdom, "You are my sister,"
and to insight, "You are my relative."

I am at a period and time in my life that I want to experience the fullest of God's glory, grace, and mercy. As I think back over my life and this book from the start to the finish, there is one thing that has never changed, and that is God. There has been one thing that has been at a constant change throughout my life and that has been my level of faith. I now realize that every situation that I have been through in life is what I call a faith builder. God gave me the freedom of choice, and I took full advantage of it.

I can remember praying at my desk months before I quit my job and asking God for my purpose in life. It seemed as if God then took me and alienated me from all of my friends and family. Once I was alone, he stripped me from all of the worldly things that I had achieved and told me to be still. It was again, in that moment that my silence started screaming so loud that I could not bear it, and I picked up the gun. God then told me again to "pause and be still." In that stillness, I could see my world crumbling around me and every person that I thought that I loved talk against me, and it was mind blowing. As a result, I decided to seek help through Christian counseling. My counselor consistently told me to read the Word. Well, that was the last thing that I wanted to do! I wanted the hurt and the pain to go away. I wanted to see the brighter days and not walk in the darkness. However, I surrendered and I began to read the Word. Then, I felt like God opened my spirit and spoke to me telling me to move, so I went out to California for about three months into further isolation. I had no clue why I was there at first, but once I made it there I realized that I had a friend who had an evil spirit riding on their shoulders as well. We then challenged God in the sense that we fasted, prayed, and went to church like never before. As usual God provided and answered every question that we had through the preachers at the churches we attended. God answered every question in the exact order that we asked them in. It was almost scary. After about three months, I felt like my journey was coming to a close in California. It was like God wanted me to make a decision. Once I made it back to Springfield, Missouri I felt like God placed another decision in front of me. Just like in Luke 9:23 the disciples were faced with the challenge, "Whoever wants to be my disciple must deny themselves and take up their cross daily and follow me. For whoever wants to save their life will lose it, but whoever loses their life for me will save it." I felt as if I had no choice but to move out of Springfield (take up my cross). Most of my friends were thinking that I was having a mid-life crisis and others thought that I had fallen off the rocker and bumped my head. They couldn't believe that I would leave a perfectly good-paying job to move to Atlanta, Georgia and live in my cousin's basement. They thought that I was even crazier when I answered their question about not having a job lined up by telling them that I was walking on faith. To be honest I didn't understand it either, but I just felt deep down in my soul that it was something that I had to do. Eventually, I gave my letter of resignation to my place of employment. I gave the majority of my household belongings away and packed my car with the remaining items and drove to Atlanta. My family in Atlanta was very supportive of me seeking God, but I was unsure of what I was doing. I had no plan but only to seek God and walk through doors that I felt He was opening. As soon as I made it to Atlanta, my cousin's wife Kim invited me to attend North Point Church with them. That wasn't the first time that I had attended that church with them. When I would come down on my vacation days, we would attend their church so I was familiar with its fellowship. I have to say that this time was different though, because it was the first time that I was attending it with my heart torn wide open. As usual Pastor Andy had an amazing and encouraging word for my soul. As we were walking out of the service Kim informed me that the church had days where they have the people that were jobless come together in hopes of networking and opening doors for job opportunities. Well, I decided to attend a couple of those sessions and I remembered thinking, "God is this really what you want me to do?" Did you really want me to leave the secular working atmosphere to possibly rejoin it again in Atlanta? I know that I have to make a living. According to my friends, in order for me to get a paid position at a church, I will have to have some type of a degree in the ministry field. With no direction in sight, I started to pray, "Father, please turn your ear towards my heart because I am lost in the darkness with nowhere to go. Please help me." As I sat in those meetings, we were divided into small groups to explore each other's minds for vital information to help get yourself or others on the right path. It didn't take long for God to answer me as I was in that meeting. I had the pleasure of meeting Jeremy, a friend that would walk a term with me during my struggle. Sitting at the table he talked about how he wanted to work with Christian camps, and he had an opportunity to do so the following week. I can remember thinking, "Man that would be so cool to do." Well, I decided to take a chance and walk up to this guy and ask him if I could attend camp with him. Much to my delight, he said, "Yes!" and we exchanged cell phone numbers. I can remember meeting up with him and following him to the camp. We had about a two-hour drive ahead of us. I didn't want to ride in his car because my thoughts were, "I don't know him, plus he could be a serial killer or something. What was I thinking getting myself in this mess?" Later I found out that he was thinking something very similar. This friend blessed me with the opportunity of attending and volunteering at my first Christian camp. Once we made it to the camp, God poured out his blessing on me. I have never been so embraced by so many people in my life, even though I was an adult volunteer at a kids' youth camp. The kid inside of me took in and learned so much during that week. Developing and understanding the different levels of faith was the lesson that I felt God wanted me to learn. When I looked into everyone's eyes, there was a level of faith inside of them that I envied. Again, I had never experienced camp before so I was blown away. I think that the most important thing that made me continue to walk in my faith and landed me where I am today was a lesson that was taught during one of the services. It was at the 10:00 a.m. service on a hot summer morning. There were about thirty kids sitting under a pavilion listening intently to the Word. You could hear the birds chirping in the trees as a couple of bees were buzzing between our chairs. The Pastor took what looked like a one hundred foot rope and he held one end. He called a student up to retrieve the other end and told the kid, "Take off and walk until you feel a tug on the rope. Once you feel the tug then place that end of the rope down on the ground and come back." Well the kid performed an about-face and off he went down a hill until he was out of our sight. After what seemed like forever there was a tug indicating the end of the rope. Finally the kid made his journey back to the Bible study site. The Pastor proceeded to take his end of the rope and held it up in the air. On his end of the rope was a piece of tan tape that was about three inches wide. That tape was a representation of the span of a human's life. The tape seemed spotless on the end closest to his end of the rope. Now on the opposite end of that three inch tape that was facing in the direction the kid walked, was a line where he placed a mark about 1/8 of an inch with a black permanent marker indicating, "The part of life that most people dedicate to God." The speaker was giving us a visual of how we walk throughout life living for the world and then when we become old, right before we die, we try and get to know the Lord. More importantly beyond that tape and that permanent mark on the tape was the rest of the rope. That remainder of the rope was a representation of the rest of your life in eternity. That illustration made so much sense to me that I vowed to take my 1/8 permanent marker line that I was setting myself up for and stretch it as far as I could over the current part of my life. I wanted to stop playing church and become a walking church. I wanted to stop leaning on my religion and embrace His relationship.

The camp session lasted for another four days and then I drove back to my cousin's house. As I pulled into their driveway and turned off the car I started to pray because I felt like God had revealed something to me, but I wasn't sure what it was yet. I felt like I had purpose in life, but I was still jobless. I felt as though I should be pursing the ministry, but my degree was in computer science. I continued to pray with all of the faith that I could muster up in my body. I had a vision but no details. I never would have guessed that His purpose would lead me to move to Chicago to do His work and bring me back for a visit in Atlanta five months later.

I never thought that my prayers would eventually lead me back to a special Sunday service at North Point, but God already had it in His plans, and on December 22, 2013, I attended church with Kim and A.O. As I sat on the front row in the West auditorium of the Alpharetta, Georgia campus, and listened to Pastor Andy wrap up his sermon, "Christmas, The End of The Line," my heart once again felt full and satisfied from the Word that was served on that day. Then, it hit me! I noticed a couple of people standing off to the right of the stage lighting candles. My curiosity drew my full attention in their direction. The speaker in the auditorium announced that they were going to light a candle. The burning candle was a representation and celebration of a year of change. It didn't matter how big or small the change was, only that it happened or was in the process of happening. The basket of candles was about three feet away from my body. I looked around and no one was approaching the baskets yet. I glanced over at Kim who was sitting two seats to my left in hopes of her giving me an encouraging nod or smile. It seemed that she was hypnotized by the speaker who was still informing the congregation about the candles. I took a step of faith and found myself standing at the basket retrieving one of the candles. I took the candle and placed it to the fire of the candle that was in the usher's opposite hand. I took three steps back to my seat and then glanced over at Kim. Once again she displayed her sisterly smile and I looked down at the flame again. While staring at the candle, I could see the orange, red, and blue flame dancing within each other. I also had a flash back in my mind of how close I was to death. I realized that I was so lucky to be standing here next to A.O. and Kim. I also realized how I had been entangled with my worst fears in life, and God intervened. As tears started to form in my eyes from my once selfish thoughts, I traded seats with AO and I whispered to Kim, "It's crazy that I almost killed myself! I almost missed the opportunity of holding this candle on this day as a representation of change." I couldn't bear to look at Kim as I said those words so my eyes were glued on the flame. I knew that she understood my pain as I felt her eyes burning a hole in the side of my head. I could see her lips moving in my peripheral vision, but she was at a loss for words. I could tell by her tone once her lips found her voice that she was in tears also. Once she pulled herself together she said, "This candle represents the changes that God has made in your life and the changes that He is going to make within our family and friends through you." As she took this picture below, those words gave way to endless thoughts and countless possibilities, but most of all confirmation that He is with me.

There are times within this walk with God that people have asked me how I was able to take up my cross and walk with God? It truly wasn't easy to surrender my life that I had become comfortable living to a God that I was so angry at most of my life. As I answered the very first person who asked me that question, these words flowed from my mouth, "If Our Father allowed one of your loved ones who has since gone to heaven to revisit you in life for a very short period of time, what would you do? What would you say? What if they told you that Heaven is real and God is Love? That the only way into to heaven is through His Son. That the Bible is truly everything that our forefathers like Matthew, Mark, Luke, and John has said it was. What if they said, 'Heaven is all that you have heard about and the streets are filled with praises and loving spirits.' That darkness never settles on the light and sadness is never conceived within our hearts. What if they told you that you need to take this life seriously and seek God with all of your mind, body, and soul? Lastly, that they are all waiting with open wings for you to enter the gates of Heaven. Would you change the way you are living today to line up within their truths?"

I know that I can honestly tell you that if WJ or my mom came back and had that talk with me that things would have been different. I figured why wait for the dead to tell me these things. Why not just listen to the people who have had a second chance at life and how our encounters with death open our eyes to life. I have heard that a person is not truly ready to live until he or she is willing to die. It gives you a new perspective on life. Now I am truly ready to live my life for my Lord. I also live by the motto, "In order to get what I have never had in life, I will have to do the things that I have never done." I will have to challenge myself to become a better person in all walks of life. If I have to pray harder, fast longer, sacrifice my ways, and develop a servant's heart, then that is what I will strive to do.

People, we have to make decisions within our lives that will complement our lives. The Prodigal Son received an inheritance from his father and decided to go get into some mess. He decided to travel and take up in a foreign land. In modern day terms of mess he probably moved in with a girl and hung out with guys he thought were his friends. They were probably staying out late, going to clubs, drinking, and smoking together. Before you knew it he had a crowd that followed him around everywhere he went until the money ran out. It says in Luke 15:16-20 "He longed to fill his stomach with the pods that the pigs were eating, but no one gave him anything. "When he came to his senses, he said, How many of my father's hired servants have food to spare, and here I am starving to death! I will set out and go back to my father and say to him: Father, I have sinned against heaven and against you. I am no longer worthy to be called your son; make me like one of your hired servants. So he got up and went to his father." Sometimes in life when we are going through our trials and tribulations we have to make a decision! At some point we all will come to a crossroad within our life where we have to choose to either go left or go right! We have to decide whether to stay and continue taking the abuse or leave? Do I turn the ventilator off or leave it on? Do I tell someone about what happened to me or do I just live with the lies within my secrets? Should I pull the trigger or not? You see at some point within our lives we all will have to make a choice – a conscious decision that will go something like this: "Do I stay here and waddle in this mess or do I stand up, dust myself off, and get my life right? Do I continue playing church or shall I put on the full armor of God?" I knew what I had to choose. The Lord also gave me the wisdom to know that I would need to prepare myself spiritually to continue to fight through the spiritual battles that life would continue to throw at me. The Lord was faithful and brought me Christian friends and family members to walk with. He showed me that I needed to surround myself with these people so that I could ask someone to pray with me as I put on my Helmet of Salvation; hold me up as I string on the breastplate of righteousness, Watch my back as I bend over so that my feet are shod with the preparation of the gospel of peace. Stand next to me as I put on my belt of truth. Walk with me as I retrieve my shield of faith, and pass me my weapons so I can grab the sword of the Spirit. (Ephesians 6:13-17) It was these realizations and God's steadfast faithfulness that allowed me to take up my cross and surrender my life to the Lord.

Now, after reading the stories in this book and feeling the emotions pouring out of my heart, I want to encourage you that you can do the same. Friends, even though you are prepared with the weapons of destructions for spiritual warfare you still have to make a decision! Do I stay here and waddle in this mess within my life or do I stand up, dust myself off, and get my life right!

The first thing that you should do is standup! Stand up so that you can see what's around you. You need to do some reconnaissance or reflecting on the area that surrounds your situation. You have to notice that you are surrounded by pigs! Just like the Prodigal Son...You have to realize that you maybe in your darkest hour and all of your so called friends have left you alone! Where are they at? Why don't they understand! You have to realize that even in your mess that you are still blessed!

Secondly, after you stand up, you need to dust yourself off! You need to get over the fact that people may be talking or have talked about you. You have to let go of the hurt feeling that your family or friends have left you/used you! You need to let go of the fact that you have made mistakes and messed up in life even though you may feel as if you have lost everything of any value in your life.

Lastly, you need to get your life right. MAKE YOUR DECISION to straighten out your life. Sometimes God allows the famines to sweep through your life to get you out of the mess you are in! God wants the hurt and pain, the feelings of loneness and self-pity to leave so that HIS love, mercy, and grace can fill those voids.

In the beginning of the book, I talked about my darkest hour. There was not one particular incident or change within my life that sent me over the edge. During the months leading up to my darkest hour, my life was pretty normal. I still had my job, girlfriend, and support system. Everything seemed pretty normal during that time of my life, so I thought. One day, six months prior to my darkest hour, I was sitting on my couch in my apartment, and God placed a vision in my head that my car was going to break down and nothing was going to be wrong with it. I just smiled and stored that vision in the back of my head. I started spending more time at the gym and keeping busy. My mind was still really busy, because I was spending a lot of time with all of my friends. Well, that vision would resurface in my mind probably about once a month. Again, I would think that it was crazy. How can my car break down and, nothing will be wrong with it? I would soon find the answers to my question. I can remember waking up on a Saturday morning eager to meet a couple of my friends at Missouri State University to participate in our weekly exercise group. As I left my house driving towards the stadium, the vision resurfaced within my mind again. Just like normal, I shook it off and drove to my destination. After running the stairs at the stadium for an hour we exited the stadium and walked over to our cars. We said our goodbyes and I entered my car. As I put the key in the ignition with full faith that my car would start and proceeded to turn the key, my car started, but it immediately shut itself back off. I tried it about three more times, and then I quickly I flagged one of my friends down before he exited the parking lot. We called a tow truck and they took my car to the shop. They advised me that they would run a couple of diagnostic tests on my car and contact me later on that Saturday evening. It seemed as if it took a lifetime for them to call me as I anxiously awaited their phone call. Finally, the time arrived as he gave me some disturbing news. I was told that the diagnostic reports all lead them to believe that my car is dead. As in it's not responding to anything at all. They advised me that it seems as if the car has locked down or has a kill switch somewhere in/on the car. He advised me that they will get the car over to the Dodge center to take a look at it. Possibly in three days since they were closed on Sunday and Monday was a holiday. It was during that period of time when I was at home from that Saturday evening, Sunday, and Monday that I met my darkest hour. It wasn't that my car broke down that sent me over the edge, it was the fact that God made me be still. I honestly called everyone in my phone, and not one person answered. It was like I was driving in the Daytona 500, and I was leading the pack of cars at speeds up to 212 miles per hour. Each of the 38 cars behind me represent a part of my past that I have never dealt with and suddenly without warning, God applied the brakes to my life. The psychological collision and damage was catastrophic and unbearable. I later realized that the vision that was revealed to me was never about my car. It was about me having an intimate encounter with my Father and Him meeting me in the midst of my pain.

The Dodge center kept my car for a week and could not find the source of the problem. Later they determined that I just needed another ignition key because my codes within my key went bad. Hence the vision of my car breaking down and nothing was really wrong with it.

Now, I'd like to answer the last question that may be wandering through your mind. Why did Joe kill WJ? I think in order for me to answer that question honestly. I would have to remove myself out of my current situation of being the victim. I would have to place myself in the position of a proud parent, in the shoes of Joe and most other parents in this world. Parents raise their children up in this world to prepare them for life. They sacrifice everything so that their children will not lack for anything. Many of their investments, hopes, and dreams are tied up into one decision – who their child will choose to be with in life. Will it be someone that they approve of, like, love, or would even choose for their child? Would they be able to withhold their parental advice and allow their child to work through their marital issues? Can they allow them to make mistakes and create solutions without taking over their child's life again? Can they give Godly advice without providing a human solution that will cause added hurt and pain? In Mark 10:7 it states, "For this reason a man will leave his father and mother and be united to his wife, and the two will become one flesh. So they are no longer two, but one flesh." Too many adults under one roof can become a disaster, so at times the physical detachment is easier than the mental. I think that the mental part of this is where the feuds between in-laws are created. Simply because the mother and/or father may want to be number one in their child's life. Whereas their wife or husband has taken that position and now there is an unspoken tension in the air. Now it comes down to how far everyone will take it. I have heard of some situations where the married couples have disowned their parents and/or in-laws. In some cases the parents and in-laws are missing out on their grandkids growing up in life. Other situations can carry it to the extreme.

I will not lie about my brother; yes, he got in a couple of physical altercations with his wife, unfortunately he was still fairly young in age. He was only 21 years old when he died. The truth is that most young people don't know what they don't know about life. In other words, they won't have extensive knowledge about life because they are just discovering/ figuring things out for themselves. Parents and adults have to provide Godly solutions and pray that their knowledge would transform into wisdom. No problem deserves a solution that leads to the road of death. I think that Joe could see a better future for his daughter and, he was thinking only if he could help in some sort of way. Now, I don't think that Joe had planned to kill my brother prior to that night, but when you mix love, fear, and rage together without pausing, the worst can come out in people even if they regret it later in life.

A month before this book was published Joe passed away due to health complications. I pray and hope that he had the opportunity to give his life over to our Lord. Most of my life I looked forward to the day of his death and what it would bring me. Honestly, it brought a lot of mixed emotions and when the smoke cleared it transformed into sadness. Simply speaking, in death it's hard to find happiness. In complete darkness there is no light, in absolute chaos there is no love, and in revenge there is no life, only emptiness and unresolved feelings. What I thought would have brought happiness ended up bringing me sadness because a cycle of sadness and depression started all over again. Instead of it eating at my heart it has transferred to the hearts of his loved ones, family members, and friends. That is why it is so important to pause within your life, so that you can allow God's love and wisdom to take over the hateful thoughts that can occur. I am sure that God had to press pause when He looked down from heaven as our sins beat His Son and nailed Him to the cross. He may have even asked, "What would Jesus want Him to do?" Just as Jesus pressed paused when He was about to come Face to

Face with His purpose. It states in Luke 22:42, "Father, if you are willing, take this cup from Me; yet not My will, but Yours be done." I am sure that Jesus had our lives in mind when He proceeded with His Father's plan.

God allowed our sins to be nailed on the Cross with Jesus back on Calvary and they are forgiven! Now we just need to learn how to forgive ourselves, our offenders, and most of all, realize that God isn't the source of our pain. Once we realize that point we will understand the reason why our Father will be waiting for us with His arms open. We will understand that we are a child of the Most High! We will walk inside of our purpose in life. We will experience true love from our father. As my mentor, Pastor Spencer Jones, has always said, "People are either in a storm, just coming out of a storm, or about to enter into a storm." Either way the Father is standing with open arms. Finally, we will learn to appreciate our trials and tribulations in life because they are the gateway to an amazing testimony once we make the decision to stand up, dust ourselves off, and get our lives right!

Again, I thank God for my Uncle Chester and Momma Mia for opening up their homes and taking in a troubled kid, Kathy Carlyle, and many others for taking me by the hand and showing me the path to His glory. I know that our testimonies have served as proof that there are many victorious defeats behind us. We still have many battles ahead of us as we climb the ladder to be one of the devil's most wanted victims. The more we spread our testimonies, the more trials we will endure and the more testimonies we will give. It states in Revelation 12:11(NIV) "They triumphed over him by the blood of the Lamb and by the word of their testimony." The devil has been defeated on more than one occasion and will continue to lose battles as long as we continue to give our testimonies. The sharing of our secrets of what our Father has done within our lives. Winning the battle is only the first part of the war; now we have to lean on the Lord for our strength because we know from whom our help comes. There is no ending to this book because our stories in life will always say, "To be continued" so that our deaths, just like my mom's and brother's, will even serve the Lord. Death will not stop the stories of our life, it will only compliment, "The Endless Journey within our Faith."

Prayers

Philippians 1:19 (NIV)

For I know that through your prayers and God's provision of the Spirit of Jesus Christ what has happened to me will turn out for my deliverance

I am personally so thankful that you have taken the time to read this book and journey through my life and many of my friend's stories. I am confident that this book will have impacted your heart and life in many ways.

I want you to know that the many positive changes that I have experienced in my life, as well as the peace and understanding that I now have in my life, can also be a part of your life.

It all starts with prayer. If you are already a prayer warrior, I commend you and encourage you to always remember to pray for exactly what you need because God truly is a loving Father who has your best interest at heart. Pray for your friends and family, too. Never stop praying. I know that I am where I am in life now because I have had a grandma, mom, and aunts that have prayed for me.

If you are reading this and you haven't prayed in a long time, or maybe you have never prayed, I want to tell you that it is ok. There is no magic formula, or words that you have to say. Just talk to God like He is your Friend and Father. Share your heart with Him. Share your brokenness and hurt with Him. Share your anxiety and fears with Him. Share your praise and love with Him. He wants to hear it all. I am going to leave you with some prayers that may help you get started. Most importantly, I am going to leave you with the sinner's prayer so that if you would like help asking Jesus to forgive you from your sins and to be your Savior you can pray this prayer. You can ask Him in your own words, too!

My prayer for you is that you will seek a personal relationship with the Lord if you do not already have one. Whether you have had a relationship with the Lord for your whole life, or you are just starting one today, I pray you will constantly seek to strengthen and deepen that relationship by spending time in prayer and reading scripture each and every day. Remember, when you PRAY, you are talking to God. When you Study His Word through reading of the bible or scripture, God is talking to you. And finally, when you share his word with others, or witness, you are talking for God. Each of these, Praying, Studying, and Witnessing are necessary elements to spiritual growth. I pray that this book has helped you to realize these things. May the Lord bless you and guide you.

Your brother in Christ,
Tarrance

Sinner's Prayer

Father God, I know that I am a sinner and I need Your forgiveness. I truly believe that Jesus Christ died on the cross for my sins and arose on the third day. I am willing to turn away from my sins and I repent. Jesus will you come and reside in my heart and my life as my personal Lord and Savior!

Prayer for Wisdom, Safety and Healing

In the name of Jesus, Father, I ask that you build a hedge of protection around my immediate loved ones, distant family, and friends. Father, I ask that you give me the wisdom of King Solomon and the strength of Samson. Father God, I ask that you give me the relationship that you once had with our forefathers Abraham, Isaac, and Jacob. Father God, my heart yearns for the visions that you gave Daniel and Joseph. Can you also give me the wisdom to understand those dreams and visions once they are bestowed upon my life? Father God, I ask that you give me a peace of mind and such calmness like you gave Daniel in the lion's den. So that I may look in the face of the enemy and know that their mouths have been wired shut and their hunger and thirst has been quenched by you. Father God, I ask that where we have been weakened that you strengthen us. Where we are torn down please build us back up. Father God, I ask that you go behind me and fix my past, walk with me in my present times, and lead me into my future as you fight my battles for me. These things I ask in your Son's name. Amen!

Breaking Generational Curses

Father God, I now rebuke, break, and loose myself and my family and friends from any and all evil curses and/or generational curses and sins. I am praying back to ten generations on both sides of my family. I break loose myself from any, and all, connected or related spirits from any person, or persons. Father God, take the lifestyles of drinking, drugs, prostitution, promiscuous behavior and any unforeseen curses out of our lives. Remove the spirits of laziness, sadness, and depression off of our lives. Replace them with the spirits of love, laughter, and happiness. Give me purpose in life and help me to walk within those boundaries. These things I ask in Jesus' name. Amen!

Breaking Physical/Mental/Spiritual Bondage

Father God, I now renounce, break free and loose myself and family from all demonic holds, and bondages of physical and mental illnesses, family and marital, as well as, other types of bondages upon us. I pray back to ten generations on my father and mother's sides of our families resulting from sins and transgressions. I pray against the spirits of suicide, life-threating handicaps, and strong holds on our lives. I ask, Father, that you remove this burden off and out of my life. I ask that you take my yoke and help me to put on your yoke because you have declared that your yoke is light. Release my mind, body, and soul to Your will, Father. In Jesus' name, I pray. Amen!

CPSIA information can be obtained
at www.ICGtesting.com
Printed in the USA
FFOW03n1354171215
19434FF

9 781498 412544